Edmund Quincy

**Wensley, and other Stories**

Edmund Quincy

**Wensley, and other Stories**

ISBN/EAN: 9783743305847

Manufactured in Europe, USA, Canada, Australia, Japa

Cover: Foto ©ninafisch / pixelio.de

Manufactured and distributed by brebook publishing software (www.brebook.com)

Edmund Quincy

**Wensley, and other Stories**

IN PRESS,

*Uniform with this Volume,*

## THE HAUNTED ADJUTANT

𝔄𝔫𝔡 𝔒𝔱𝔥𝔢𝔯 𝔖𝔱𝔬𝔯𝔦𝔢𝔰.

BY EDMUND QUINCY.

*EDITED BY HIS SON, EDMUND QUINCY.*

**One vol. 12mo. $1.50.**

———◆———

For sale by all booksellers. Sent postpaid, upon receipt of price, by the publishers,

JAMES R. OSGOOD & CO.,

**BOSTON.**

# WENSLEY

## And Other Stories

By EDMUND QUINCY

EDITED BY HIS SON, EDMUND QUINCY

BOSTON
JAMES R. OSGOOD AND COMPANY
1885

*Copyright, 1885,*
BY EDMUND QUINCY.

*All rights reserved.*

University Press:
JOHN WILSON AND SON, CAMBRIDGE.

# EDITOR'S PREFACE.

IT is not without some hesitation and misgiving, that the editor ventures to withdraw some of the lighter writings of the late Edmund Quincy from the pages of half-forgotten magazines, and give them again to the public, together with the only novel he ever wrote. In the whirl of the present day, it cannot be expected that many will stop long enough to read stories of so quiet and unexciting a nature; still there may be some to whom very accurate pictures of a way of life long passed away, and tales, all of which have a certain foundation in fact, may not be wholly without interest. The history of the octogenary, Colonel Wyborne, for instance, is in the main facts a true one; and his nocturnal visit to Boston, after an absence of fifty years, was an actual occurrence. Mr. Quincy was always of opinion that his essay on "Old Houses," published in 1837, might have suggested to Hawthorne that great magician's wonderful "Tales of the Province House," published some time after.

The best years of Mr. Quincy's life, as many of his contemporaries will remember, were given to the antislavery cause; and his writings on that subject, if published together, would make many volumes, and might furnish a contribution not without value to the history of that momentous struggle. The time for such a republication is not yet come, perhaps never will come. A few specimens only are given, at the end of this volume, of what Mr. Quincy wrote on the subject so near his heart. They were chiefly contributions to an annual called the "Liberty Bell," edited by Mrs. Chapman for the antislavery fair which was held in Boston annually for many years.

# BANKSIDE.[1]

## BY JAMES RUSSELL LOWELL.

MAY 21, 1877.

I CHRISTENED you in happier days, before
These gray forebodings on my brow were seen:
You are still lovely in your new-leaved green;
The brimming river soothes his grassy shore;
The bridge is there, the rock with lichens hoar,
And the same shadows on the water lean,
Outlasting us. How many graves between
That day and this! How many shadows more
Darken my heart, their substance from these eyes
Hidden forever! So our world is made
Of life and death commingled; and the sighs
Outweigh the smiles, in equal balance laid:
What compensation? None, save that the Allwise
So schools us to love things that cannot fade.

Thank God, he saw you last in pomp of May,
Ere any leaf had felt the year's regret:
Your latest image in his memory set

---

[1] The place at Dedham where Mr. Quincy resided during all the latter years of his life was so named by Mr. Lowell.

The poem, which the editor takes the liberty to insert, was printed in the "Nation," under the date of Mr. Quincy's funeral, and is given as being a very good description of Mr. Quincy's character.

Was fair as when your landscape's peaceful sway
Charmed dearer eyes with his to make delay
On Hope's long prospect, as if They forget
The happy, they, the unspeakable ones, whose debt,
Like the hawk's shadow, haunts our brightest day.
Better it is that ye should look so fair,
Slopes that he loved, and ever-murmuring pines
That make a music out of silent air,
And bloom-heaped orchard-trees in prosperous lines:
In you the heart some sweeter hints divines,
And wiser, than in winter's dull despair.

Old friend, farewell! Your kindly door again
I enter; but the master's hand in mine
No more clasps welcome, and the temperate wine
That cheered our long night other lips must stain.
All is unchanged; but I expect in vain
The face alert, the manners free and fine,
The seventy years borne lightly as the pine
Wears its first down of snow in green disdain.
Much did he, and much well; yet most of all
I prized his skill in leisure and the ease
Of a life flowing full without a plan;
For most are idly busy; him I call
Thrice fortunate who knew himself to please,
Learned in those arts that make a gentleman.

Nor deem he lived unto himself alone;
His was the public spirit of his sire,
And in those eyes, soft with domestic fire,
A quenchless light of fiercer temper shone
What time about the world our shame was blown

On every wind ; his soul would not conspire
With selfish men to soothe the mob's desire,
Veiling with garlands Moloch's bloody stone ;
The high-bred instincts of a better day
Ruled in his blood, when to be citizen
Rang Roman yet, and a Free People's sway
Was not the exchequer of impoverished men,
Nor statesmanship with loaded votes to play,
Nor public office a tramp's boozing ken.

# AUTHOR'S PREFACE

TO THE ORIGINAL EDITION OF WENSLEY.

---

AS the last sheets of this work were passing through the press, my friend in Boston, who is kind enough to read the proofs for me, was asked by the competent authorities of the printing-office for the preface. Now, it had never occurred to me to write a preface; and I do not believe I should ever have thought of it, had it not been for this official reminder. But, when I came to think the matter over, it seemed to me quite likely that the "gentle readers and still gentler purchasers" (may their name be Legion!) might possibly marvel within themselves why I should have thought it worth my while and theirs to confide to them the passages of my life herein recorded. So perhaps, as it has been put into my head, I may as well tell just how it all came to pass.

I am sure, if anybody wonders at finding himself (or herself) the depositary of personal confidences on my part, I am much more astonished to find myself making them. It fell out on this wise. In the early part of August, 1852, while the monthly bearing the superscription of Mr. Putnam, 10 Park Place, New York, was as yet only in supposition, a gentleman now prominently connected with the management of that excellent periodical chanced to be my guest for a while. An accident which befell him while on a pedestrian tour among the Appalachians, the particulars of which are immaterial to my present purpose, though sufficiently interesting in themselves, obliged him to remain for some time under my roof. The many who enjoy his acquaintanceship will think it a very natural consequence of this adventure that he should have made me a friend; while the few who possess mine will esteem it a very odd one that he should have made me an author. But so it was.

And thus it was. Confiding to me the project of the intended magazine, he kindly invited me to contribute something for its pages. Now, I had always wished to leave behind me some sketch, however imperfect, in the lack of a more skilful limner, of my revered and beloved friend Mr. Bulkley; and here seemed to be the occasion and the repository offered ready to my hand. So in due time I wrote, and forwarded to New York, the substance of what the reader will find in the first two chapters of the book before him; that is, if he have not already read the book on the supposition that he had laid hold of a novel (a species of literature which I have no wish, as there is certainly no occasion, to encourage), and now turned back to the preface last of all, as Sir Walter Scott tells us is the way with that class of students, to find out what the author would be at.

The kindness with which this outline was welcomed, and the friendly encouragement I received to fill it up, induced me to enlarge my canvas, and to paint in the other figures that seemed likely to illustrate my main design. It was throughout my purpose to have Mr. Bulkley the central figure of the group, and to make him the chief object of observation and interest. I say thus much to excuse myself to those readers who object to the appearance of egotism, which is inseparable from the autobiographic form which my narrative naturally assumed. I say *naturally*, because it seems to me more simple to recount any passages in which one took a part one's self in the first person rather than in the third; though, to be sure, there are illustrious examples to the contrary—as Julius Cæsar of Rome, and Major-General Heath of Massachusetts, in their respective Commentaries. The first of these military authors says, "Cæsar did so and so;" and the other, "This being the opinion of our general, he did this and that." But, as I was never suspected of being a hero, I prefer the more plain and straightforward form of speech, which, if it savor more of vanity (which I doubt) than the other, at least smacks less of affectation, which is worse yet.

Thus it was that my narration grew up to its present bulk, and extended itself through all the numbers of a whole volume of Putnam, instead of occupying a modest corner of one. After it had run its race in that arena, I supposed that there was an end of the whole thing; when, one day a while ago, I received a letter from the eminent publishers, Messrs. TICKNOR AND FIELDS of Boston, proposing to print it in book-form. At first I could account for the proposition only on the hypothesis that that respectable firm had been seized with a sudden paroxysm of insanity — a theory rendered the more probable by the accounts the Boston newspapers were then giving of the untimely raging of the dogstar in those latitudes, driving great numbers even of the canine race out of their wits. But finding, on inquiry, that no commission of lunacy had as yet been issued against those worthy gentlemen, I was prevailed upon to yield my opinion to theirs, and to consent to their proposal, the rather that it included inducements which no true-born, well-brought-up, and intelligent American citizen could find it in his heart to resist.

This is the way by which Wensley has come into the hands of the reader in its present shape. I can hardly help laughing to see myself in such relations with the public, after so many years of absolute retirement. But then, to be sure, it is very likely that the critics, should they get hold of me, will make me laugh the other side of my mouth. If my publishers were indeed in the rabid condition above suggested, when they proposed giving it this form and pressure, I must hope, for their sake merely, that they may suceeed in *biting* uncounted multitudes throughout the country. But if they should not, and they should find that they have made a loss by the operation, the responsibility as well as the loss will be theirs alone. I never asked them to undertake it. But should the public, which I acknowledge as the tribunal of the last appeal, in passing upon my part of the matter before them, pronounce judgment against it, I shall bow reverently to the decree; and all that I shall have to say in mitigation of sentence, and extenuation of my fault, will be expressed in the formulas of the ancient pleas of the nursery and the schoolroom: "I did not mean to do it; I am sorry for it; and I will never do so again."

St. Philipsburgh, Monongahela County,
    Penn., April 1, 1854.

# CONTENTS.

|  | PAGE |
|---|---|
| Editor's Preface | iii |
| Bankside, by James Russell Lowell | v |
| Author's Preface | ix |
| Wensley | 3 |
| Mount Verney | 279 |
| Who Paid for the Prima Donna? | 321 |

# WENSLEY.

1

# WENSLEY:

## A STORY WITHOUT A MORAL.

---

### CHAPTER I.

#### HOW I CAME TO GO TO WENSLEY.

I BELIEVE I have a natural affinity — it may be only an elective one — for odd people. At any rate, allowing for my limited opportunities, it has been my hap to fall in with my share of them during the time past of my pilgrimage. And I began betimes too. I dare say not many of my readers ever heard of the Rev. Mr. Adrian Bulkley of Wensley, in Massachusetts; and yet I will make bold to assure them that they have not had many acquaintances better worth knowing than he; or, if they have, their luck has been more than mine. It is a thousand pities that he had not fallen in the way of Charles Lamb or De Quincey. They, or Hawthorne, would have delighted in making him immortal. But for the lack of a sacred bard he must needs be forgotten, like the heroes that lived before Agamemnon, and be as if he had never been. Possibly his name may yet be one of the household words of the little inland town over which he predominated for so many years; and perhaps the genial eccentricities of his life and speech may still make the staple of a winter's tale round a farmer's fireside there. But, beyond these narrow bounds and the not much wider sphere of his clerical exchanges, he was but little known while he lived; and even within them his memory must, by the natural laws of decay, be gradually mouldering away, along with his dust in the Minister's Tomb, out of men's minds. So that it will not be many years before his name will survive only in the homely annals of the parish records, on the tablet lately erected by the Wensley Sewing Circle to the deceased ministers of the town, and in the triennial catalogue of Harvard College.

I well remember my first sight of him. And well I may; for it was connected with a little incident in my life such as usually makes a deep impression on any ingenuous youth whom it befalls. Not to mince the matter, the government of the college charged with my education were misled by a train of untoward circumstances to the conclusion that a residence of some months in a rural district, remote from the temptations incident to academic life, would be at once beneficial to me, and of good example, by way of warning, to the rest of the university. I need hardly say to any one who knew me at that time, or who enjoys that advantage now, that they were entirely mistaken, and rested their conclusions upon very erroneous premises. The facts were these: there was at that time a sodality, or voluntary association of youth for mutual improvement, the object of which was to combine abstract with practical science. Their purpose was to imitate, at a humble distance, the example of the divine Socrates, and to call philosophy down from heaven to minister to the necessities of man. They delighted in nicely observing the effects of fire, for instance, on certain animal and vegetable substances. They curiously watched the chemical changes resulting from the mixture of divers liquids one with another. And they speculated profoundly on the laws of pneumatics, whereby, through the agency of fire at the one end and of a gentle suction at the other, a desiccated vegetable convolution could be returned to its original elements of air and earth in the form of smoke and ashes, — *pulvis et umbra*, as Horace would have said touching it, had he not died before the sight.

This harmless, not to say praiseworthy, fraternity appropriately denominated themselves "the Deipnosophoi," or supper philosophers, — a term which very aptly described the practical nature of their scientific pursuits. It did sometimes happen to them, as it hath to the ardent followers of science in all times, that they pursued their investigations a little too far, and that occasionally the supper was rather too much for the philosophy. It was the gloss of the rulers of the university, that the night which was the immediate cause of my introduction to Mr. Bulkley was one of these exceptional occasions. I neither admit nor deny the imputation. It was affirmed on behalf of the prosecution that songs of a lively character, interspersed with laughter of a vociferous nature and an occasional shout of triumph, disturbed the stillness of the night. It did also happen that the windows of an unpopular tutor (since a very eminent literary and public man) were broken in a most emphatic and unqualified manner that particular night. But I defy the world to the proof that any of our party had anything to do with that. But, suppose both these charges could have been substantiated, I appeal to every impartial and well-regulated mind whether any inference could be drawn from them to the disadvantage of young votaries of science, who could not refrain from seizing a favorable moment for testing the principles of acoustics, or were unable to resist an eminently tempting opportunity to reduce to practice the laws governing projectiles. These liberal views, unfortunately, did not inspire the proctors when they gave hot chase to our party, who, resorting to the laws regulating muscular locomotion with great energy, all made their escape, with the exception of my unlucky self. But I, after practically experiencing the law of the resistance of matter by striking my foot against a stone, exemplified that of gravitation by measuring my length on my mother earth.

Of course there was no use of resistance or disguise

when the enemy had me at such a deadly advantage. Wellington, Napoleon, General Taylor himself, would have surrendered under such circumstances. I was seized and identified, and then ordered to go to my rooms. This was quite superfluous, as I had no intention of going anywhere else. So I went thither, cursing my ill luck, and having a particularly ill opinion of supper-eating combined with philosophy. Nor did this unfortunate conjunction rise in my estimation when I was summoned before the college government in full conclave the next morning, to answer for the deeds done the night before. Honest old souls! Not one of them left! I hated some of them then, but I think tenderly and reverently of them all now. Of course I admitted what could not be denied, but resolutely refused to give any information that should implicate any one else. So I was thought to have got off very easily when the President sent for me soon after, and read to me my credentials (then popularly known as my *walking-ticket*), stating that the government, in consideration of Osborne's having assisted at a festive entertainment on such a night, sentenced him to be suspended for nine months, to pass the same under the charge of the Rev. Adrian Bulkley of Wensley.

After a little advice, given in the kindly and friendly tone which has given him a place in the hearts of all his academic sons, the President dismissed me with "a merry twinkle in his eye," as if he did not regard me as a sinner above all others, enjoining it upon me to leave town within an hour. Having expected this, and having escaped much better than I had feared, a chum of mine drove me to Boston as fast as Read's best horse could carry us. Here I reported my misfortune to my guardian (having been an orphan since infancy); and after receiving, like Don Juan, "a lecture and some money," I took my place on the top of the stage-coach which passed through Wensley on its way to Haverford, and found myself, about five o'clock on a fine afternoon in June, whirling up to the door of Grimes's tavern, well renowned in all the region round about for flip, the loggerhead whereof never grew cold.

Old Grimes — I beg his pardon, I mean Major Grimes — squinted a welcome to me out of his one eye, while his copper nose glowed with anticipated hospitality as he assisted me to descend from my elevation. But his hopes of immediate advantage from my advent were dampened by my inquiring, as soon as I had complied with the custom of the time, and done my best to qualify the coachman for breaking the necks of the travellers I left behind me, by a stiff glass of toddy, — by my inquiring, I say, for the house of the Rev. Mr. Bulkley.

"Mr. Bulkley!" repeated the Major, wiping his toddy-stick as he spoke, and laying it reverently aside for the next occasion, sure soon to recur; "you are a relation of his, perhaps, sir?"

"None whatever, that I know of," was my curt response.

"Ah, only an acquaintance, then?" persisted the gallant toddy mixer.

"Never saw him in my life," said I.

"Only know him by reputation?" suggested the Major.

"Never heard of his existence till this morning," I returned rather snappishly; "but for all that I wish to see him, and shall be obliged to you if you will tell me where he lives."

"Oh, I understand," drawled out mine host, cocking his eye afresh at me with an indescribably knowing leer, which was also indescribably provoking, "now I understand it all. When did you leave Cambridge, sir?"

"Cambridge be d——d!" said I in my haste (I do not justify this summary disposition of that ancient seat of learning, but historical accuracy compels me to record that this was the precise formula I made use of): "is it any business of yours, I should like to know, where I came from? What I want of you is to know where I'm to go."

"Not the least business of mine in the world," responded my interrogator with the most quiet equanimity, still regarding me out of the corner of his eye with an expression in which fun and toddy seemed to be mixed half and half; "but I have directed several young gentlemen to Priest Bulkley's in my time, though it is a good while since the last one. I know how they look, sir: there's no mistaking 'em." And he chuckled till I felt inclined to close up the one organ he had left for making such observations on the rising generation under difficulties. But, restraining my wrath, I contented myself with saying, —

"I should like to know what the devil you have to do with my affairs, sir. If you can answer my question without any more impertinence, answer it; if not, I will try and find my way by myself."

"Oh, I beg your pardon, sir," replied the Yankee Boniface; "I meant no offence. I know that young gentlemen will get into scrapes, sir; though it seems to me that the beauty of a scholar is to keep out of the scrapes, sir. Not a bad scrape, I hope, sir?"

"Go to the devil!" I bounced out in a towering passion, and at the same time bounced out of the tavern-door to find my own way. But I soon heard the inquiring Major hobbling after me; for he was damaged in one leg as well as in his visual orb.

"I say, sir," he called out after me,— "I say, sir, don't be mad with a fellow. I meant no harm. Why, Judge Waldo, and Parson Tisdale, and General Shaw, and half a dozen others I could tell you of, have been sent to the old priest since I have lived here, just as you are now, and nobody thinks any the worse of 'em for it. Halloo, sir!" he exclaimed, seeing me only hurry on the faster to get out of the reach of the catalogue of my illustrious predecessors, — "halloo, sir! You ain't going the right way! You'll bring up at old Dr. Fitch's, in Southfield, instead of Priest Bulkley's, the way you're going. But perhaps he'd do just as well."

This brought me up standing; and I soon put my course about, and returned to the tavern-door, the Major talking all the while without stopping to draw breath, or even to spit. When at the door, summoning all the dignity of incensed nineteen into my face, I said, —

"Now, sir, I will thank you to put me in my way without any more words."

"Can't be done without 'em, sir," replied my imperturbable tormentor; "must use 'em, unless I go along with you. Perhaps I had better."

"Tell me the way, if you can, and be hanged to you!" I exclaimed in a rage. "I want none of your company. I've had enough of it already."

"Oh, very well," replied the placable man of war with perfect good-humor; "you will just keep straight on through the village till you come to the meeting-house; and the priest's house is the third beyond it, on your left hand, just at the head of the road."

"And why could you not have told me this an hour ago?" said I, setting off at a round pace, the Major sending his winged words after me as long as I was within hearing, and I dare say a good while longer.

"You'll find the parson at home, sir. I saw him ride by just before you came; and if his old horse has n't fell to pieces, he's to home by this time. I'll take good care of your trunk, sir. The priest'll send black Jasp after it for you. Hope you'll give me a call, sir. Best of wine and spirits. No such flip in the country, sir, nor punch, neither. Priest Bulkley tries to keep his scholars away from me; but it's of no use, sir. They will come. And so will you, I hope, sir," etc.

And, when I turned my head to transfix the loquacious sinner with a Parthian look of indignant contempt, I saw him laughing with all his might as he halted back to his dominions. I felt very much as if I should have liked to kill him just then; but we became very good friends before long. Perhaps there was more danger of his killing me.

So I passed on through the main street of the village, which, indeed, was no street at all, but a country road sprinkled with farm-houses, none of which seemed to have been built since the old French war, with fine old elms and buttonwood-trees in front of most of them. Near the bridge which spanned the pretty little Quasheen, which ran through the town, was the grocer's shop, which also contained the post-office, from which favorite retreat and the bench in front of it stared forth whatever loungers the village could boast; but in sooth they were not many, and were mostly made so by the potent spirits of which Major Grimes had boasted himself. But in those days a certain allowance of topers was thought as necessary a result of the institutions of New England, in every town, as a due proportion of militia officers or of church-members.

Just over the bridge on the other side of the way, " under a spreading chestnut-tree," stood the village smithy, which was about the only other place that showed signs of animation, with its glowing forge, flying sparks, regular sharp strokes that made the anvil quiver, and with the farmers waiting with their horses and wagons for their turn of the Cyclopean art. Still, so rare was the sight of a stranger that for a moment even the anvil had rest, and the weary lungs of the bellows ceased to fan, like the breath of a mischief-maker, fires that were hot enough before into tenfold fury, while they all took a good look at me, and then, no doubt, discussed all the possibilities of my personal identity and antecedents, substantially very much as such phenomena are treated in the bow-windows of English clubs or the smoking-rooms of American hotels.

I soon came to the meeting-house, leaving which on my left hand, I approached, much faster than I liked, my destination. The parsonage was full in sight of the meeting-house; but though, as the Major had informed me, there were but two houses between them, it was a good third of a mile to it. The road taking a bend just there, the ministers had apparently taken it up as a good raking position, commanding the church and the green about it, and thus serving as a sort of outpost, or tower of observation, appurtenant to the walls of their Zion. I confess that I did not regard the edifice before me with any violent emotions of pleasure. To be delivered up for nine mortal months to the tender mercies of a Calvinistic minister of the very straitest sect (for such I had ascertained him to be), seemed rather a severe retribution for one night of supping philosophy. But it is in vain to contend with inexorable fate. I strode on, resolving to face mine with the best grace I could. But, as often happens, I found the frown which I had dreaded turn into a most attractive smile. For this acquaintance thus forced upon me, and thus unpromising in anticipation, proved one of the chiefest pleasures of my youth and early manhood, and ended in a friendship which lasted as long as his life, and which certainly was not buried with him. But I am now close upon him, and will introduce him to the reader as soon as I have made his acquaintance myself. A new chapter, however, is the least compliment I can pay to either party.

## CHAPTER II.

### THE MINISTER AND HIS MAN.

THE parsonage was merely a plain, unpainted farm-house some hundred and fifty years old, with its roof sloping to the ground behind, and overgrown with moss. The grass grew green up to the broad doorstone, which was divided from the high-road by no fence. The house was overshadowed by a magnificent elm, which had taken root apparently before Columbus had begun to dream of a western passage to the India of Marco Polo and Sir John Mandeville. On a rough seat which ran round this tree sat a gentleman, who, I knew at the first glance, must be my fate for nine months at least. As I approached near enough to give him assurance that my visit was meant for him, he laid aside the pipe with which he was solacing himself, and rose to receive me. He advanced, erect and a little formal, but with an air of one that had seen the world, for which I was not prepared, as I knew nothing of his history. His dress, I am bound to say, bore no marks of inordinate care, and possibly might have been the better for a judicious application of needle and thread in some of its departments. But, for all that, he had eminently the look of a gentleman of the old school.

The hat which he raised when I approached was, I regret to say, one of the profane round abominations which came in with the French Revolution, and which still deform the heads of the nineteenth century. And it was his own white hair (for he was then near seventy) that it covered.

His cocked hat, not long relinquished, yet hung behind the study-door; and his wig, which had anticipated his hat by some years in its flight from before the innovating spirit of the age, still stood in its box on the bookcase to your right as you faced the fireplace. His knee-breeches, I rejoice to say, he lived in to the last — and for that matter died in too. Later in our acquaintance, when, in spite of the difference in our ages, —

> "We talked with open heart and tongue,
> Affectionate and true,
> A pair of friends," —

Mr. Bulkley would sometimes assume, for my edification, these ancient symbols of clerical dignity, and, with his gold-headed cane in his hand, step as it were out of the middle of the last century, every inch a minister of a time when the New England clergy were, indeed, what M. Kossuth wished the United States to become, — "a power on earth.'

Upon my introducing myself, and presenting the letters introductory with which my Alma Mater had favored me, he courteously welcomed me to Wensley, and then, glancing at the document, looked at me, with a comic expression, out of the corner of his eye, over his spectacles, which he had donned for the nonce, and said, —

"A festive entertainment, eh? That's what they call 'em now, is it? Bad things, festive entertainments, Mr. Osborne."

"Oh, sir!" I interpolated, "it was quite a mistake; a very innocent affair, I assure you."

"No doubt, no doubt," responded he. "The college government is subject to error, like all human bodies; and it is rather remarkable that they have happened to be mistaken in the case of every young gentleman that they have ever sent to me. Quite a Massacre of the Innocents, I do assure you!" and he laughed so cordially and good-naturedly that I could not help joining him.

"For all that, sir," I replied, "mine was a very harmless business, as I believe you will allow when I tell you the particulars; if, indeed, you consent to receive me."

"It is a long time," he said, "since I have afforded a city of refuge to the ill-used sons of Mother Harvard, — if she may not be rather entitled to be called stepmother, an *injusta noverca*, you know, in such cases, — and I had about made up my mind to shut up my sanctuary for good. But may I ask if you are the son of the late Hon. Joseph Osborne of Boston?"

"I have the honor to be Mr. Osborne's son," I answered; "though he died before my remembrance."

"Of course he must have," Mr. Bulkley continued. "But you have a trick of his face that reminds me of him. As the country-people say in these parts, you *favor* him decidedly."

"You knew my father, then, sir?" I asked.

"Knew him? Why, my dear sir, he was my very old and very good friend. He was a year before me in college; but, for all that, we were intimates of the closest description. Ten thousand pipes have we smoked together;" and he sighed as his mind reverted to those fleeting joys. "But our friendship did not end in smoke, if it began in it," he continued, with a melancholy kind of smile: "it lasted until he died, — too soon for his friends and his country, though he had served both long and well."

My heart warmed to the old man at hearing him thus speak of my father, for whose memory I cherished the strongest admiration and reverence; and I began to feel a wish growing within me that he might accept me as an abiding guest during my term of exile. So I said, —

"I hope, then, sir, you will not refuse to receive my father's son under your roof. It would be a great satisfaction to me to live under the care of a friend of his; and I will endeavor to give you as little trouble as possible."

"It is not the trouble I am thinking of, Mr. Osborne," he replied; "but I doubt whether I can make you comfortable in my strange bachelor way of living. It suits me; but I am afraid that it may not suit a young gentleman like you."

I was proceeding to assure him that he need give

himself no uneasiness on that score, when he interrupted me with, —

"Well, sir, you will stay with me to-night at least, and to-morrow we will decide as to the rest of the time. Here, Jasper, Jasper!" he called out, clapping his hands, as the Orientals do for lack of bells.

And at the word, Jasper appeared, issuing from the front-door. He was black as ebony, and his blackness was set off by the perfect whiteness of his hair, which had scarcely a perceptible wave in it, and by the glitter of his teeth. He was a remarkably handsome old man for all his complexion. His features were more Caucasian than African, as usually seen; his nose straight, though a little thicker than the Apollo's; and his lips not larger than those of multitudes of men calling themselves white. He evidently came of a comelier race, such as travellers assure us exists in the interior of Africa, than that furnished by the Guinea coast, the southern hive from which have swarmed the involuntary emigrations of the negro race. He stood two or three inches over six feet in his stockings, and was not at all bent by his threescore and ten years. He stood firm and erect, awaiting his orders.

"Jasper," said Mr. Bulkley, "you remember Mr. Osborne, who used to come here twenty years ago?"

"Lawyer Osborne of Boston," answered Jasper, in a tone of deliberate recollection, "who got off Pomp Jaffrey from being hanged in the year three?" Mr. Bulkley nodded. "Yes, sir, I remember him."

"This young gentleman," proceeded his master, indicating me with the stem of his pipe, which he had resumed, "is his son, and will spend the night here."

"Proud to see you here, sir," replied Jasper, still remaining perfectly erect, but bringing up his hand to the military salute in the most respectful manner.

"Take your wheelbarrow, Jasper, after tea, and go and fetch Mr. Osborne's trunk from Grimes's. — You left it there, I suppose?" turning to me.

I assented, of course; and Jasper bent his whole body a few degrees in token that he understood his orders. He then faced to the right about, and marched back to the parsonage. We followed him almost immediately, and found him rearranging the tea-table to meet the rare emergency of company. This was laid in the study, the room on the left as you entered the front-door, and the only room occupied by the minister by day (he slept in the one opposite), and which was drawing-room and dining-room as well. It deserved, indeed, to be called the library; for its walls were covered with a collection of books which would be thought large for a private one even at this day of larger things. They were, like their master, of no very modern date or dress, but of sterling and various merit, — good substantial friends of all ages and of many climes. Latin, Greek, Hebrew, French, and Italian were there good store, and English down to the end of the last century. There he stopped; for, as he said, of buying as well as of making books there was no end. I remember he had never heard of Lord Byron until I introduced him to his acquaintance. And he would not like him then, in spite of my boyish enthusiasm for the Harolds, Manfreds, Laras, Conrads, and other *aliases* under which it was his lordship's pleasure to disguise himself. But down to his own time he was thoroughly well read, and a discriminating and entertaining critic, though something odd in his taste, as it was then accounted oddity. I recollect he first brought me acquainted with old Burton, and with Ben Jonson and the earlier dramatists.

Jasper soon furnished forth an ample New England tea, to which I was quite prepared to do an ample justice. But while I am discussing in imagination the excellent johnny-cake and rye-and-Indian bread, and while Jasper waits upon us with the gravity and decorum of the butler of a duke, let me pause, and dwell for a moment on the images of the two men, inseparable to my mind's eye as it glances back at those happy days. Don Quixote and Sancho Panza, Tom Jones and Partridge, Peregrine Pickle and Pipes, Roderick Random and Strap, Uncle Toby and Trim are not more one and indivisible in the general mind of English readers than are (with all reverence be it spoken) the Rev. Mr. Adrian Bulkley and Jasper, his man-of-all-work, in mine. Maid-of-all-work he might also be denominated; for he was both maid and man to the worthy minister, and performed all feminine as well as virile offices in the household and domain of his master. I do not know whether Jasper's cooking and sweeping and bed-making would have come up to the highest ideal of the more fanatical of the sect of the housekeepers. I am not quite sure whether I myself should relish their results now as I did thirty odd years ago in the undiscriminating freshness of nineteen. But they answered Mr. Bulkley's purposes; and, such being the case, I shall not stir the question of details, conceiving that they are none of the reader's business.

The fairer portion of my readers would have divined by this time, even if I had not inadvertently let the fact slip a few paragraphs ago, that Mr. Bulkley was a bachelor. But let them not condemn him too summarily or too severely for this blemish in his character; for I believe there was an excuse for it the validity of which they should admit, though I could never get at the precise facts, as it was a subject to which he would bear no allusion. It is enough to say, that, according to the unbroken tradition of Wensley, he had an early and unhappy passion for the beautiful Miss Julia Mansfield, who was the toast of every mess table during the siege of Boston. It was the old story of Crabbe's Patron over again, as far as I could gather; only that Mr. Bulkley was not so easily killed as poor poet John. He came into Mr. Mansfield's family as tutor to his youngest son, Thomas (afterwards the Colonel Mansfield who was killed by a shell, in his tent, before

Badajos) soon after leaving college; and, finding there the most lovely young woman in the province,—gay, thoughtless, coquettish, and seventeen, — is it any wonder that he found his fate there too? He did not know that she was vain, cold-hearted, and selfish (perhaps he never knew it) until the mischief was done.

It was done, however; and poor Bulkley had taken leave forever of the unkind Julia and of his dream of happiness, and was finding what consolation he might in the pursuit of divinity (a very different mistress) before the war broke out. At the evacuation, Miss Julia accompanied her father (who, all the world knows, was one of Governor Hutchinson's mandamus councillors) into exile; and she married, not long afterwards, Colonel Ferguson, the receiver-general of Jamaica. It was not a well-assorted marriage, and its history is not one that I care to record. The lovers of Old-World scandals can mouse out the details from the contemporary chronicles of such matters for themselves, as I did, if they must know them. But the old Wensley people used to say that the minister was plunged into a deeper dejection by the news, in the year eighty-seven, of the duel in which her husband shot Sir James Carlton on her account, near Spanishtown, than even at that of her death, which arrived soon afterwards. He seemed to feel it as a personal dishonor. It was a cruel iconoclasm,—that shot, which broke in pieces the idol he had privily worshipped in the secret places of his heart for so many melancholy years.

After Jasper had cleared away the tea-things, Mr. Bulkley and I sat by the window, and entered into a long conversation, which I have not time to record, though I remember a great deal of it. We began with the college and the latest news therefrom, including, of course, my own *escapade*, which my new Mentor did not seem to look upon as a crime of the blackest dye. He laughed merrily at the details I gave him of my adventure, which I did, unconsciously, with as much freedom as if I were talking with one of my own contemporaries. There was that about this gentleman which put one at perfect ease with him on the first acquaintance, and there was nothing in his tone or manner which asserted his claims as a superior by virtue of age and experience. Of course, as in duty bound, he stood by the college government as touching the necessity of inflicting the discipline they did, having had the misfortune to make the unlucky discovery. But he evidently rather *cottoned* (to use a Fanny Kembleism) to the Deipnosophoi, and would have thought it good luck, and no great harm, if they had all escaped with a whole skin, even if some of them should have done it with a *full* one. The temperance movement had not, at that time, begun to play the mischief with the old drinking usages of New England; and a slight convivial exuberance occasionally was looked upon as no very heinous offence even by the graver classes of society.

Mr. Bulkley belonged to a grave class of society, certainly; but he was no very grave member of it when he unbent himself from the serious business of his profession. A merrier man "within the limit of becoming mirth," one does not often talk withal in one's journey through this working-day world. I think he had the finest voice for a story (and, like most of his cloth at that time, he abounded in them) that I ever heard. It was as good fun as seeing Mathews to hear him tell one. And then his laugh! He did indeed "laugh the heart's laugh," before which no blue devils, however resolute, could hold their ground. From this latest piece of college history he made a transition to his own times, and told many piquant anecdotes concerning the customs of those times and the adventures of men afterwards famous. The hardest sort of drinking seemed to have been quite the general rule of his day; and his stories showed that some advances had been made in refinement, at least, between his time and mine. The Deipnosophoi, I am happy to say, could furnish no parallels to some of the instances he related of the potatory achievements of our grandfathers. I had begun a paragraph to tell of some of them; but, on the whole, I believe I will not "draw their frailties from their dread abode." Let one brief specimen, by no means one of the best or the most characteristic, suffice.

"I remember poor Tom Frost," said he, "whom you must have heard of. He turned Democrat; and

Jefferson sent him consul to Tripoli, where he died of the plague." I intimated that I had heard him mentioned; and Mr. Bulkley continued, "I remember, one Commencement Day, he fell into the company of a set of jolly blades, — being, in general, a very steady-going fellow, — and got most undeniably and unequivocally drunk. It was with some difficulty that he was put to bed; but at last he was fairly between the sheets, and we thought he was disposed of for the night. But we had not been gone long, when we heard a heavy sound in his chamber, and, hastening thither, found that he had fallen out of bed. After replacing him, one of his friends remonstrated pretty sharply with him for giving us this new trouble. 'Why, I'll tell you how it was, fellows,' said poor Tom with drunken gravity; 'it was not my fault. I held on to the cursed bed as long as it could be done. For, as soon as you had gone out, it began to whirl round one way, and then it spun round the other; and then the head of the bed was lifted up to the ceiling, and then the foot; and then it rocked from one side to the other like a raving-distracted cradle. And I held on to it like a good fellow. It could n't shake me out, let it do its worst. But, when the d——d thing turned upside down, the devil himself could hold on no longer, and no more could I!'" And the minister laughed his musical laugh till all rang again.

"Your friend," said I, "certainly fulfilled the conditions laid down by an English Cantab in Blackwood lately, who says that he thinks it most unfair and ungenerous to call a man drunk as long as he can hold on by the sheets. But, if he will persist in tumbling out of bed as fast as you put him into it, then the most candid must admit that it is no abuse of language or of charity to pronounce him drunk."

Mr. Bulkley laughed, and the conversation took a new departure, and ranged far and wide over books and politics, and Old-World family histories, until the late summer evening closed in about us. After it grew dark, Jasper entered, holding one of his own dips in his hand, with which he made a sort of military salute to me, saying, "Your trunk is in your chamber, sir," and then, placing his candle on a stand near the opposite window (for the study filled the entire breadth of the house, having windows on the two sides), and taking a large folio from a lower shelf, put on his heavy iron-bound spectacles, and set himself diligently to read it. It was evident, from the perfect simplicity with which it was done, that it was nothing out of the common course of events; but it took all my scanty stock of good breeding to conceal the astonishment I felt at such a phenomenon. Had the minister's old horse (which, like Yorick's, was "full brother to Rozinante, as far as similitude congenial could make him") walked in from the stable, and squatted himself on his haunches, like a Houyhnhm, beside me, I could not have been more taken aback. I fully assented to the general reputation which pronounced Parson Bulkley a very odd man.

Poor Jasper read, with the help of his forefinger and with a laborious murmur of the lips, like one whose reading had not "come by nature," but by hard work, after he was grown up; and I had a suspicion that this lecture was rather for my edification than for his own, though, when I discovered afterwards that it was a volume of "Hakluyt's Voyages" he was encountering, I was somewhat shaken in it. There was a comical expression in Mr. Bulkley's eye, too, which showed that he was not without the same surmise. We talked on, without regarding Jasper's presence, until nine o'clock, when the minister read a chapter in the Bible, and prayed, according to the ancient custom of New England. After prayers, Jasper put up his book, and took himself and his dip off to bed, making us a military salute at the door by way of good-night.

When he was gone, and Mr. Bulkley had lighted the pipe, which was to wind up the labors of the day, he said to me, —

"I noticed that you were a little surprised at seeing Jasper make himself so much at home here."

I made a dubious sort of a bow, hardly knowing whether I should acknowledge such a feeling about a matter which was clearly none of my business.

"It was natural enough," he continued, "that you should have wondered at it. But Jasper and I have slept too many years under the same tent for me to mind having him in the same room with me when he has done his work."

"Under the same tent, sir?" I repeated interrogatively.

"Certainly," he replied. "He has never left me since he came to my rescue at Brandywine, when I was lying flat on the field with an ounce of lead in me, which, for that matter, I carry about with me still. The bayonet was raised that would have finished the business, had not Jasper despatched the grenadier that stood over me, and carried me off on his back to the rear."

"So you served in the Revolutionary War, sir?" I exclaimed. "Were you long in the service?"

"Pretty well," he answered, smiling. "I began at Lexington, and ended at Yorktown. I don't know that any one can say more than that. You see that old firelock," he continued, pointing to a fowling-piece of formidable length and venerable age, which was crossed over the fireplace with a silver-hilted sword: "that was the gun with which I left Parson Sanborne's study for Lexington on the morning of the 19th of April, and the old sword is one I picked up on the Boston road that day, and wore for the next seven years."

"In what capacity did you serve, sir?" I inquired, a little bewildered by this new flood of ideas.

"Why, I began as chaplain," he replied. "But as there was more need of the arm of flesh, and as there was an especial lack of educated men for officers, I took a commission from General Washington; and I ended as a captain, doing the duty of brigade-major.

My health was not firm at that time, and I thought a campaign would do me good; and, being once in for it, I found it hard to break off, and so kept on to the end."

"And Jasper?" I suggested.

"Oh, Jasper was born the slave of Colonel Cuyler of New Jersey, who emancipated him on his consenting to enlist, and afterwards employed him as his servant, a soldier being allowed to every officer, for that purpose. Colonel Cuyler dying of a fever consequent on the exposures of the campaign in the Jerseys, Jasper remained in the ranks until he was taken by me, at his request, as my servant. It was of some advantage to him in the way of mounting guard and the regular drills; though he was still on the rolls, and required to return to active duty whenever in the neighborhood of the enemy."

"And he has been with you ever since?" I inquired.

"Ever since," he replied. "And now I think it would be rather hard to oblige him to mope by himself in his kitchen when he has done his day's work. His greatest pleasure is to sit in the corner of my fireplace in winter, and watch me as I read or write. He does not come so regularly in summer; but he comes when he pleases, and I think I should be a beast to deny so cheap a pleasure to my old companion-in-arms and most faithful friend. At any rate, I do not intend doing so. Indeed, in my solitude, his presence in the long winter evenings, though not society, is human companionship, and I am confident I am the better for it."

I cordially expressed my concurrence of opinion on all these points; and then Mr. Bulkley, knocking out the last ashes of his pipe (he never lapsed into the later heresy of cigars), laid it in its place, and proposed to show me the way to my chamber. This done, he shook hands with me as he bade me goodnight; and I lay awake for some time after I had gone to bed, ruminating over the revolution which the last fifteen minutes had wrought in my first ideas of the minister and his man.

## CHAPTER III.

#### THE TORY AND HIS DAUGHTER.

"PRAYER-BELL rung yet, Charley?" said I, gaping fearfully, the next morning, awakened by hearing somebody putting down my shoes by my bedside, and catching a glimpse of a black face through my half-shut eyes. "Not the second bell, I hope."

"It's me, sir; it's Jasper," said that worthy functionary, as he moved softly towards the door. "The young college gentlemen always ask me that the first morning, sir. We don't ring no bell, sir; but master breakfasts at six, and has prayers afterwards. It's just five, now, sir."

And the truth streamed in upon me, with the sun through the uncurtained windows, that I was an exile from college; that this was Wensley, and not Cambridge; and that the sable form which had just quietly vanished was a revolutionary hero, and not Charley Richmond, — a cadet of an ancient family of color which had served for several generations the wealthier sort of students in the capacity of what the English Cantabs call a *gyp*, and the Oxonians a *scout;* which Mr. Thackeray, when he rolled the two single universities into one as Oxbridge, also amalgamated into a *skip*.

As I had an hour before me, there was no occasion for hurrying myself: so I lay still, and revolved in my mind the current chapter of my history. A quarter of an hour was all that was thought necessary in those good old days, before shower-baths and hair gloves, for anybody's toilet: so I had time enough and to spare. Bless my soul, I must have a good hour and a half to get myself up for the day now! These hygienic and physiological new lights have a great deal of other people's time to answer for. I lay still; and, as I lay, that mysterious homesick feeling which always comes over me (I wonder whether it does over other people) the first time I wake in a strange place took full possession of me. I had left no home; my parents were both dead; I had neither brother nor sister; I hated college, or fancied I did, and had just as much business to be in Wensley as anywhere else: and yet I felt the strongest disposition to cry at finding myself there. And, if I did actually cry, men do more unmanly things than that, and pretend they are not ashamed of themselves, every day of their lives. Perhaps the excitement of finding myself in a new place, quickening the flow of my ideas, brought these facts, or the emotions they naturally excite, with a fresh shock to my mind; and surely they were enough to make anybody cry.

But I am no metaphysician, and shall make no

attempt to puzzle other people by trying to explain what I do not understand myself. But such is the psychological fact, whether it belongs to my special idiosyncrasy or not. I never felt the emotion more strongly than I did, years afterwards, the first morning I opened my eyes in London, and, casting them out of the window of my chamber on the roof of the Adelphi, saw the great dome of St. Paul's rising, as it were, out of a surging sea of fog, and heard the ceaseless rush and roar of life chafing in the channels far beneath me. It was a moment which I had been looking forward to for long years, as the Christian pilgrim to that of the first glimpse of the holy sepulchre, or the Mussulman to the supreme instant that gives him the vision of the tomb of the Prophet. I had reached "the Mecca of *my* mind," and yet I thought of everything rather than of it. I have heard it said, that, when a man is drowning, the whole of his past life rushes before his dying eyes in an instantaneous phantasmagoria. Well, it seemed as if my plunge into the boiling ocean of London worked the same miracle with me. The roar of its tide was in my ears; but I heard it not. All of my past life, especially every sad and tender image, came streaming through my mind in a flash of thought, and oppressed me with a bitter pang of homesickness — Heaven knows why. So it was, though I don't pretend to expound the philosophy of it. But then, as it has nothing in particular to do with my story, it is of the less consequence.

But the bluest of devils cannot long withstand the genial influences of early sunlight and of youth,— that early sunlight of life, God bless it! though the benediction is quite superfluous, for God *will* bless it whether or no; and mine vanished before their potent exorcism by the time I was half dressed. And by the time my toilet was finished I felt no more longing to hear the cracked voice of the chapel-bell, or the stamping to and fro over my head, and the scuffling of feet backwards and forwards in the entry and on the college-stairs,— the familiar sounds which I had yearned for when I first awoke, — and was well content to accept in their stead the riotous vivacity of the birds and the undertoned hum of the insects in the trees on both sides of my chamber. For it filled the entire breadth of the house, and it was not very broad, for all that, and had two windows on one side, and one on the other; the one behind occupying a deep cut into the sloping roof, and looking directly into the thick boughs of a lime-tree buzzing with insect life. The walls were plastered and white-washed; a thick beam ran lengthwise through the ceiling; and so queer was the shape of the room from the obliquities of the roof, that it would have puzzled a better mathematician than I was to calculate its contents. There was a strip of carpet by the bedside, the floor (the face of whose scenery was of a rather *rolling* character) being otherwise bare. A few wooden chairs and a pine table made up the furniture. But what cared I for those things? God made us men, before we made ourselves upholsterers; and I had not yet passed into the factitious and out of the natural state.

"Well, Mr. Osborne," said Mr. Bulkley as we sat at breakfast, "do you like your quarters well enough still to wish to remain in them?"

"I like both my quarters and my company, sir," I replied, "and should be very sorry should you determine not to take me."

"And that would be a pity," he said, — "would it not be, Jasper?" Jasper inclined his assent. "In fact," the minister went on, "Jasper has been interceding for you; and the prime minister, you know, does what he likes at court; and I suppose I must let him have his way."

"I am greatly indebted to him for his interest," said I, bowing with mock gravity towards Jasper, "and shall endeavor to show myself worthy of his good opinion."

The minister smiled; but his man took it all in perfectly good faith, and with serious grace acknowledged my little speech with his military salute as he stood firm and erect behind his master's chair.

"Jasper having given his sanction to your remaining," Mr. Bulkley resumed, "and you continuing to wish it after having a taste of our bachelor's way of life, I suppose I may as well acknowledge to having no particular objection to it myself: so we will consider that as arranged, if you please." And we shook hands across the table to close the bargain. Though what he said about Jasper's consent was spoken jestingly, yet I found afterwards that it was literally true that he would not have received me, had Jasper disliked the plan.

"As to-day is Saturday," the minister proceeded, "we will defer our plans of study until Monday. Saturday is my working-day, and shall be your holiday. Perhaps you would like to get a little acquainted with the Siberia to which you have been banished. Or you may use my study just as if I were not here; or establish yourself in your own chamber, as you like. We dine at twelve, and drink tea at six; at which hours you will report yourself, if you please."

After which, Jasper brought the great Bible, and we had prayers; which done, I whiled away the time as best I could with old books and cigars, and in sauntering round the premises in quest of amusement, which did not seem very easy to be found, till dinner-time. After dinner, as the sun was a little mitigated by clouds, I set forth upon a voyage of discovery into the unknown regions round about. I passed through the village, where my apparition again caused a general suspension of labor, and variation of idleness, as long as I was in sight. So I took myself out of sight as speedily as possible, turning into the road to your right just after you have crossed the Quasheen, and winding along its banks. It was a most charming walk, solitary, shady, with glimpses of rich pastures dotted with cattle by the water-side.

There was no discordant jar of machinery. The innocent little stream had not yet been compelled by the genius of the lamp or of the ring to help build the palaces of our New England Aladdins; it yet ran sparkling and dimpling to the sea, without having to buffet with mill-wheels, and to fling itself headlong, as it fled, over injurious dams in desperate waterfalls. Cows stood up to the middle in its shady little bays; ducks led out their flotilla of ducklings upon its waters; and swallows dipped in it with none to molest, or make them afraid. It was a delicious walk, as I said before.

Here and there along the road was a farm-house of the oldest description of New England rustic architecture, but not many of them. It seemed as if this little town were a nook which the tide of improvement, as we are pleased to call it, had swept round, and left it overlooked in its haste, leaving it just as it was a century before. Nor was this effect diminished by a glance I got at a house, having decidedly the look of a gentleman's seat, off at my left; for such were always sprinkled over the face of the New England landscape. It was a square wooden house, having a porch in front, with seats on either side, flaunting with honeysuckles, as I could see at that distance, with windows in the roof, and an ornamental balustrade running round it. The ground sloped up to the house, and, being fine mowing-land, had as lawnish a look as land can well have in our climate. A few aboriginal oaks stood singly here and there; and there were clusters of shrubbery near the house, but apparently kept low for the benefit of the prospect. Beyond the house it seemed as if there was an old-fashioned avenue of elms running down the other side of the hill to parts unknown. I passed about a mile and a half farther, pondering as to who could be its inhabitants, but meeting no one of whom I could make the inquiry.

But when I had gone, by my estimation, about three miles from the village, the clouds, which had at first invited me to go out, now more strongly urged me to go back. They rolled up blacker and thicker, and seemed almost to touch the tops of the trees, among which the road sometimes wound. There was evidently a thunder-shower altogether too near at hand for my advantage: so I set my face homewards, and made what speed I could, though with little hope of escape. I came, however, in sight of the capital mansion and messuage (as an auctioneer might say) just described, before the critical moment arrived. Still I hurried on, and soon found there were other people in haste besides myself; for just then I heard the sound of hoofs behind me, and an elderly gentleman and a young lady on horseback galloped past me. As they passed, they gave a glance of surprise at me, and presently reined up, and had evidently a brief exchange of words; or rather the gentleman said something to his companion, and I could see that the tassel of her riding-cap waved an affirmative. He then turned his horse's head towards me, and, putting spurs to his sides, pulled up before me in an instant.

"Young gentleman," said he, touching his hat as I raised mine, "there is a violent shower at hand. Let me beg you to take shelter in my house there," indicating the capital mansion aforesaid with his riding-whip. "Pray do not hesitate, for I feel the first drops already. By striking across that field, you will be at the door nearly as soon as we."

He touched his hat again, and, wheeling round, galloped off, and he and his companion were the next instant hid from my sight by a turn of the road. I was a bashful boy, and felt as awkwardly as such animals are apt to do in an emergency like this. But still I had a little rather not spoil my new hat; and, moreover, the thing had a spice of adventure about it which could not but make it relishing: so I leaped the stone wall, and then "set down my feet, and ran," to such good purpose that I did actually reach the house before the pair dashed up, just as the rain was coming down in good earnest. As there was no time for ceremony, I stepped up, blushing like the morn, lifted the young lady off her horse, and set her down safely under the porch. I had had some little practice in this line before, having often performed this office for ——; but on the whole it is no concern of yours who it was for. It is enough that I had had practice. The young lady hastily bowed her thanks, and, after giving her habit a good shake, hurried into the house.

The gentleman, having given over the horses to the servant who ran up to take them, now joined me, and courteously invited me to walk in. He was a man of middle height, and well proportioned, though of rather a slight figure. He was between sixty and seventy; but as he wore powder it was not easy to tell to which extreme of the decade he inclined. Perhaps he was about halfway between the two. He had a cultivated and well-bred voice, as well as deportment; and his tones were more English than American in their modulations. And yet he did not look like an Englishman. His face must have once been very handsome; though time, and perhaps sorrow, had made their mark upon it. He gave one the impression of a man that had suffered, and through suffering had lived more than his years. He led me into a good-sized and well-furnished room on the right of the hall-door, and then through a narrow, arched door, by the farther side of the fireplace, into a larger back room, which appeared to be his library, though his collection was not much. Here I found a wood-fire burning, though it was hot summer, but which, nevertheless, was exceedingly acceptable to a damp stranger like myself. Inviting me to be seated, and sitting down himself, he said, pointing to the blaze, —

"I trust you will find this whim of mine, as I find it is thought to be hereabouts, not a bad one to-day. You remember, perhaps, the Spanish proverb, that nobody ever suffers from cold, except a fool or a beggar. And as I hope I am not quite a fool, and as I know that I am not absolutely a beggar, I am resolved to guard myself against the inclemency of your summers as well as of your winters."

"My winters!" thought I to myself: "I should suppose they were as much yours as mine, my good sir." But I *said*, " Many people, I believe, sir, would be glad to imitate your example, if they had but the strength of mind."

He smiled, and said, "Indeed, it does require some resolution. I know I had to put forth a good deal before I could overcome the opposition of Mrs. Warner, my housekeeper. She would have put out all my fires on the first of May, and not allowed me another spark until the first of November, had I not raised an insurrection in the house."

"Your victory seems to have been complete, sir," said I.

"Oh, a perfect Waterloo, my dear sir!" he replied; " and that, although my undutiful child was inclined to side with the enemy. A diversion from my own camp, by Jove!"

"His child!" thought I again; " then she *is* his daughter! Well, it's much better than being his wife." But I *said*, " I am sure, sir, I have reason to rejoice at your courage and success. And I imagine the young lady herself would not be disposed to question your wisdom, any more than your generalship, this afternoon."

"I dare say not," he rejoined. "I wonder she has not come down yet. I think that she likes my fire, as well as myself, in her heart; for I often find her nestling down by it in the mornings and evenings. Jupiter! what a flash!"

And it was a flash indeed, followed by an almost simultaneous crash of long-rattling thunder. We instinctively rose, and approached the window; but the darkness of the shower had settled down again over the landscape, almost as black as night; while the heavy drops fell like shot on the roof, and poured down on all sides in sheets, the spouts being entirely unequal to the occasion.

"That flash struck not far off," observed my host. "I hope it has done my trees no damage."

"Your hope comes too late, papa," said a voice behind us; "for I saw one of the oaks on the lawn struck as I came down stairs."

"Not the Sachem's Oak!" exclaimed papa. "I had almost as lief have had the house struck as that."

"I believe not," she returned; "but I could not tell certainly, it is so thick and dark. I think it was the next one to it."

"I will go and see," he said quickly, "if this gentleman will excuse me." And, without waiting to see whether I would or not, he hurried out of the room.

I have had greater calamities befall me since then than being left alone with a pretty woman. In fact, I have long since ceased to regard it as a misfortune at all. But, at that particular juncture of my life,

I would a little rather that papa had remained with us. I was getting on pretty well with him; and, with him to back me, I think I could have encountered this new form of danger with tolerable presence of mind. And I must do the enemy the justice to say that she did not seem to have any particularly hostile designs towards me. She seated herself near the fire, but yet sidewise to it, and with her face turned round, looking out of the window at the driving storm with an abstracted air, as if she were thinking not much of that, and still less of poor me. I don't know whether her attitude as I have described it will appear to have been a graceful one to my readers; but, if it do not, they may be assured it is entirely their fault or mine. The attitude was perfect, and the more perfect because entirely unstudied and unconscious.

"And so she was handsome?" you will all say. Handsome! to be sure she was. Do you suppose I should be writing about her at this present if she had not been? Currer Bell may broach and preach her damnable heresy of homely heroines with pug noses and carroty hair, if she please. The republic of letters has no established church; and, if she can build up a sect on that foundation, she may. But I belong to the good old orthodox school. None of your Jane Eyres or Lucy Snowes for my money! To be sure, this is not a novel, but a veracious history; and so I have nothing to do but to tell the simple truth. But I might have held my tongue, I suppose. There is a great deal of talk nowadays about woman's rights, and I am told clever things are written about them on both sides. And then reverend gentlemen write treatises on "the true sphere of woman," and "woman's mission," "the duty of woman," and so on. Now, I am a practical philosopher, and never meddle with abstract discussions; but my private notion of the sphere, the mission, and the duty of woman, is, that every woman ought to be handsome. It is a duty she owes to society. That's my simple moral philosophy, and, till somebody can show me a better, I shall stand by it.

I think, if you could have seen my heroine,— for the dullest reader must have discovered before this that we have found my heroine at last,— you would have acknowledged that she filled her sphere, fulfilled her mission, and performed her duty; for she was marvellously handsome. But I am not going to give an inventory of her charms. It's of no use; and I do not intend making a fool of myself by making the attempt. All I shall say is, that her hair was of a tinge very uncommon in America, and what I suppose poetical people mean when they talk about "golden locks" and "sunny tresses" (not *red;* I vow and protest it was not red; the most malicious rival could not have called it so); while her eyes and eyelashes were as near black as they could be without actually being so. Her complexion was the *véritable peau de lys,* as smooth and pure as the petal of a lily, and, though with the expression of perfect health, generally as colorless. But, when passion or emotion did summon the "blushing apparitions" into her cheek, it was a sight, indeed, that Raphael might have dreamed of. And as to her mouth and her teeth, if nature or art could have improved upon them, I should like to see the handiwork.

> "Quivi due filze son di perle elette,
> Che chiude e apre un bello e dolce labro."

And I would go a good way to see a finer arm and hand and foot than hers. But I won't describe her. Only I will say that the effect of the contrast of her dark eyes with her hair and skin was as odd as it was fine. I have never seen more than two or three of the kind in the course of a pretty extensive and careful study of the subject.

I thought I must say something, though I dare say she would not have missed it, if I had not; and so I ventured to suggest, —

"I hope you are not afraid of thunder and lightning."

"What, I?" she exclaimed, starting from her revery, and turning towards me. "Oh, no, indeed! I delight in them."

Delight in thunder and lightning! I must say I could not sympathize with my fair friend in this taste. I have not learned to like those unpleasant explosions yet, and had still less fancy for them then. But the horrid idea flashed into my mind that she might suspect as much. So turning with as composed an air as I could command to a portrait which hung over the fireplace, but which I could see but very indistinctly in the gloom of the day and the room, I said, —

"A portrait of your father, I presume?"

"A portrait of papa!" she replied, smiling, and shaking her head. "Oh, dear, no! Don't you recognize it as that of his late Majesty?"

His late Majesty! Old Farmer George, whom Byron had just left practising the Hundredth Psalm when his "Vision of Judgment" ended; whose only merit, according to the same infallible authority, was

"That household virtue, most uncommon,
Of constancy to a bad, ugly woman"—

what business had he here, in the heart of his revolted province? Who could these people be? Before I could ponder this problem further, the master of the house came in, saying,—

"It was not the Sachem's Oak, my dear, but the old one I have been trying to persuade myself to cut down these two years. But the lightning has taken it into its own hands now, and has settled the question forever. It is breaking away, however, and the shower is passing off to the westward. I have not heard such thunder since that storm among the Bernese Alps."

The Bernese Alps! Had they been there too? I looked at them with new respect; for you will remember foreign travel was not as vulgar then as it has become since. It was a distinction, at that time, to have been abroad : now, the distinction is to have staid at home. We have become a match for the English in our migratory habits. James Smith, I believe it was, who said, *apropos* to their invasion of the Continent after it was first opened, that soon there would be a sight set up of an Englishman who had *not* been to Rome. I should think it might be worth Mr. Barnum's while to add to his other curiosities an American who had not overrun Europe. But he must make haste, though, or there will not be one left to be caught.

This, however, gave us something to talk about, or rather for him to talk, and for me to listen about. He talked like a man of sense and education ; and I should have been well content to have listened to him, and to have looked at his daughter, for an indefinite time. She took no part in the conversation, except when appealed to by her father, but sat looking abstractedly into the fire. I could not but feel that she was not thinking about me. Indeed, I could not flatter myself that she would ever think of me again after I had passed out of her sight. I felt as "young" as David Copperfield did when the father of the eldest Miss Larkins asked him "how his schoolfellows did."

But, as we talked, the storm, which had "scowled o'er the darkened landscape," passed away, and the "radiant sun" extended his evening beam over it with farewell sweet. I had no longer any excuse for staying. My host rang the bell, and an elderly matron, whom I suspected to be the housekeeper, of whose leaning to the anti-Vulcanian theory I had heard, entered, bringing wine. After partaking of this then universal hospitality (for as yet temperance societies were not), I took my leave with many grateful acknowledgments. The young lady rose, and graciously returned my parting bow, while her father accompanied me to the door, and wished me a pleasant walk.

I passed on under the dripping trees vocal with birds, and over the saturated turf which the slant sun glorified into beatific diamonds and emeralds, and through the clear, cool, moist air, but thinking more of those whom I had left than of the sights and sounds about me. Nothing had escaped them which indicated who or what they were. They had shown no curiosity as to my poor self, had asked no questions as to my name, home, or business. They evidently only regarded me in the light of a lad whom they had saved from a ducking, and should see no more. Who could they be? Of course I should pluck out the heart of the mystery when I reached the parsonage, for Mr. Bulkley must know all about them. So I made what haste I could, and soon found myself at the worthy minister's door.

4

# CHAPTER IV.

#### IN WHICH I LEARN WHO THEY ARE.

I WAS soon at the parsonage; and, as it was too early for the minister to have relaxed from his task of sermon-work, I walked round to the garden at the back of the house. There I found Jasper, hoe in hand, whistling merrily as he waged war against the weeds, which had apparently availed themselves of a temporary suspension of hostilities, and made a stand against the foreign intruders upon their native soil.

"Jasper," said I, "who is it that lives in the large house on the river road, about two miles from here?"

"The big house with the two rows of trees behind it?" he asked, in his turn.

"To be sure," said I. "There is but one that I can mean. Who lives there?"

"Queer man, sir; queer man, sir!" he replied, shaking his head mysteriously, and resuming his work with great gravity.

"Queer or not," I answered, "I suppose he has a name, has n't he?"

"Name!" he responded. "Name enough, sir, for the matter of that! Bad name, too, sir."

"Well, what is it, then? It won't hurt me, will it? Tell me: I'm not afraid of it," said I.

"Mr. Miles Allerton is his name, sir. They call him Colonel Allerton; but I don't think he's any business to be called so here."

"Why not? Why shouldn't he be called so, if he be a colonel?" I asked.

"I don't think they ought to call such sort of folks so," he replied: "it ain't right. It makes me mad to hear 'em."

"Why, what's the matter with him, Jasper?" I asked, my curiosity being a good deal aroused. "He's an honest man, I suppose, isn't he?"

"I don't know that," he replied, with an emphatic stroke of the hoe into the ground. "We didn't use to think such kind of folks none too honest. But times is changed from what they used to be."

"He pays his debts, don't he? He isn't a swindler, I hope?" said I, laughing.

"O Lord, yes, sir! He pays his debts well enough. Why, he's the richest man this side Boston, they say!"

"Well, then, in the devil's name, what ails him? He isn't a Democrat, is he?" I persisted; for I had moused out that Mr. Bulkley was a stanch Federalist of the extremist sort, like most of his profession in New England at that time, and that Jasper was no whit behind him in zeal.

"O Lord, no, sir!" he exclaimed with a sort of deprecating tone, as if he had really gone too far in having excited such a suspicion; "not a *Dimocrat!* He ain't so bad as that, sir! He's only an old Tory."

I laughed heartily at Jasper's distinction; for, like Yorick, I do love a good one, in my heart. And, after all, there is something respectable in a well-preserved, good old prejudice, always provided that it is old enough. An old gentleman in breeches and hair-powder is a respectable object in all eyes; while a man in a five-year-old coat is one justly contemptible to every well-regulated mind. There was something very comic in this conflict of prejudices in Jasper's mind. But on the ethical theory of somebody,— I forget who,— of doing the duty that lay nearest him, he honestly hated the Democrat of the present generation more than the Tory of the last.

"What amuses you so much?" said a voice behind me. And, looking round, I saw Mr. Bulkley, who had come out to take a turn before tea. "Has Jasper been saying something witty?"

"Rather wise, sir, than witty," I replied; for I was a fierce Federalist too. And I told the minister what had passed between us, and the occasion.

"Ah, that's one of the few points of difference between me and Jasper," said Mr. Bulkley, smiling. "He has no charity for the Tories, and thinks it a weakness in people, that they are beginning to forget to hate them.— But everybody has not such a memory as you, Jasper. It does n't last for fifty years, generally."

## IN WHICH I LEARN WHO THEY ARE. 53

"I shall never get to like a Tory," replied Jasper doggedly, "if I live fifty years more. They're too mean."

"Nor a Democrat either, I suppose," said the minister, laughing.

"No, indeed, sir!" answered Jasper, *con spirito*, — "not if I live a hundred."

Mr. Bulkley and I laughed again, and then paced up and down, side by side, the centre walk of the garden, which was nicely edged with box, and hard with well-rolled gravel.

"So you took shelter at Colonel Allerton's," said he, "during the thunder-shower. You were in luck; for it is not easy to get admission there. And did you see Miss Eleanor, too?"

I told him all the circumstances of my adventure, and concluded by begging him to let me know who these mysterious people were.

"All I know about them," he replied, "is soon told. You must have heard of the famous Tory, John Allerton, so notorious in colonial history before the Revolution. He was attorney-general, and afterwards judge of admiralty, under the crown, in Hutchinson's time, and went away with the Tories. Well, this gentleman is his son, who, at the time the siege was formed, was in college, and, not being recalled in season, was cut off from the town, and prevented from joining his family. We kept him, together with other members of Tory families in the same predicament, — women and children chiefly, — in a sort of honorable captivity, as hostages for the good treatment of the families of the patriots who were detained in Boston. I was acquainted with Judge Allerton's family, and was able to make the young man more comfortable than he would have been otherwise."

"Was there no communication between these prisoners at large, in and out of the town, and their families, all that time?" I inquired.

"When a flag was sent in or out on other business," he replied, "open letters, to be inspected by the authorities on either side, might be exchanged. That was all that could be allowed. I tried to get permission for young Allerton to go into the town when it became tolerably certain that it must be evacuated; but the apprehension of the mischief that the British troops might do as they retreated prevented our parting with any pledge of their good behavior. He was sent to Halifax, however, in the first cartel that came in for exchange of prisoners afterwards."

"And what was his history after that?" I asked.

"I merely know its outlines," replied Mr. Bulkley. "The British Government behaved well, as you know, to the loyalists who had suffered in its cause. Judge Allerton received a liberal compensation (though necessarily not a full one) for his losses, and was appointed chief justice of Barbadoes, where he died. This son, the only child he had, received a commission in the army, and rose early to the rank of lieutenant-colonel. He resigned, however, many years ago, on his marriage with Esther Arbuthnot."

"And who was she, sir?" I inquired.

"She was the daughter of Peter Arbuthnot, another famous Tory. He was registrar-general. I remember her well, before the siege, as a pretty little girl. Her father was made a commissary, and afterwards became a contractor, and made a large fortune in Mr. Pitt's first war against the French Revolution. This, I presume, all went to his daughter, Mrs. Allerton; for his only son died before him, in Jamaica, of the yellow-fever. I knew him well, poor fellow; and so did your father."

"And Mrs. Allerton is dead too, I suppose," said I.

"Yes, she died, ten years or more ago, in the south of England, where they lived after their marriage, chiefly."

"And how came they in this country again?" I inquired. "And when did they come?"

"They came about two years ago," he replied. "But the why and wherefore I do not profess to know. Mr. Hayley, his man of business in Boston, told me that it was to look after the landed estates of his great-uncle, Ralph Clarke, who died without heirs, just as Madison's war began, in 1812, and which escheated to the State. He has sent in a petition to the General Court, and is prosecuting it; but the estates are hardly valuable enough to account for such an exertion, even if his chance for getting them were better than it is like to be."

"But how came they here?" I asked. "What

particular attraction drew them to Wensley, of all places in the world?"

"Why, I believe I must do my modesty the violence to say that I consider myself a main cause of that," responded the minister. "I was in Boston, attending the convention,[1] during election week, just at the time he came to town from New York, where he arrived from England, and happened to meet him at dinner at General Bradstreet's. He remembered our old acquaintanceship, which was renewed the sooner that I was almost the only one surviving of his former friends. He came up to visit me; and just at that time the estate where he now lives was for sale. Old Mr. Remington, whose father built it early in the last century, was just dead; and his third wife, promoted to be his widow, preferred living in Boston, where her wisdom has been justified," he went on laughing, "by her marrying, the other day, Dr. Hobart of the New East Church."

"And so he bought the Remington estate," suggested I, to bring him back from this episode.

"Yes," he replied. "Its solitariness seemed to suit him; and there was something about the lay of the land and the disposition of the trees which reminded him of Walford Hall, his house in Devonshire. I flatter myself that my being his neighbor was no objection in his eyes; but I am quite sure that there

[1] Of Congregational ministers, held that week in Boston, from time immemorial.

being no other within seven miles was a still greater inducement."

"It must be rather dull for the young lady," said I.

"One would think so," said he; "but she seems perfectly well content with their way of life. She is a charming creature, although a most loyal subject, like her father, to his Britannic Majesty. Still, she has won all hearts in the town by her beauty and graciousness. Even Jasper has surrendered to her; though he still holds out against the old Tory, her father."

"And is he the only one of the Wensleyans that holds fast to the faith that their fathers delivered to them, — of hating the Tories?" I inquired.

"Almost the only one," he replied. "Colonel Allerton's liberality, and kindness of heart, have succeeded in driving away the prejudices and suspicions with which he was at first regarded. Even Jasper's professions of dislike I fancy to be rather a point of honor than of feeling with him. Corporal Berry himself, although he has limped through life cursing the Tories, ever since he was shot through the leg at the time of Arnold's attack on New London, could not withstand the battery of blankets, flannels, meat, wine, and firewood, that was kept up on his citadel at the north part of the town, when he was close besieged by the rheumatism last winter. He even calls his benefactor 'colonel;' which Jasper has not made up his mouth to do yet," he added, laughing.

"You give them a good character, sir," I said.

"No better than they deserve," he answered. "I have unlimited authority to call upon him in case of any distress in the town. And, what is better, he and his daughter often visit in person poor people in sickness or other trouble, to see for themselves what they really most need. He says it is a habit they formed at home — by which he means England, of course. And what else do you think he is going to do for the town, sir?" — and he rubbed his hands gleefully at the thought, — "a clock, sir, a clock for the meeting-house! He had old Willard up here last month, and has given him an order for one of his best. It will set the poor old thing quite on its legs again." And he looked affectionately at the tower, as if he beheld in vision its future glories.

"Deacon Holt," he went on, "objected to it as unscriptural, at first; but I put him down with the dial of Ahaz, and clinched the argument by the examples of the Old South and other sound churches of Boston. So it is all settled now, sir, and the orthodoxy of the clock is fully established."

And he laughed out one of his ringing, musical laughs, which I still hear in my mind's ear (why should not the mind have an ear as well as an eye? it certainly should be allowed the full possession of all its senses), and then led the way into the house to tea. As the sabbath began at Wensley on Saturday night at sundown, ceasing at sundown on Sunday, I retired to my chamber after tea, and spent the evening in preparing an epistle to the Deipnosophoi, describing the adventures of which their enthusiasm for the vital principles of their foundation had been the remote cause. This finished, and directed to Tom Stacey, the worthy head of the order, I went to bed with even a better opinion of Wensley, as a place of academic retirement, than I had the night before.

## CHAPTER V.

### MY FIRST SUNDAY IN WENSLEY.

THE next morning was a truly delicious one. The shower of the afternoon before had cleared the air, and breathed a fresh life of verdure into the trees and grass. White, fleecy *Ruysdaelesque* clouds floated in the azure depths, relieved in sharp perspective against the blue; and their gigantic shadows gave a fresh grace to the landscape as they glided over meadow, stream, and tufted hill. I sat at my window, after breakfast, and revelled in the affluence of rural sights and sounds and smells which were poured out around me. I had left the minister in sole possession of his study, both that he might give, if he chose, a finer edge and point to the spiritual shafts he had been forging the day before, to be aimed on this at the hearts of his flock, and also because, though there was nothing in the least grim about his piety, he maintained a uniformity of seriousness in his deportment on Sundays very different from his working-day manner, which made it more agreeable to me to sabbatize by myself in my own room.

We often hear of the sabbath stillness of a day or place; and it seems to be generally taken for granted, because Sunday is a day of rest, that it is therefore a day of unusual quietness. Now, it was not so at Wensley. On the other six days of the week the very spirit of repose seemed to be brooding over the town. Sitting at my back window, which commanded a lovely bend of the Quasheen, always brimming to the brink, but never overflowing, with rich fields sprinkled with timber sloping down green and firm to its very margin, and, on the farther side, with the sweetest little wooded knoll lying clasped in its embrace, — sitting there, I say, one might imagine one's self leagues away from any habitation or haunt of men. No sight or sound was there that was not intensely rural. The silence was audible, and made only the more palpable to the mind by the chirping of birds, the hum of insects, the quiver of the leaves, and the rippling of the waters. And on the street side it was only now and then that an ox-cart came creaking lazily along the road, or a barefooted urchin loitered whistling by as he drove the cows to pasture, or home again. It always seemed to me as if it were an outlying dependency of the Castle of Indolence, just beyond the park-palings, and that one might see its dreamy turrets rising above the woods in the distance, if one would but take the trouble to look for them. I dare say it was not a great way off.

But on Sunday it was quite another thing. Then there were sights and sounds that gave a human interest to the scene. As long as Mr. Bulkley lived, there was no schism in Wensley. Methodists, Baptists, and Universalists refused to disturb the quiet of his parish while it was his. But, when he slept with his predecessors, the revolutionary spirit, which had been controlled by the personal affection felt for him, broke forth ; and its monuments are to be seen in three or four ugly little wooden conventicles, which perk their pert cupolas in the face of the good old meeting-house, like so many irreverent Quakers or Anabaptists, giving themselves airs of equality in the presence of an ancient, substantial, steeple-crowned Puritan magistrate. But in my time there was no open dissent. The meeting-house at the Centre was the only one in the town. It was a large building, with two galleries, and every part of it was entirely filled every Sunday. It was a sight which has not been seen in New England, I suppose, for twenty years at least, if, indeed, this were not the last surviving example of an absolutely unbroken parish.

After the first bell had rung, the roads leading to the meeting-house, which was fully commanded by my window, began to be alive with church-goers, and to pour an increasing tide upon the green on which the building stood. Some came on horseback, but more in bellows-top chaises, or gigs with leathern heads, that shut back with springs, and had a certain resemblance to the follicular convenience from which they derived their name. A few were conveyed in vehicles which have been long numbered among the extinct races, and which had come down from the middle of the last century. Square-top chaises they were denominated, or gigs with immovable leathern heads, and little windows at the back and sides. Some of them had a seat in front for a boy to sit upon, and drive. But modern Wensley (or young Wensley, as it would be called now) turned up its nose at these venerable relics of a former generation, and (to anachronize a little *slang*) voted them " slow;" which, indeed, they were.

But the greater part of the people, young and old, honestly trudged on foot. They came trooping along in families, and sometimes in pairs, the latter not unfrequently looking rather sheepish and conscious; though I am sure I don't know why they should. They were perfectly well-behaved young men and women, for all I could see. Arrived at the church, the "leathern conveniences" were put in the horse-sheds, which formed a sort of outwork on three sides of the meeting-house. The women all entered the house as they arrived, and were seen no more by me for the time; but the men remained without, standing about the door, or dispersed in groups over the green, discussing the weather, the crops, or the next election. It was their weekly exchange.

As I watched this lively scene, the second bell began to ring. Presently Jasper tapped at my door to let me know that the minister was ready to proceed, and I incontinently joined him. The moment the door of the parsonage opened, and the minister was seen to issue forth, the bell began to toll, and the men about the church-door to hurry in. Mr. Bulkley, leaning upon my arm, walked on erect and stately; while Jasper, no less stately and erect, followed us, a few paces behind, with a music-book under his arm. As we advanced in this state, I saw a plain carriage and pair drive up from the direction of the bridge, and stop at the meeting-house door. Of course I knew that it must contain my hosts of the thunder-shower. The horses were spirited and restive; and, before the elderly coachman could descend from his box, a white-headed old man hobbled up, and opened the carriage-door, and let down the steps. The minister pressed my arm, and said, with rather a week-dayish look out of the corner of his eye, in a low tone, —

"Corporal Berry opening Colonel Allerton's carriage-door! Toryism is triumphant in Wensley, I'm afraid — or would be, but for Jasper."

A guttural ejaculation, rather emphatic than distinct, and which, we will charitably hope, had no element of profanity in it, was heard behind us, expressive of the patriotic consistency of that veteran's opinions. There was a slight symptom of incipient rebellion in the region round about the minister's mouth; but he resolutely quelled the insurrectionary tendency, and arrived at the church-door the very personification of gravity.

Mr. Bulkley strode up the broad aisle with majestic self-possession, the whole congregation remaining standing to receive him. I, who was not accustomed to be the target at which such volleys of eyeshot were directed as were now aimed at me, followed him with less ease and a good deal more self-consciousness. Arrived at the pulpit-end of the aisle, he opened the door of his pew, the front one on the lefthand side, and, waving me into it, ascended the pulpit-stairs as a king might mount to his ancestral throne. As soon as he had disappeared in its vast recesses, a noise not unlike an irregular volley of musketry was heard over the house, being that of the seats slamming down, which had been turned back on their hinges, for room's sake. It was a fortunate hearing for me; for, not being acquainted with this fact in the natural history of the old parish churches in the country, I should have infallibly seated myself on the floor, but for the warning sound. This same salute was repeated every time that the congregation resumed their seats after rising for any of the services, and was generally executed with a fervor commensurate, as I suppose, with the warmth of their devotion.

Jasper I had missed as soon as we entered the house; and I was pleased to discern him belaboring a huge bass-viol in the choir (for that innovation had reached even the seclusion of Wensley) when we stood up at singing-time. I also discerned that the Allerton pew was on the opposite side of the aisle, answering to the minister's. But devout church-goers need not to be told that this is one of the most unfavorable situations for personal observations of an edifying nature, that the economy of an ecclesiastical interior affords. A place in the deacon's seat — where Deacon Holt and Deacon Williams, the one burly and red-faced, and the other lank, lean, and squinting in every direction, sat with their backs to the pulpit, overlooking the audience — would have been a much more eligible position for enjoying some of the incidental advantages of public worship. As it was, I could only observe that Miss Allerton was quietly attentive to what was going on; while her father, like an old soldier as he was, fairly dropped asleep with a cannonade of the heaviest sort thundering over his head, aimed at the errors of the Church of England, of which communion he and his daughter were the only two members within a dozen miles. But the serene height, away up under the sounding-board, from which he manœuvred his ecclesiastical artillery, saved the good parson from the mortification of seeing how his hot shot passed over the head of the enemy.

Dear old man! he never held back his hand from smiting the heretical Philistines that infested the region round about. His were good old-fashioned polemical sermons, well fortified with texts of Scripture, and garnished with quotations in the original tongues, which were none the less relished by the congregation because they did not understand them. It confirmed them in the faith, which was only second to that they entertained for Holy Writ, that he was the most learned man in the world. To be sure, there must have been all this time an undercurrent of heresy loosening the hold of some of his people upon their old anchorage, as we know from its breaking openly forth as soon as his restraining power was removed, and scattering abroad the barks which had remained peacefully in the old harbor as long as he had command of the fleet. But, during that period, no piratical Universalist, nor buccaneering Methodist, ventured to hoist a flag in the calm waters of Wensley. But he kept his batteries pounding away at them, and at all dissentients from the strictest rule of the ancient faith of New England, all the same as if they were within point-blank range of his guns. I have often thought whether this persistent warfare upon his theological enemies, and the constant statement of their arguments, which was necessary to give force to his refutations, might not have had something to do in bringing about that dispersion which followed so soon after his death.

Mr. Bulkley was, as I have said, a Calvinist of the very straitest sect; and he was none the less earnest a one for having become such, as the Quakers say, "by way of convincement." He was born and bred in the Arminian, or Latitudinarian, school of the last century; and when that form of faith lapsed into Unitarianism, at the beginning of this, he was at first carried by the tide into those waters. The investigation, however, which the Unitarian controversy induced, led him ere long to cut away from his old moorings, and to drop his anchor where he thought it would take a firmer hold. But, surely, never did a more genial and affectionate spirit qualify the severe necessities of religious logic. A milder and kinder soul never looked forward to the ultimate damnation of the vast majority of mankind, including all heathendom, ancient and modern, and all unregenerate infancy; for he was not a man to shrink from the logical consequences of his premises. He pitied the Unitarians; but he cordially despised those divines, claiming to hold the good old Orthodox faith, who devised ways of escape from the stern results of the doctrines of election and reprobation, of original sin, and redemption by grace. He used to call them ———; but, on the whole, it's no matter what he used to call them. It was not a complimentary epithet.

But not only did he keep at bay during his time all avowed adversaries of the faith that was in him, but he kept at a distance, also, all irregular practitioners even of the regular school. "How many years have you preached here, sir?" I asked him one day. "I have *reigned* here," he replied, nodding his head cornerwise at me, with an indescribable look of fun out of his gray eyes,—"I have *reigned* here forty years save one." And it was very much so. It was his business to take care of the souls of his parish; and he would have no assistance but such as he chose to call in on his own responsibility. No strolling revivalist, or starveling evangelist, ever ventured to set foot on the remotest corner of his territories as long as his sway lasted. Had he heard of such an incursion, I will not say that he would have taken down the firelock of Lexington, or drawn the sword of Yorktown, from their honorable retirement over his fireplace, to vindicate the integrity of his soil; but I do think he would have charged the invader, at the head of Jasper, gold-headed cane in hand, and driven him over the border, an example to all such intruders for the time to come. And the whole parish would have stood by him.

For my own part, I had many a sermon launched at my head during the time I lived with him, as I sat defenceless under the shadow of his pulpit. For I was (to use another Quakerism) a "birthright" Unitarian; and he doubtless felt it to be his duty to set in order before me the errors of my hereditary faith. But it was all in vain. I knew nothing of the arguments on my side of the question: indeed, I could not well see that there was any such thing as standing up before the battalions of texts, and squadrons of syllogisms, with which he bore down upon me, and rode furiously over me. But, though he could overrun me, he could not keep possession of me. All I knew was that my father and mother had been Unitarians; and I regarded it as a point of honor, binding upon me as a gentleman, not to forsake the faith in which they had lived and died. I was by no means clear that my Mentor was not right, and that the doom which he so fervidly described as that of all such misbelievers did not impend over my head. But that made no difference. It merely gave me a kind of exhilaration of spirits (I neither account for the phenomenon, nor defend it: I merely describe the sensation), such as a suspicion of danger, or the knowledge that he is considered as exposed to it, is apt to inspire in a lad of spirit. And I rather think I was quite as well fitted to die for my faith, in a war of religion, or at the stake, as a good many heroes and saints who have won for themselves the crown of martyrdom. But all Mr. Bulkley's prelections for my benefit were confined to Sunday and the pulpit. He never labored for my conversion in private. Either he saw that I had a good share of that virtue which we call firmness in another when it answers our purposes, and obstinacy when it thwarts them, and so knew it would be of no use, or else he thought that his Sunday labors would be more likely to act favorably on my mind if he left them to their natural influences during the week, without disgusting me with his zeal by making it a perpetual annoyance. Whatever his motive might have been, I was very happy to compound for the result.

When the services were at last over (and it was an *at last*, for Mr. Bulkley was none of your twenty-minute men), and the benediction was pronounced, I hastily gathered together my hat and gloves, and was for joining in the precipitate retreat I had always seen expected from all the churches I had ever attended before. But I had no sooner thrown open the pew-door, and put one foot out of it, than I saw that all the rest of the congregation remained standing, with their faces turned towards the broad aisle. I drew back, and, raising my eyes, encountered those of Colonel Allerton, who stood facing me. He smiled at me, as if understanding my case (very likely it had been his own once), and bowed, as if recalling our interview of the day before. I returned his bow, not a little abashed at finding myself again the centre of all the eyes Wensley had in its head, and, abiding the result, presently perceived that it was the custom of the town (once universal throughout New England) to wait, and let the minister go out first. Presently Mr. Bulkley descended the pulpit-stairs, not having apparently hurried himself at all, and passed slowly down the aisle, bowing royally from side to side in acknowledgment of the rustic salutations which he received. As soon as he approached me, he made me a sign to follow him, and then shook hands with Colonel Allerton, who joined him in his progress through the capital of his dominions.

It was a necessary consequence of this order of procession, that Miss Allerton and I came out face to face into the aisle. She graciously returned my bow; and we walked after the elders, side by side, kindling yet more speculation in all the eyes of Wensley, eager to spy out what I could be. As we came out into the porch, the two gentlemen remained a little on one side, in conversation, and I proceeded to put the young lady into the carriage, which stood ready drawn up at the door. I hoped that she had experienced no harm from the shower yesterday afternoon; which hope, she was able to inform me, had become fruition. I then informed her that it was an uncommonly fine day, and on this point I am happy to say our views cordially coincided. What I should have stated next, I can hardly imagine; for the congregation were now swarming out, and many were lingering within earshot to discover what sweet influences this "bright particular star" of theirs was shedding upon me; and the consciousness of this fact did not help to concentrate my ideas. But, fortunately, just at that moment her father approached, and, as he stood with one foot on the carriage-step, he offered me his hand, saying, —

"Mr. Osborne, I am happy to know your father's son. I met him often, and knew him well, at Paris, when I was there during the peace of Amiens."

I bowed, and blushed my acknowledgments for his goodness.

"I hope," he continued, "that I shall have the pleasure of seeing you at Woodside at some time when you can have a less stormy reception than that you had yesterday."

"I could not have a kinder one, I am sure, sir," I replied, "nor one that I should be more happy to experience again, if you will allow me to pay my respects to you and to Miss Allerton."

"With all my heart," said he, smiling; "only without the thunder and lightning, if you please. We three may meet again, I hope, but not, I trust, in thunder, lightning, and in rain. So good-morning."

And they drove away, leaving me upon the steps. And now, I suppose, the sagacious reader will expect an account of my sensations; for of course he (or she) takes it for granted that I fell fearfully in love with the fair Eleanor at first sight. But they must wait a while. I am not quite ready to go into the confessional just yet, with his (or her) ear glued to the grating. Perhaps I scarcely knew how I felt myself; for I have more than once acknowledged my inaptitude for the dissections and demonstrations of metaphysical anatomy. And perhaps it is hardly fair to require a man to conduct his own autopsy. But, whatever may have been my own state of mind, one fact, mortifying as it may be, I must needs confess. It must be admitted that the beautiful Eleanor did not fall in love with me either at first or second sight. Perhaps it was no proof of her taste or discernment; but the fact cannot be denied. Her deportment towards me was perfectly kind and wellbred; but I could not help feeling that my image might never again occur to her, if not recalled by my bodily presence. Of course, such a conviction was not flattering to my vanity (if, indeed, I or any *man* was ever subject to such a weakness); but did it go near breaking my heart? It is altogether too near the end of a chapter to enter into an inquiry of this intricacy, and so it must be adjourned to a day future. I am none of your epic writers, who dive at once into the middle of things, and then plunge and splash about until they have somehow or another brought the beginning and end together. I am a plain narrator of a simple passage of biography, and tell things just as they happened, and must be allowed to take my own way, or I shall be sure to make a botch of the whole thing. When they were gone, Mr. Bulkley put his arm in mine, and we walked off towards the parsonage together. He told me, what I had surmised before, that I was what they were talking about, he having asked Colonel Allerton if he had not known my father during his public life in Europe. He had then told the Colonel who I was, and, as I surmised, the occasion of my residence in Wensley; but he did not say so, nor did I ask, as the day, if not the subject, was too serious for a joke, and it would have been too much for his human nature or mine to have suppressed one under such favorable circumstances. The order of our return home was the reverse of that which had distinguished our march to the meetinghouse; for Jasper, instead of bringing up our rear, was discerned far in our van, and, in fact, just entering the parsonage. This apparent breach of subordination, however, would have been pardoned by a stricter martinet than I, on beholding the excellent cold dinner which he had set out in the study, ready for us on our arrival: at least it would have been, if the martinet in supposition had been as hungry as the worthy parson's diatribe against bishops had made me.

# CHAPTER VI.

### AN INVITATION AND A DINNER AT WENSLEY.

THE Allerton pew was empty in the afternoon. I was not sure that it was not the morning's onslaught upon the Anglican Church that had driven away its inhabitants, until Jasper assured me that they never went to meeting in the afternoon. This he resented as a slight to his master, and as one of the many mischiefs of the Church of England, for which the worthy Afrite had much the same mysterious horror that many excellent people feel for the Church of Rome, and probably with about the same degree of knowledge. I discovered afterwards, that it was the belief of Wensley that there was a chapel fitted up at Woodside, where the Colonel read the service of the church to his daughter and her maid, Ann Petchell, the only other member of that communion in Wensley. This was some explanation of the phenomenon to its curious inhabitants, and perhaps made them easier under it, on Priest Bulkley's account, of whose honor they were as jealous as Jasper himself. I am bound to say, however, that a tolerably intimate acquaintance with the house in after-times never revealed to me any such secret place of worship; and

Colonel Allerton, with all his various excellences, seemed to me as little likely to become an amateur chaplain as any possible man, when I came to know him better.

These facts, or myths, I learned that evening from the conversation of Deacon Williams and Major Grimes, and one or two of the parish besides, who called in to see the parson, and possibly to take a look at me also. When the sun went down on the day which bears his name, all the sabbatical shade of seriousness which rested upon it passed away with him. By this time, Mr. Bulkley's spirits seemed to rebound from the pressure of unwonted solemnity, and to be elastic and joyous as usual. His stories were more and better, he fought his old battles over again with new vigor; and his jest was more frequent, and his laugh more resonant, than ever. Sunday evening was the time when his parishioners usually came to call on him. Then they were mutually at each other's service. They had nothing to do; and he was well content to do nothing in their company after the labors of the day.

He was a student of men as well as of books; and I have never known any one better versed in the niceties of Yankee character and dialect than he. He could draw them out with marvellous skill, of which the subjects were perfectly unsuspicious, and all with no shadow of ill-nature, or purpose of satire. It was simply the study of man, in which he delighted, and for which he must use such materials as

## AN INVITATION AND A DINNER AT WENSLEY. 77

came in his way. As we sat round the wall in summer, waging internecine war with the mosquitoes or round the fire in cold weather, discussing all manner of public and parish politics, with the apples and cider, which formed the staple entertainment, there were odd traits of character, and curiosities of expression, enough to have made the fortunes of a score of Yankee Hills or Haliburtons. I wonder whether there are any such people left anywhere in New England now. I am afraid that they have had all their sharpnesses ground down by the mill-wheels, and that they are all reduced to undistinguishable particles; or that their originality has been all crushed out of them by the locomotives that fly, screaming like so many devils, all over the country.

Major Grimes, I must do him the justice to say, had changed his mode of address towards me since he had put me in the right way two days before. He was perfectly respectful and deferential, now that he found that the old priest had actually received me under his roof, and had discovered, furthermore, who I was.

"You find Priest Bulkley a fine man, sir," said he, when he had an opportunity for an aside, "don't you?" using the epithet "fine," as almost all Americans do, to denote mental and moral qualities, and not, as an Englishman uniformly does, to express fine presence and personal beauty. You may hear an Englishman say, "He is a very fine man: what a pity that he is such a fool!" and an American, "She is a very fine woman : what a pity she should be so homely!" But this is parenthetical.

"From what little I have seen of him, I judge him to be a very fine man," I answered coolly.

"You will think more and more of him, sir, the more you see of him," replied the Major. "I did n't think he meant to take in any more young college gentlemen; but when I heard who you were, from Jasper, when he came after your things, I knew he would."

"Indeed!" said I. "You knew more of my influence over him than I did, then."

"Oh, but your father and he used to be so thick together!" rejoined the martial dispenser of toddy. "They were the greatest cronies you ever saw. And the old priest is n't a man to forget his friends, alive or dead, I can tell you. That's why he took you, sir."

"I'm very glad of it, whatever brought it about," said I.

"Your father used always to put up his horses at my place when he came to Wensley. He used to drive a phaeton and pair; and good horses they were, I can tell you, sir. Are you fond of horses, sir?" he went on.

"I like them well enough when I have occasion for them. I am no judge of them, and have nothing of the fancy for them that some men have."

"Because, if you ever want a saddle-horse, I don't believe you can find a better in Boston than my Turk; and, for a chaise (*videlicet,* gig), you won't often sit behind a better beast than my mare Black Sally. Colonel Allerton wanted to buy her; but it was of no use. I wouldn't part with her."

"The Colonel is a judge of horses, then, I suppose," said I.

"A judge! I believe you!" he replied briskly. "There isn't a man in New England that knows horse-flesh better. Why, he keeps five himself here; and I have heard say that he had near twenty in England."

"It's no wonder, then," I said, "that he fell in love with Black Sally. I should have thought he would have had her at any rate."

"Well," returned her fortunate possessor, rather drawlingly, "you see he wasn't willing to give me quite as much as I thought he ought to for her. At the same time that I offered her (reasonable, too) to the Colonel, I told him he might have Turk for three hundred. But he didn't want a saddle-horse just then, he said. And I'm glad of it, for I should have missed him training-days. He'll stand cannon, musketry, music, anything. General Smithett would give me five dollars a day for him any muster, if I didn't want him myself."

I was just telling my military friend that I would certainly try the quality of his stud on my first occasion, when a quick double knock was heard at the door, and in another moment the personage whose name was the last word in our mouths was ushered into the presence by Jasper. Colonel Allerton entered nimbly, and shook hands cordially with the minister, and afterwards with me; and then, bowing kindly to the other guests, all of whom rose on his entrance, he sat down by me.

"The Parson gave us a capital sermon this morning, Deacon," said he, addressing that functionary, whose eyes seemed to be more than ever in all places at the same time. "Rather hard upon me and my daughter, perhaps. But it is a positive pleasure to be flogged by some people, it is so cleverly done."

I thought the Deacon might have said that it was well for some other people, that, like tops, the more they were whipped, the better they slept. But he did not. Perhaps the dispersion of his vision over the remoter regions of the meeting-house prevented his seeing what was so directly under his nose. What he said was, —

"I'm glad you liked it, sir."

"Liked it! To be sure I did," rejoined the Colonel. "And, egad, Parson! I should be sorry to be required to answer you. But I'm not converted, for all that, you know. You can't suppose me such a pitiful fellow as to be driven from my religion merely because I can't defend it against a militant minister, armed to the teeth, like you. No, no! You must make another breach before you'll carry me by storm, much less Eleanor."

"I shall try for it, you may be sure," said Mr. Bulkley, smiling; "for I am sure, that, if you are hard to carry, you will be easy to hold. There'll be no backsliding in your case, or Miss Eleanor's, either."

"I think you're right, by Jove!" returned the Colonel, "and, that we may keep your good opinion the better, I think we'll not backslide from where we stand now. But do all you can to unsettle us, pray. You are perfectly welcome to do so, if you can, I do assure you."

I felt that if he always had the invention blessed by Sancho about him, to wrap himself in, and to serve as

"Feather-bed 'twixt castle-wall
And heavy brunt of cannon-ball,"

he was really in no great danger from the good parson's theological gunnery.

After a little more talk between them, in which no one else joined, unless appealed to, the Deacon and the Major, followed by the other village visitors, rose, and took their leave. As soon as they were gone, the Colonel said to the minister, —

"Well, Parson, to show that I bear no malice, I have walked down this fine night to ask you and Mr. Osborne to come and dine with me as soon as you can. When shall it be? To-morrow?"

"To-morrow is rather soon," Mr. Bulkley replied, "as Mr. Osborne and I have not yet reduced ourselves into our order of studies. We had fixed upon to-morrow to begin."

"Very well. If not to-morrow, fix a day for yourself. Only let it be some day this week."

"Shall it be Thursday?" inquired Mr. Bulkley, looking over to me.

I intimated that all days were alike to me, and that Thursday suited me perfectly well. So the dinner was fixed for Thursday.

"I wish to have you come this week," said the Colonel, rising to depart, "because I shall have to go to Boston next week, and may not be able to return until the very end of it, or the beginning of the week after. On Thursday, then, I shall expect you."

And he was taking his leave, when the Parson and I thought that we would walk with him, the night being extremely fine, as far as the bridge. Our society was gladly accepted, and we walked merrily along the road, accompanied by many a story and jest, and followed by many a laugh. No doubt, as we passed by the scattered houses of the village, people said, "That's Priest Bulkley's voice! I should know it among a thousand. I wonder if anybody's been took sick. It can't be, though, or he would n't laugh so."

At the bridge we parted; the Colonel pursuing his way by the river road, and the Parson and I going back over our steps.

"It was so like him!" said Mr. Bulkley, as soon as we were fairly out of hearing.

"What do you mean, sir?" I asked. "What was so like him?"

"His coming so instantly to invite you," said he.

"He never hangs fire — the Colonel. He always goes off at half-cock."

"Well, sir," I replied, "provided he hits as well as he has to-night, it's not a bad way of going off."

"Not at all, not at all," he returned: "a short aim is generally the best. But he's a queer man, sir, as Jasper told you — an odd compound of openness and reserve. He seems so transparent, that you would think you could see straight through him at a glance. But you will find yourself mistaken. You may look your eyes blind, without really making him out."

"Do you suppose, sir," I asked, "that he has anything really to conceal, or that he does not choose to make talk of his private affairs, merely because they are private?"

"I can't tell," he replied. "I can only say, that intimate as I have been with him, and the only person he really associates with for the greatest part of his time, he has never let a word drop as to any of them; not even as to his motive for coming to this country, or the probable length of his stay. It must be systematic to be so uniform."

"Is he as close as to his life in Europe?" I asked.

"Very nearly," he replied; "that is, as to the more recent part of it. He talks fast enough about old times, and very well too. However, it's none of my business; and I suppose he is of the same opinion. But you will find him a charming companion, as well as Miss Eleanor; and I am glad you have got admission to the house."

"Is she as sly as her father?" I inquired. "She does not seem to have as much to say, at any rate, judging by the little I saw of her."

"I hardly see enough of her by herself to judge," he answered. "And, besides, I am afraid I am hardly the confidant she would be likely to choose if she had anything to tell. But it would not have been strange if her father had sometimes, by chance, let fall to me something of his history or plans that might not be proclaimed in Grimes's bar-room. But no such chance has ever happened. You know as much of them as I do; and what I have told you I obtained from other sources than themselves."

We were now at home, and I bade him good-night, smiling a little, privily, at the good man's curiosity (of which he did not seem at all suspicious) to know of his neighbor's affairs; which, however, I am given to understand, was no idiosyncrasy of his particular constitution, nor even one confined to small rural parishes like Wensley. There was a shade, however, of wounded feeling in his expression, as if he had not received quite a just return for the fulness of confidence he was ready to pour into the bosom of his friend, at which I had no disposition to smile. But is there any of us that has not some Bluebeard's chamber in his heart, which he keeps close shut, even to his nearest and dearest? I do not pretend to know more than my neighbors; but, from what I have seen and heard, I surmise that there are married men even, who would be ready to play Bluebeard in good earnest, if they should find that the very wives of their bosoms had found a cranny through which to peer into those prohibited recesses. I wonder what they would see there. And Mr. Bulkley himself — would he have exposed to the eye of his dearest friend the sacred though dishonored image of his fatal Julia, and the troop of recollections, emotions, and agonies, that waited upon it? I think not, even to have the veil lifted from the most secret places of any other life.

Thursday arrived, as it usually does, as nearly in the middle of the week as possible. And, moreover, it was a very fine day; so that Mr. Bulkley and I chose to go to Woodside on foot, rather than disturb the bones of Smiler, the minister's cross old horse, from their repose in the stable. Jasper had brushed up his master's buckles, and made him as smart as his best coat and breeches (it would hardly be historically correct to call them his *new* ones) could make him; and, as he was a vigorous walker, we were soon at the hospitable door, which stood open to welcome us. On the threshold stood the master of the house, ready to give us a most cordial reception, and to usher us into the presence of his daughter. She looked handsomer than ever; and as she sat in the window (which she had had cut down to the ground, an astonishment to all Wensley) opening into her flower-garden, in the light of that lovely day, she did look as lovely as the day itself.

The dinner was excellent, such as wealthy gentlemen of that day used to set before their guests. The table furniture was handsome but plain, and all display of wealth was evidently repressed. The table linen was of the finest of damask, and the service of Nankin china. The silver forks were the first that had penetrated to Wensley, and were a marvel, and a mystery to its oldest inhabitants, who had never heard of the like. At that time this luxury, which has now become almost a necessity, was confined, even in the cities, to the very rich, and, indeed, not always in daily use with them. So that it is no wonder that their advent caused a sensation in Wensley, nor that Jonathan Snell, the Colonel's coachman, should have condescended one day to take a specimen in his pocket to show to the astonished inhabitants, at their special instance, after custom had bred familiarity with that great man. Mr. Bulkley would never give in to this *new fanglement*, as he called it. So he was always supplied with a good old-fashioned three-pronged steel fork, with which — " *sævitque tridenti* " — he did manful execution.

Mr. Bulkley, of course, took Miss Allerton in to dinner, which ceremony he performed by bearing her hand aloft, with an Old-World grace, like a septuagenarian Sir Charles Grandison. He would have scorned the custom, had he been cognizant of it, of clapping a lady's hand under his arm like a brown paper parcel from the grocer's. The Colonel and I followed after them ; and though he made no sign of remarking the good man's gallantry, he could not control a little twitching of the muscles about the corners of the mouth. During dinner I had but little to say to Miss Allerton beyond taking wine with her, and assisting her in the dispensation of the dishes at her end of the table. With two elders at table who talked so much and so well as her father and Mr. Bulkley, there was little occasion or opportunity for us to display any conversational gifts we might possess, except that greatest one of listening well, — that "*grand talent pour le silence*" which Talleyrand (or whoever it was) showed more wit than sense in laughing at. What would he have done, I should like to know, if there were not some people willing to hold their tongues?

It was entertainment enough to sit and hear the two men talk, and to look at the lovely mistress of the house. Colonel Allerton had seen all the public and literary men of the end of the last century and the beginning of this, and had known many of them personally. It was something to hear a man talk who had seen Garrick during his last season, and had had the vision of Dr. Johnson rolling along Fleet Street, though he had never met him face to face as an acquaintance. He had breakfasted in company with Gibbon, and had dined at the same table with Sheridan; and, of all the orators and authors and beauties of that period, he had had opportunities of personal observation, and could make report of them from what his own eyes had seen. Whatever secret reserve he might have to his best friends, of which Mr. Bulkley had complained, there was no sign of it in his conversation. Nothing could be more free and flowing than his stream of talk. It seemed as if you had only to give it a direction, and it would waft directly to your feet all the facts of his experience. But he was not in the least an overpowering talker. He did not compel you, as Carlyle says Coleridge did, "to sit as a passive bucket, and be pumped into, whether you consent or not;" which, he goes on to say justly, "can, in the long-run, be exhilarating to no creature." On the contrary, he carefully drew out Mr. Bulkley, and made him appear to his best advantage, and was very far from neglecting me.

Mr. Bulkley, indeed, was not a man to be easily put down. Just to others, he was just also to himself, and it would have been a clever man that could rob him of his fair share of what talk was going on. But nobody who had ever heard him talk (your oppressive talkers never hear anybody but themselves) would ever wish that he should talk any less. Though he had lived in retirement so long, still his seven-years' apprenticeship to the world, during the war, had made him a master of that craft, and had furnished him with inexhaustible stores of personal recollections, all connected with the most interesting times and people. Then the very quaintness of manner and speech which his solitary life had bred, set off by his extensive though odd reading, gave a rare raciness to his talk. His intimate acquaintance, too, with the peculiarities of character and dialect of the country-people whom he had made his study for so long, and his uncommon powers of mimicry, which he would exert in safe societies, made him, I think, the most entertaining companion I ever met in the course of a pretty long acquaintance with the world.

"The choir sung very well last Sunday, Parson," said Colonel Allerton, with the slightest possible glance at his daughter and me. But, if there were any irony in the tone, the Parson did not notice it.

"Yes, I think they improve," he said. "I'm sure I take pains enough with them."

"Do you know," returned the Colonel, "that I was rather disappointed, on coming here, at finding the noses of good old Sternhold and Hopkins put out of joint by Dr. Watts? I was in hopes of hearing once more sung, line by line, by the whole congregation, as of old, 'The Lord will come, and he will not;' and then, as a distinct proposition, puzzling to my infancy, 'Keep silence, but speak out!'"

"If you had come only five years sooner, you would have had your wish," replied Mr. Bulkley. "I believe Wensley was the last town that yielded to the innovation. I withstood it as long as I could; but the Association [1] would give me no rest till I fell in with it. But I found it hard work, I assure you."

[1] In New England, from the earliest times, the Congregational ministers within a convenient distance of each other form associations, which meet at regular intervals.

"What! were the people unwilling to make the change?" exclaimed the Colonel. "I respect them for it."

"Loath enough at first," responded the Parson. "Most of the old women actually believed that those were the very strains which King David sang to his harp, and looked on the change proposed as little short of blasphemy."

"And how did you manage it?" asked Miss Allerton.

"Why, to tell you the truth, my dear young lady," returned the minister, "I found the young people my best allies. The allurement of a singing-school for the winter nights, and the glories of the singing gallery on the sabbath, were more than they could resist: so, by playing off the vanities of the young against the prejudices of the old, I gradually brought all round, except Deacon Holt. The Deacon maintained the faith long after all the rest had given in."

"And how did you overcome him?" inquired the Colonel.

"I'll tell you," pursued the Parson. "I knew that he was as self-willed as one of his own bullocks; and so I left him until the very last of the opponents had submitted. Then, supposing he must have been somewhat mollified by the change of opinion in the parish, I moved up to the attack myself. I found the Deacon sitting at his front-door one fine sabbath evening about sundown. The delicious west wind did, to be sure, bring with it an occasional whiff from his slaughter-house hard by; but the Deacon liked it none the worse for that. So, by way of making my approaches regularly, I said, 'An uncommonly fine evening, Deacon.' — 'Ya-as, Parson,' he replied : 'the weather is dreadful fine, as you say. It somehow makes a fellow feel kind o' nohow. I was just a-saying to Miss (*Nov-Anglice* for *Mrs.*) Holt, it was such-a-most-a-beautiful *arternoon*, if it was n't that it's Sa-a-ba-a-day, I feel just as if I should like to *sla-a-ter suthin'* (slaughter something)."

The Colonel and I roared at this, of which no print can give any idea of the perfection of the Parson's twang. Miss Allerton laughed too, but with some exclamation of horror at the Deacon's association of ideas.

"But, my dear Miss Eleanor," expostulated Mr. Bulkley, "you should allow for an artist's enthusiasm. *I* did, and, waiting sympathizingly until it had exhaled, I thought that now was my time; and so I broached the subject at once. 'Deacon,' said I, 'I am surprised to find that a man of your piety and discretion should oppose the substitution of Watts's for the old version,' and then proceeded to give the reasons in favor of the one over the other. He shook his head. 'Parson Bulkley,' said he, 'I'll tell you what : I've two good reasons why I won't never agree to it.' — 'May I ask,' said I, 'what they are?' — 'My first objection is,' said he, 'that Watts isn't an *expired* man.'— 'Watts not an *expired* man!' I exclaimed. 'My dear sir, I am astonished to hear a man of your intelligence say such a thing. I do assure you that there is nothing more certain than that he is an *expired* man.'— 'Be you sartain?' the astonished Deacon asked, somewhat shaken by my confidence. 'I am not more certain of my own existence,' I replied. 'It is a perfectly well-established fact.'— 'Well,' said he slowly, 'if you be sartain sure, I s'pose I must give up that *pint.*'"

We all laughed merrily at this; and the Colonel said, "And what was the other point, Parson?"

"That's just what I asked the Deacon," he replied; "and the Deacon said, 'My second *pint* is, that there's a word in it that is n't in *Scriptur.*'— 'Indeed!' said I: 'that *is* vital. Pray, what is the word?' —'PAUSE!' said the Deacon. 'There's the word *pause* in it; and it ain't nowhere in the Bible!' and he looked triumphantly at me, as if he had cornered me now.[1] 'My good friend,' I replied, 'I am more astonished at this objection than at the other. *Pause* not in the Bible! Please just reach it to me. Look here, now (1 Sam. xvii. 37), "The Lord hath delivered me out of the *paw* of the lion, and out of the *paw* of the bear." The paw of the lion and the paw of the bear, taken together, make "*paws*," don't

---

[1] The non-evangelical reader, if, unfortunately, there are any such, may need to be informed that Dr. Watts hath divided his longer psalms and hymns into two or more portions by the interposition of the word "PAUSE."

they? How can you say, then, and you so well read in the Bible, that the word *paws* is n't in it?'"

We all shouted with laughter at this new exegesis; and Miss Eleanor fairly clapped her hands, saying, "And was the Deacon silenced?"

"Completely," replied Mr. Bulkley. "He has never been heard to say a word against Dr. Watts or his psalms from that day to this. My victory was complete. But this is the first time I ever told the particulars, and you will see that I have put myself in your power. It is a secret of the confessional. But I am not afraid to trust you."

The cloth being removed, Colonel Allerton said, that, out of regard to Mr. Bulkley's feelings, he would give the President's health first; but it was on condition that the King's should be duly honored afterwards. As the wine was excellent, of course the minister made no objection to this; only, when the toast was given, he slyly improved it, as he drank it, thus: "The King's health — *and amendment!*" And even these his loyal subjects, in view of the recent developments consequent on the Queen's trial, could hardly say that his Majesty was absolutely beyond the reach of such an aspiration.

Miss Allerton soon withdrew, and as the two gentlemen began to talk politics earnestly, about which I cared nothing, I overcame the opposition of my natural bashfulness, and yielded to the influence of the more attractive metal in the drawing-room, — or parlor, as it was called in those days, — and soon joined her.

She made room for me by her window, and, the excellences and oddities of Mr. Bulkley giving us a beginning, we soon went off into a brisk conversation. Perhaps she found that I was not quite such a booby boy as she might have taken it for granted I was. I did not waste much of my time at the university, to be sure, upon the stupid routine laid down by the authorities; but then I was extremely well read in many authors not contained in the college course. The respective merits of Lord Byron and Walter Scott, the mystery hanging over the Waverley novels, the relative rank to be assigned to those delightful fictions, the comparison of our opinions as to our favorite characters, gave us plenty to say.

We did not always agree, by any means. For instance, she was a warm admirer of Wordsworth; whereas I was entirely too bigoted a devotee of the Byronic school to allow him more than a very small modicum of merit. I remember that I made her lift up her hands and eyes by denying that he was the founder of any school at all, only a duller sort of Cowper, with Cowper's knack at landscape-painting, but without his wit. She retorted, however, by asserting that Byron plagiarized from Wordsworth in the third canto of "Childe Harold," which I stoutly denied; declaring, however, that, if he had, Wordsworth should be forever obliged to him for the honor done him. This was all said playfully and banteringly on both sides; and, when the two gentlemen came in to coffee, we were on the easiest terms imaginable.

After coffee, Miss Allerton gave us some music. In those days, people had not grown too fine to like Tom Moore; and she sung "Oft in the Stilly Night" and the "Last Rose" with a roundness of voice, and pathos of tone, which made the tears roll down Parson Bulkley's withered cheeks. Moore was as fresh to him as Byron, and he could not deny his lyric power. He was never tired of hearing his Melodies sung even by me, much less by the fair Eleanor. But as there must be an end of all things, however pleasant, so the time came in due course when we had to take our leave. Mr. Bulkley made the move about eight o'clock. Miss Allerton cordially offered me her hand at parting, and joined in her father's hearty and repeated invitation to visit Woodside as often as I could.

Mr. Bulkley said, as we went along, that I was a lucky dog to find such a solace to my exile in that out-of-the-way place, and, indeed, I was very much inclined to think that my reverend friend was not far wrong in his opinion. We talked the day over merrily as we walked home, where we found Jasper waiting for us in the study. I went to bed early, and fell asleep in a confused whirl of ideas and images. I remember that I could hardly believe that it was only a week since the scientific session of the Deipnosophoi had resulted in my finding myself where I was. It seemed an age since then. I don't see why it should. Why should my making the acquaintance of two old gentlemen and one young lady (for I don't believe Jasper had anything to do with it) make that week seem so long? I am sure it had been a pleasant one enough. But, as I have said formerly, I am no metaphysician, and only state facts in psychology, without pretending to explain them.

## CHAPTER VII.

BEING ONE OF ACCIDENTS.

MY acquaintance with Miss Allerton went on prosperously from that time forward. The next Sunday evening, I walked over to Woodside to call upon its inhabitants after their hospitality, and was invited to join their riding-party the next afternoon. This enabled me to redeem my promise to Major Grimes, that I would improve the first opportunity that offered of putting the virtues of Turk to the test of experience. Perhaps I did not feel as much surprise, after this taste of his quality, at Colonel Allerton's refusal to come up to the worthy Major's terms at the time the treaty for the possession of that valuable animal was pending, as his gallant proprietor expressed when he gave me the history of the negotiation. But I forbear to dilate on his personal qualities. Such a digression would be foreign to the purpose of this work. If his performance did not absolutely come up to the promise of the Major, still I imagine that officer was not the first military commander whose bulletin was more brilliant than his campaign. If he did not excel all other steeds in swiftness, he might be pardoned as a comfortable exception to the celerities of the fast age in which he lived; though indeed, at that time, it was but just getting its speed up. If he did stumble a little now and then, let the biped that hath never done the same thing, and with less provocation and on a smoother road, throw the first stone at poor Turk. I remember him with emotions of tenderness; for he is associated with the beginning of a memorable acquaintanceship, and of a succession of charming rides, that lovely summer, through a country as lovely, in my eyes, as the summer itself.

Philosophers differ as to the very most advantageous position in which one can be placed in relation to a charming young lady on whom one has no specific objection to making an agreeable impression. Some think that a walk "by moon or glittering starlight" is the very best invention that the wit of man hath ever hit upon; other some, that the corner of a blazing wood-fire on a winter's evening is indeed "a coigne of vantage," if rightly improved by a judicious mind. There are who hold that a sleigh-ride in a clear, cold, crackling winter's night, is not incapable of being turned to a good account, with all its manifold exhilarations and excitations. And there are not wanting who maintain that a ball-room, with all its heat and crush and bustle, —

"When music softens, and when dancing fires," —

furnishes that exact combination of proximity and isolation, which constitutes the most congenial atmosphere for civilized love to grow in, from the first incipiency of flirtation to the final desperation of proposal. There was much to be said in behalf of this theory in the days before the incursions of barbarian dances had shaken the institutions of civilized ball-rooms to their foundations. The country-dances of our ancestors, and the quadrilles of our own times, were not unfavorable to the gentle flutterings of the hovering Loves. But it must be a stout Cupid indeed, of a robust constitution and a hardy disposition, that can stand up before the frantic rush of a polka or redowa, and not be swept away into utter annihilation by the very tempest and whirlwind of those whisking petticoats.

But it is my notion that a *tête-à-tête* ride on horseback, through lonely lanes and solitary wood-paths, is not the worst way of being brought into confidential communications with a lovely young woman. Sometimes, you know, one cannot avoid guiding her bridle-hand in some emergent difficulty; and cases have come to my knowledge in which an enlightened philanthropy could not be satisfied without supporting her jimp waist with a sustaining arm in narrow and perilous passes. A painful and dangerous position, indeed; but then, you must allow, one could not suffer her to run the risk of falling from her horse. I wonder the Humane Society does not reward such heroic risks by the awarding of gold medals to the virtuous adventurers. Merely plunging into the water to pull out a stupid boy or blundering man were a safe and easy feat in the comparison.

My Monday's ride with Colonel Allerton and his daughter was blessed to me in this very form and manner. Finding that I was a tolerable horseman, and withal a very modest and discreet youth, the Colonel proposed to me that I should accompany the young lady in her rides during the rest of the week, which, as he had previously informed me, he should be obliged to pass in Boston.

"And, by the by," said he in reply to my blushing acceptance of his proposition, — "by the by, I think you had better make use of my Prince here. I fancy he will carry you better than the beast you have under you. Is n't that the horse Grimes wanted me to buy?"

"The horse you wanted to buy of him, rather," I replied, laughing; "for that was the statement the Major made to me of the case."

"Was it, indeed!" he answered, laughing in his turn. "I certainly ought to have wanted to buy him if he had had half the virtues vouched for him by the Major, and he would have been cheap at twice the money. But it was he proposed the *trade*, and he had the impudence to ask three hundred dollars for him."

"So I inferred, from what dropped from him afterwards," said I. "But your refusal, sir, raised you many degrees in his estimation. He thinks you a doctor in the science he esteems the highest of all, — the science of horse-flesh."

"I could hardly help picking up the elements," he replied, "considering I was for more than twenty years in a cavalry regiment. I do not profess to be a doctor, or even a master, in the art; but I know enough to know that such a brute as that is not worth the half of three hundred dollars."

The next day, Colonel Allerton departed for Boston, and in the afternoon I walked over to Woodside, and found Miss Eleanor all ready, waiting for me; her Fairy and her father's Prince pawing the gravel before the hall-door. We were soon in the saddle, and, as she was perfectly well acquainted with the country for ten miles round, we were not long in reaching as sweet a winding and wooded by-road as any country could furnish. The mania for improvement, so deeply seated in the character of New England, which, at the beginning of this century, found its relief in cutting infinitely extended straight lines of turnpike roads in every direction over the country, had spared this remote corner of its domain. Even the road to Haverford, by which I had journeyed to Wensley, was the old road, which, avoiding the turnpike (as the road itself is invariably called in New England), meandered about from village to village, according as the early settlers had arranged the division of the soil when they first helped themselves to it. And so the by-roads through which our course lay wound themselves around the homesteads and outlying fields of the farmers, or swept by the skirts of their woodlands (wood-lots they call them there), like Schiller's river, —

"Honoring the holy bounds of property."

"Is this ride anything like those you had in Devonshire, Miss Allerton?" I inquired of my fair companion, as the road plunged into a depth of wood thick with brushwood, the branches of the pines almost making it impassable for two riding abreast, so broad and long did they stretch themselves. "You are too civilized there, I take it, to permit such impediments as these to cross your path."

"Yes," she replied. "England has been inhabited rather too long to have left many such primitive scenes as this — at least in the south, where I have mostly lived. I never saw that, for instance," she said, pointing with her riding-whip to the tangled undergrowth which choked up the passages between the trunks of the trees, — "I never saw anything like that till I came here."

"And you wish it away, as a deformity, I suppose," said I.

"No, not as a deformity," she replied. "It is characteristic of an aboriginal wood, as I suppose this really is; for, though the ancestors of these trees may have been cut away once or twice, I fancy it has never been anything but a forest; and it is picturesque and beautiful in itself. But I own I long for an opening now and then under the trees, by which one might escape from the beaten road, like a damsel or knight of fairy in quest of adventures."

"We must first find a well-disposed magician, or benevolent enchantress, to clear our way for us," I answered; "for I fear that we shall never find the undergrowth cleared away by any Yankee, until the caitiff is ready to hew down the trees too, as, indeed, he is but too well inclined to do. We are but beginning to outgrow the antipathy which our fathers instilled into us against trees and Indians. As they grow scarce, we may grow merciful to the aborigines of both kinds."

Talking thus, we rode along; and my companion entertained me with descriptions of the neighborhood of Walford Hall, and the differences between those scenes of ancient civilization and exact culture, and the rough and half-reclaimed country around us. Presently she drew rein at a narrow opening into the forest which the woodcutters might be supposed to have made for their own occasions.

"Come," said she, "what say you to trying our luck down that path? Who knows but it may lead us to some adventure? I know all these roads by heart; and, if you will back me, I will try and find out a new one."

"I imagine you will find it a passage, like those in the Long Story, that leads to nothing," I answered. "But still, if you are for the trial, I'll not fail you. Only let me have the honor of leading the van, and facing the perils of the enterprise first, as becomes a good knight."

I turned my horse's head for the purpose of preceding her, and, in the first place, of removing two or three bars which crossed the entrance; but she was too quick for me. Giving her mare a smart blow with her riding-whip, like another Di Vernon she made her leap the low fence, and so secured the lead; for the pathway was too narrow to admit of my passing her. Now, though I was a tolerable horseman, as I have already said, I had had no particular experience in leaping fences, that being a freedom in which we are not much indulged in this land of liberty. But still, like Frank Osbaldistone, I was piqued to show my horsemanship by such an example, and accordingly pressed my steed to the point, not without a secret misgiving that I might find myself performing a mathematical curve of some unknown description over his head. It was lucky for me that I was backing Prince at this critical moment; for I should have been sorry to put Turk up to such a trial of his mettle. But Prince took the fence as if he were used to much greater feats than this, and thought but little of it. So I followed my fair leader, who shook her golden curls, which had escaped from under the control of her riding-cap, and shot me through and through with her laughing glances as she looked back at me.

She was in the highest spirits, and talked and laughed in a most bewitching manner. We could not proceed very rapidly; and, as I followed in her track, I had an excellent opportunity of admiring her firm, erect figure, and the admirable manner in which she sat her horse. Still she often turned her face half round to me, and chatted away in the liveliest way possible. The absence of mind which I had observed at my first interview, and of which there had been an occasional trace at the few times I had seen her since, was entirely gone. The exhilaration of the fine, clear sky; the delicious air, fragrant with the spicy smell of the pines, and growing cool as the sun dipped lower and lower; the excitement of the exercise, joined to the sense of pleasure which must always, I suppose, attend an exploring expedition on however minute a scale, — all united to make her seem a totally different creature from what I had imagined her from my previous observations.

And possibly it might have been that the companionship of the only young creature she had seen for so many months helped to unlock her spirits by the secret magic of youthful sympathy. She must have discerned that I was a harmless as well as a sheepish youth, without the least mixture of the lady-killer in my composition. She could not but know that I admired her extremely; and, in that desert, even the admiration of a college lad like me was something. Moreover, I had made no demonstrations of a love-making nature. I was by far too modest for that, had I had any constitutional tendency to that complaint, or rather vice. Making love, indeed! A vile phrase — as bad as that of "falling in love," which Yorick justly reprobates as implying that "love is something *beneath* a man." No, no! Love is none of your confounded manufactures. It is an indigenous growth. You cannot *make* it. You may tend and cherish and foster it, and sit in its shadow, and crown yourself with its blossoms, and feast upon its fruits unto everlasting life; but you can no more make it than you can make a rosebush or a grapevine.

And now I suppose my readers would like to know whether this magic growth had sprung up in my heart, and taken possession of me. A very natural curiosity, I admit, but one which I hardly think it time yet to satisfy. I fully concede the reciprocal rights and duties of this confessional, of which these lines, at which the reader looks and listens to me, may represent the bars, or lattice; and I shall be ready to make a clean breast of it in due time. Perhaps I am not, at this point of my narrative, in a sufficiently penitential frame of mind. Possibly I am not clear in my own mind how it was with me at that precise point of time. You know that my acquaintance with her was very young. "Ah, yes!" you will reply; "and so is Dan Cupid very young too. We all know from authentic story, if not from our own experience, — we all know that he springs to life, all armed, at a single glance of an eye." I admit the general proposition; but then, I have already assured you that she had not shown the faintest symptom of falling in love with me. But here you shake your heads with one consent, and agree that that is nothing to the purpose. Why, what would become of the whole tribe of novel-writers and story-tellers, if the course of true love ran smooth all the time? Are they not obliged to cast about, every mother's son of them, for sticks and stones to throw into the stream, so as to make it chafe and murmur the more musically rough in its passage to the tranquil lake of matrimony, which they have spread out to receive it at last?

This, again, I cannot gainsay. But, then, I have not told you yet the fatal truth, that I had formed the decided opinion that she was at least a year, if not two years, older than I. I positively looked upon her with a certain sensation of respect for her advanced years, and, whatever sentiment I entertained for her, it was qualified by a feeling of reverence for her age. I thought she must be at least as much as twenty. And here, once more, you all look arch and knowing, and ask me if I don't know that a man always falls in love, for the first time, with a woman older than himself. You are right again, my friends. Your observation is founded in the nature of things, and is just as well as original. But, then, how do you know *that it was the first time?* Have I opened to you the seals of all the books of my whole past history . Did I tell you who it was that I used to lift off her horse, when it was on the very tip of my tongue, in narrating one of the most surprising adventures of this true history? If you only patiently bide your times, you will be told all things that are fit and edifying for you to know.

In this manner we fared onwards, finding it very often hard enough to keep our saddles, so difficult was it in places to make our way good through the boughs interlacing across our pathway. Presently, however, she called cheerily to me to make haste after her, for she had come within sight of land. I was soon by her side, and found that our narrow way emptied, so to speak, into a wide clearing, which showed signs of having been cultivated at some former time, though then in a sluggardly condition. Here and there charred stumps raised themselves above the level of the field; but they looked as if the rains of many summers, and the snows of many winters, had been blanching their grim skeletons since they were first submitted to the ordeal of fire. But the greater part of the plain was perfectly cleared, and furnished a sufficiently hard surface for riding purposes. It was nearly surrounded by wooded hills; the pine-trees sloping upwards to the hill-tops, and looking like spectators in some vast amphitheatre, peering over one another's heads at the arena in which we were the sole actors.

"A race, a race!" she exclaimed; and, suiting the action to the word, she put her mare to her speed, and I was not slow to do the same good office by Prince. The horses sprang forward over the turf in the direction of the only opening in the amphitheatre of hills, which appeared to be about a quarter of a mile distant.

My horse was much stronger and heavier than hers, and in a long run he would, undoubtedly, have had the advantage. But for a short distance Fairy was more than a match for him; and, besides, her mistress was perfectly well acquainted with her ways, and could command her best speed, as I could not well do the first time I had ever been upon Prince's back.

So my companion had fairly the start of me, and was entering the gap in the hills, which was the goal at which we aimed, when I had not cleared much more than two-thirds of the distance. She was hid from me for an instant by the shape of the ground; and the next moment I was horror-stricken to hear a sudden splash and scream from the direction where she had disappeared. I struck my spurs "up to the rowel-head" into the sides of my horse, who leaped forward as if intelligent of the distress, and in an instant I was on the spot from which the cry came. The first glance showed the nature and occasion of the accident. The Quasheen, which washed the wood on that side, was so near the opening at which I had lost sight of my companion, that, before she could check her speed, her horse carried her into the middle of the stream, where, by the suddenness of the shock, she lost her seat, and was plunged into the river.

The stream, though not wide, was deep, and quite sufficient to drown a stouter person than Miss Allerton. But, though she had lost her seat, she had not lost her presence of mind; and she held fast by Fairy's mane, being well assured that she would bring her through her peril. I threw myself from my horse, and was already in the water, when my hopes of being the preserver of my fair charge were unexpectedly disappointed. A man suddenly stepped into the river opposite where she was (for Fairy had swum a little way down the stream), and, seizing Miss Allerton by her floating riding-habit, drew her towards him, and then carried her in his arms to the landing-place whence she had made her plunge.

Oh, shouldn't I have liked to have killed him at that moment! And then to be obliged to thank him for having robbed me of my unquestionable prerogative! But any such emotions as these were soon put to flight by the effect which the sight of her rescuer produced upon Miss Allerton when she had fairly recovered herself enough to look at him, which was as soon as he had set her down, dripping like a Naiad, upon her feet. Clearly, all recollection of her recent danger and of her obligation to the man before her was lost in stronger emotions. She seemed struck mute with amazement, and to be pale with some yet stronger passion. It seemed to me that it looked like fear. The man was obviously a gentleman; though he was roughly dressed for trout-fishing, in a coarse sailor's jacket, boots which came up above his knees, and a weather-beaten, broad-brimmed hat. His face was as pale as hers, but calm with a calmness that concealed deep feelings of some sort. In the surprise and suddenness of the whole thing, I could not read his features very accurately; but, as I remembered them afterwards, it seemed to me that they conveyed a strange expression of exultation and defiance, with some deeper passion under all; but I could not make out whether it were love or hate. I remember I thought it could hardly be the first. He must have long since survived that passion at the age he had reached. He was, probably, about five or six and thirty.

As soon as Miss Allerton could command her voice, she said to him, with a tone in which was mingled no gratitude for the service he had done her, but only coldness and aversion, and, as it still seemed to me, some dash of terror, — "And so you have followed us hither, too?"

"*You* I have followed hither, and will follow farther than this, as you might have guessed. But" — He paused, and, turning to me, said, "Perhaps this young gentleman will be good enough to catch your horse for you, or it may get out of reach down the stream."

I understood the drift of his suggestion, and looked at Miss Allerton for instructions.

"Do," said she, inclining her head to me. So I had nothing left for it but to go and leave them together, to my most cruel disappointment; for the adventure seemed to be fast reaching its climax. I hurried along the bank of the river, sometimes having to wade in it up to my middle, as the trees often grew so close to the water's edge that there was no room to stand on. I had toiled on in this way for about a quarter of a mile, before I came to poor Fairy, who had not yet found rest for the sole of her foot. She was just trying to scramble up a steep bank on the opposite side of the river when I came upon her: so I had fairly to plunge in, accoutred as I was, to reach her, and thus was as thoroughly drenched in her service as I had been most desirous of being in that of her mistress. My only comfort was, that her mistress seemed as little pleased with the way of her escape as I could be myself. So, contenting myself as well as I could with these reflections, I took Fairy's bridle over my arm, and made the best of my way, like an active personage whose name it would be improper to name in this presence,

"O'er bog or steep, through strait, rough, dense, or rare,"

until I found myself at the point from which I had started.

If I had happened to be in love with the fair Eleanor, I certainly had no occasion for jealousy in the relations she seemed to hold with the stranger. They were so absorbed in what they were saying, that they did not notice my approach at first; so that I could not help hearing Miss Allerton say,—

"I owe you no thanks for that. I could have saved myself without your help; and, if not, God knows I had rather have died than owe my life to you."

"You are an ungrateful girl," he replied, with a smile which made me hate him more than ever. "But you will behave better by and by, and know that I am, if you will let me be so, your best friend." Eleanor made a gesture of impatience. "At least you know," he resumed, as if provoked, but still calmly,—"you know that it is not the first time I have saved you. It may be," he added significantly,—"it may be, that the time may come when

I will *not*. But here comes your horse," perceiving me for the first time. "Let me put you on him, and entreat you to lose no time in getting home."

He advanced towards her; but she turned from him, and, beckoning to me, invited my assistance to place her in her soaking saddle. She turned her horse's head away from him, and took no notice of the parting salutation he made her. I mounted Prince, whom the stranger had secured to a tree after I had gone in search of Fairy, and followed her, touching my hat to my unknown acquaintance, which he did not return, — not, however, from incivility, as I judged, but because he was looking so earnestly after the lady, that he did not see me. Miss Allerton disappeared first in the wood; and, as I took a parting look behind, I saw him slowly turn away, and walk towards the bank of the river. But I imagine his fishing was over for that day.

Miss Allerton and I pursued our way in silence. As I followed her, I could perceive that she was deeply agitated, and that she was indebted more to Fairy's instinct than her own care for getting safely over the narrow and uneven pathway. In one place it was just wide enough for two persons to ride abreast. She drew on one side, and walked her horse, as an invitation to me to join her.

"Mr. Osborne," she presently said in an agitated voice, "I have a favor to ask of you. It is, that you will not mention what you have seen to-day to any one."

I readily gave her the assurance she asked for.

"I cannot tell at this moment," she went on, "how far I may explain to you what you must have thought so strange — not stranger, I am sure, than it has seemed to me. But you shall know all about it some time or other."

"If I can be of any service to you, my dear Miss Allerton," said I, "tell me what you think best. But I do not desire to pry into any of your affairs, as a mere busybody in other men's matters."

I *lied* there; for I was dying to know all about them.

"Oh, Mr. Osborne," she resumed, in a voice scarcely audible from agitation, "I am an unhappy girl, no mother, no sister, no friend, and yet needing so much the sympathy and help of the wisest and tenderest friendship."

She could contain herself no longer, but fairly burst into tears on Fairy's neck — on *Fairy's*, who seemed perfectly callous to the blessing. Launce's dog could not have been more insensible to the affliction of his respectable family. Was there never another neck near that would serve her turn?

I was a tender-hearted youth at that time, and the sight of a woman crying was too much for me. Perhaps I ought to be ashamed to confess that it was all I could do to keep from bearing her company; but I am not. I was deeply moved at her distress, and would have given the world (or as much of it as usually falls to the share of any one person) to comfort her.

"But my dear Miss Allerton," I ejaculated, thinking, like a fool, that I must say something, "there is your father."

"Oh, yes!" she exclaimed, with a fresh burst of weeping,— "yes, dear papa! But, then, he"— she interrupted herself, and presently added, "I hardly know what I say, my spirits are so confused by the surprise of this afternoon. Pardon me if I say nothing; for I may say what I ought not."

As we were now approaching the high-road, she evidently made a strong effort to command herself. She dried her eyes, and, pulling down her veil, proposed that we should get over the ground as fast as possible, that we might avoid at once observation and the ill consequences of our exposures. Though she said this, I believe she was thinking as little as I of the watery plight which we were both in. I believed the strong excitement she was under would prove an effectual antidote to the wetting she had got; and, as for mine, I cared nothing for it. I would repeat the treatment every day for a month in her good company. We fortunately arrived at Woodside without meeting any of the Wensleyans, but were received by Jonathan Snell, when he came to take our horses, with the most unequivocal marks of astonishment and concern. And no wonder; for a pair of more thoroughly ducked fellow-creatures could have seldom come within the range of his philosophy.

"Mr. Osborne," said Miss Allerton to me when we alighted, "I insist upon your coming in until

Jonathan can put the horse into the gig to take you home."

I remonstrated; but she persisted. "You need not fear giving extraordinary trouble; for I must send him to the village directly, and he can take you round perfectly well."

This being the case, I yielded to her kindness, and not the less willingly from the consciousness of what a figure I should cut in passing the strait by the bridge, between the post-office and the blacksmith's shop, as well as of the gossip of which I would be the theme for the next week. So I went into Colonel Allerton's own room, where his fire was still kept trimmed and burning, notwithstanding his absence from home, and gyrated before it like an animated joint of meat primitively suspended by a string, with a *penchant* for roasting. Miss Allerton retired up stairs, and I saw her no more that day. When the master of the horse was ready, I joined him, and we set forward for the village. That eminent officer of the household, of course, was curious to know the particulars of our adventure; which I gave him, with no more of the *suppressio veri* than the case required. He was not a man of many words, and he made use of very few on this occasion; but it was quite clear to my mind, that he thought me a very incompetent person to have charge of his young lady. And perhaps he was not far wrong.

When we came to the post-office, instead of driving by, as I had hoped, he drew up at the door, which was watched, as it seemed to me, by a double corps of observation, which made ample use of its opportunities as I sat holding the reins. Jonathan, as he resigned them to my deputed care, took a letter from his pocket, which I saw at a glance was carelessly folded, and hurriedly written, and directed to Colonel Allerton. He said Miss Eleanor was earnest that it should not miss the mail-coach which would pass through from Pentland on the edge of the evening of that day.

So she had written to her father an account of the adventure she had encountered. It was, then, nothing peculiarly and especially her own. That was some consolation in my ignorance. What could be the rights or the wrongs of the matter? I had no time for protracted speculation, however; for I was soon deposited at the minister's door, who was at first alarmed by my appearance, and then diverted by my story, told, as it had been to Snell, according to Captain Absolute's directions, with "no more lies than were absolutely necessary." I thought he would never be done rallying me on my misadventures as a Squire of Dames. But I was too full of what I could not tell him to mind much his comic commentary on what I could. My boyish sensitiveness was somehow hardened over since the morning. I did not mind his fun half so much as I should have done the day before. Indeed, it was rather a relief to me.

## CHAPTER VIII.

### IN WHICH ANOTHER CHARACTER APPEARS.

"OSBORNE," said Mr. Bulkley to me the next morning, as we sat at breakfast, "do you recollect who your grandmother was?"

"My grandmother?" I repeated. "I suppose I must have had the usual allowance; but really, sir, upon my word, I"— And I shook my head. "But what is my grandmother, supposing I had one, *apropos* to — to *boots?*"

"No, no!" returned he — "to something much more to the purpose than boots. I mean your father's mother — was she not a Shuldham?"

"That was the name, I am quite sure; though I am afraid I should not have been able to recall it of myself. But what of her, sir?" I asked.

"Much, and to the purpose," he replied. "Your grandmother Shuldham's mother was a Tindall, daughter of Lieutenant-Governor Tindall, who died in office in the year 1717, or thereabouts; and his son Matthew, who was for so many years speaker of the House, had an only daughter. Do you understand?"

"Well, sir," I answered, "I cannot deny it, if I wished to. But how does it concern me?"

"Thus," he replied. "That daughter married Judge John Allerton, and was, consequently, the mother of the Colonel. D'ye see now, young man?"

"Why, yes," I answered. "I see that the Allertons and I are far-away cousins, and" —

"Far-away cousins!" he interrupted. "Only four degrees removed! Do you call that far away? When I was a young man, sir, I should have called cousins with a pretty girl like Miss Eleanor, if it were twice as many."

I laughed, and assured him that I was infinitely obliged to him for bestowing upon me so charming a relation, and that I would claim all my cousinly privileges, even though the claim were as many removes farther off. And this I subsequently did; and it gained me one great advantage when my cousinship was allowed, as it was, with much merriment, as soon as I communicated to them this result of the good parson's genealogical studies, in which, indeed, he was a great proficient. Miss Allerton and I became Cousin Eleanor and Cousin Frank from that time forward; an advantage, which if the reader doth not appreciate, he is unworthy of ever having a pretty cousin, — an institution the blessings of which should be confined to those who can properly value them. But this was not immediately acquired, as it was some time before I felt that I was intimate enough, or that Miss Allerton would relish a jocose interlude of this sort, after the tragic, or at least melodramatic, adventure of the forest and the river. Indeed, I did not see her for the rest of that week. That plaguy fellow in the jack-boots, whoever he might be, had effectually put an end to our rides together for the time being. I could not tell what influence he might have upon the fair Eleanor's fortunes; but I was sure I cursed him by my gods for his sinister interference with mine.

Colonel Allerton returned before the end of the week, recalled, doubtless, by his daughter's letter. I had called, of course, the day after our adventure, on Miss Allerton, to "humbly hope she caught no cold" from her accident; but Petchell, her maid, brought me a very kind message, saying that she should not leave her chamber for a day or two, in consequence of it; after which time she should be glad to see me. So I had perforce to wait until her father came back. After his return, I visited at Woodside as usual, and was even more cordially and kindly treated than before. Eleanor looked a little paler than usual, though her roses were usually rather Yorkist than Lancastrian, but all the more charming from the new and mysterious interest I felt in her. Nothing could be kinder than her reception of me when we first met; and after that meeting, at which her manner was necessarily a little tinged by a consciousness of what had passed when we were last together, she fell back into very much her former way of life and conversation.

Perhaps a shade more of sadness clouded her serene beauty, and perhaps her thoughts wandered oftener

## IN WHICH ANOTHER CHARACTER APPEARS.

from the things around her. Perhaps, however, this was only my imagination; and, at any rate, I had now no difficulty in accounting for and excusing those untimely flights from the ignorant present to the past or the future. What would I not have given to have been able to look down through those lustrous eyes, at the soul that looked out of them, and see what was hidden from my sight, and to have known why it was disquieted within her! What were the phantoms, the spectres, that passed before her eyes when they looked into vacancy?

> "Ah, fixed on empty space, why burn
> Her eyes with momentary wildness?
> And wherefore do they then return
> To more than woman's mildness?"

How I longed to protect her, to cherish her, to drive far away whatever it was that molested and made her afraid! But I feared that this adventure was not reserved for me.

After the Colonel's return, our rides were resumed, and Turk once more had the honor of keeping company, by their grace and favor, with Prince and Fairy. Occasionally, when her father was occupied, I was again allowed the privilege of escorting her alone. But we had no more adventures of the wood and the stream. Eleanor's passion for exploring seemed satisfied; and we kept to the highway in as humdrum a fashion as the most rabid stickler for the proprieties of life could require. She saw no more, when I was in company, of the intrusive benefactor of the Quasheen, and she never made any allusion to him or his works. So I was obliged to solace myself with the recollection of her promise, that one day I should know all about him. Indeed, I cannot deny, though Eleanor proposed no new voyages of discovery, that I may not have attempted one or two on my own account. I whipped the Quasheen for trout more than one Saturday, for miles (though neither the Quasheen nor the trout suffered much from the flagellation), in hopes of coming upon that anomalous angler yet once again. But I saw him not. He was as shy as the trout themselves.

Afterwards I visited the taverns of the neighboring towns, and made many a libation of punch and toddy on the altar of my curiosity; and not wholly in vain. Captain Pettingell, who kept the Rising Sun in Bradfield, the next town, thus invoked, told me, from the oracular recesses of his bar, that a person answering my description had staid at his place for a week or ten days; that his name was Smith; and that he was gone all day with his fishing-tackle and sometimes, he added, came back with fish enough for a week's consumption, and sometimes without having had a bite. The captain believed him to have been a Britisher; but as he paid his way well, and was a good friend to the house, he overlooked that error, as well as a way he had of profanely cursing and swearing (the captain was a professor, and a pillar of Dr. Babson's church) when anything happened to go against the grain. And, by the captain's account, he had given his vocabulary in this kind an airing extraordinary, one night when he came home dripping wet from having missed his footing, and fallen into the river. He seemed to have taken this accident, one surely ordinarily incidental to the gentle craft, so much to heart, that he had retired from the neighborhood in disgust, and taken the Pentland coach the next morning for Boston. This was all I got in repayment of much time and some liquor which I wasted in this research; and it was not much more than I had known before.

Matters went on thus for a few weeks, when my frequent complaints of the inadequacy of Turk to the exigencies of my case induced Mr. Bulkely to suggest whether it would not be better for me to have a horse of my own. This proposition met with my cordial approbation; and Jasper was forthwith called into council as to the possibility of carrying it out. As I had already established myself in his good graces by my admiration of his master, and my eager attention to his own personal narrative, — which I delighted in extracting from him, and which, to do him justice, he was ready enough to communicate, — he was not long in consenting to advise what he saw we both wished to be done. He loved a good horse, he said, and should like to take care of one of Mr. Frank's, if he only had time. This objection Mr. Bulkley made light of, and I made away with by offering to pay for the hire of as much outdoor labor as would make good his outlay in my behalf. This having been made all easy, the next thing was to obtain the consent of Mr. Moulton, my guardian, to this investment in horse-flesh. As my application was backed by the recommendation of Mr. Bulkley, and supported on the ground of my valuable health, Mr. Moulton interposed no more opposition than was essential to vindicate his authority in a matter of this moment. And his letter containing his assent included, also, a proposition by no means repugnant to my own ideas of the fitness of things. He suggested, as this was a purchase of some importance, and which it was as well should be entirely to my own mind, that I should come down to Boston for a week, and assist at the researches preliminary to its final adjustment. To this suggestion Mr. Bulkley was pleased to lend a friendly ear; and with his full consent I intercepted the Haverford coach the next morning (having, I trust it is needless to say, walked over to Woodside, where the transaction excited the interest its importance deserved, to give notice of my intended absence), which, in due time, deposited me at Mr. Moulton's door in Autumn Street.

This gentleman was no ill specimen of his class, with specific idiosyncrasies of his own. He was descended of an old New England family, which, however, had gone to decay for one or two generations. He found himself, on attaining to man's, or rather youth's, estate, in a remote country-town, with no advantages of education but such as the town-school had afforded him; with no capital but what he carried in his head, and what he had invested in an excellent character. After various struggles to rise above his hereditary position in the country, he changed the scene of action for the city (or rather the metropolis, for Boston was a town only, for years after that), where he buffeted and battled with fortune, with alternations of failure and success (which, well told, would be a curious picture of life), until he at length achieved a place among the foremost merchants of the nation. It is unnecessary to say that he was a man of eminent ability; for such is almost necessarily implied in great success of any kind. The talent that could build up a great fortune from nothing by commerce, if it had received another direction, would, in all likelihood, have achieved eminence on the bench, or in the Senate, or, perhaps, even in literature.

Mr. Moulton might, possibly, sometimes be caught tripping in his speech, and his verbs and nominative cases might not always bear that precise relation to each other that the more bigoted disciples of Priscian choose to exact; but the substance of what he said was good sense, according to the sense of his times, and most unequivocally to the point. He was not without his provincialisms and his prejudices. He verily believed that, as Massachusetts politics went, so would go the country, and, as the country, the world. He really thought that all the hope of liberal principles throughout Christendom depended on the fragment of the New England mind that had accepted for truth the Unitarian idea. He was benevolent and open-handed to the poor, and would found charities, and endow professorships; but he would take the bread out of the mouth of every Democratic lawyer, minister, doctor, or artisan, if he could, and count it to himself for righteousness. He gloried in his liberality of opinion; but he hated and despised a Calvinist in about equal proportions, and was firmly of the faith that no good thing could come out of that Nazareth. His multifarious affairs, and complicated commercial connections, made him intellectually aware of the fact that a considerable portion of the civilized world lay beyond the purlieus of State Street. And probably arithmetic would have convinced him, had he applied it to the subject, that a good deal of the mind of Christendom lay beyond the domain of the Unitarian denomination; but practically, as far as his walk and conversation were concerned, the one constituted the true State, and the other the true Church Universal. But, where his prejudices did not interpose between his natural goodness of heart and any person or class that he could benefit, he was liberal, even generous, of his money, his time, and his influence with others.

I am sure that I have good reason to speak well of him; for he took excellent care of my estate, and let me do very much as I liked. And yet he was not negligent of me, either. He had a cordial detestation of vice in all its shapes, and, without preaching, made me feel that he looked upon me as incapable of anything so low and ungentlemanlike. This confidence was, no doubt, as well judged as it was well intentioned, and, I trust, was not misplaced or unrewarded. But perhaps the kindest and wisest thing he did for me was his introducing me to the excellent society which at that time, as much as any other before or since, distinguished Boston. To be sure, my connections with the prominent members of that society entitled me to be free of it; but it was to the kind encouragement and good offices of my guardian that I owed an earlier initiation than my years demanded. His own children were grown up and married off, excepting one bachelor son at home; so that he seemed to feel, and certainly expressed in his conduct, the sort of partial yet discreet indulgence a sensible man often shows to his youngest child. All this, however, is not particularly to the purpose of my narrative, of which I am by no means the hero; and I do not know why I should suppose that the public will care about my own private concerns. But the image of this worthy gentleman rising up before me as I looked back at that particular portion of my life, I felt impelled to jot down the slight pen-and-ink sketch you see above. And, as I hate rewriting anything, we will let it stand.

"I am glad you came to-day, Frank," said Mr. Moulton, after the first cordial greetings were passed; "for I expect a youngster to dine with me not long from college."

"Indeed, sir!" I replied. "And who may he be?"

"Oh! none of your acquaintances," he answered; "none of your Yankee collegians, let me tell you.

He is from Oxford or Cambridge, one or both; and I want you to be civil to him."

"An Englishman, then, I take it for granted," said I.

"Why, yes — he is, after a fashion," Mr. Moulton replied. "That is, he was born in England; but his father was a refugee Tory, — James Markham, — who raised and commanded a company of riflemen during the Revolution."

"And what is his business here, sir?" I inquired.

"His business is his pleasure, I guess," returned Mr. Moulton. "The Bellinghams and Mildmays are a sort of cousins of his, and he has been renewing the connection. Anne Shippen [one of his married daughters] thinks that he is sweet upon Esther Mildmay."

"Indeed!" I rejoined. "And has he been long enough here for that? I never heard of him before."

"Why, as to that," he answered, "how long, think ye, does it take a young fellow to get up a flirtation? and how long do you suppose it takes for the report of it to get wind?" looking at me with a quizzical kind of significance, which made me feel as if a sudden growth of nettles were springing under favorable circumstances from the entire surface of my body. "And as to your not having heard of him before, why, if a young gentleman's health requires his going into the country, he mustn't expect to be posted up to the very last minute. However, he has been here about a fortnight. But much may be done in a fortnight, Master Frank, I would have you know."

I could not reasonably have denied this proposition if I had felt disposed to be argumentative, which I did not. I was wondering whether any rumor of my frequent visits at Woodside had reached my guardian's ears; and, if so, whether he had drawn any inferences from them to the effect that I was in love with the charming Eleanor. Like most shy people, I was as proud as Lucifer, and scorned the idea of being supposed sighing at any lady's feet, seriously, until it was known that she had consented to extend her royal hand to place me by her side. Of course I was never without some princess or other, whom I served most faithfully till she was dethroned by some fresher usurper; but nobody ever regarded these transitory submissions as even looking towards a permanent allegiance. So I was resolved to take up my very last flirtation just where I had left it off two months before, and to prosecute it with redoubled zeal by way of blinding my Argus. Whether or not it was the most effectual way, experts in the art of love must decide according to their own experience. But I must defer these passages of mine with Matilda Robinson until I have more space than I have to spare here. I have in contemplation the preparation of a work to be entitled "The Philosophy of Flirtation; its Origin, Uses, and Tendencies: with Illustrations from the Life." Should this plan be carried into effect, the reader will there find everything made clear which the stern necessities of this particular case compel me to leave under a cloud.

Dinner-time came, and brought Harry Markham with it. He was three or four years older than I, and therefore I was the more disposed to like him when he showed an inclination to be friends with me. He had taken his bachelor's degree at Oxford a year or two before with good reputation, and was therefore a personage of great dignity and high interest in my sight. I was never tired of cross-examining him as to the details of university life and discipline in England; and he had not been so long delivered from them as not to like to recount them. During the fortnight of my stay in town (for my week grew by degrees to that size), we were constant companions. By day we scoured the country round in search of points of view (for he was an excellent draughtsman) and of historical interest. In the evenings we resorted to the pleasant societies still to be found even in many town houses, although it was early in August,— for the dispersion of the summer was not then as universal as it has since become, — or else we drew rein at some of the villas within ten miles of the city, where we were sure of a hospitable entertainment. Pleasant, cheerful, happy hours they were. And why not? It were hard, indeed, if the hours between nineteen and three and twenty were not pleasant, cheerful, and happy, — and those, too, the hours of a fine August flitting over the face of a lovely country, fit residence of as lovely inhabitants; at least, some of them.

I have forgotten to mention, what was not unimportant to the prosecution of these adventures, that I had succeeded admirably in accomplishing the object of my visit to Boston. I had mounted myself to my entire satisfaction, and in this had derived material assistance from the skill of my new friend in horseflesh. He had not wasted the whole of his time at the university over Latin and Greek. He had improved a portion of his hours in more practical pursuits, among which might be reckoned the occasional pursuit of foxes and hares; and one result of these studies was a more than common knowledge of the noblest of the servants of man. Having thus secured what I had come down for, soon after my arrival, I thought it advisable to give my new purchase a full and fair trial before taking him to the distant solitudes of Wensley: hence these rides of which I have spoken, and hence the agreeable episodes I have hinted at in the course of the last paragraph. So Whitefoot — for such was the Homeric designation we bestowed upon him, from the color of his off forefoot — Whitefoot and I formed the friendship which lasted for the rest of his life, under these pleasant circumstances and in this good company. To be sure, it took some time to satisfy all my scruples as to his sufficiency; and we had to make a good many afternoon and evening excursions, not always unaccompanied by side-saddles and riding-habits, before he had vindicated to himself his claim to my entire confidence. But it was erring, if erring it were, on the side of prudence and discretion, — virtues which were early developed in my character, and which I still regard as its chiefest jewels.

I do not know what inference my readers may draw from this voluntary prolongation of my leave of absence. Perhaps I ought not to have told of it. It may not be creditable to me, that I was willing to exchange the society of Miss Allerton for that of any number of other beauties. I certainly saw none other so handsome; but then, you know, safety may lie in other multitudes than those of counsellors. In fact, although I do hate inconstancy as much as my Lord Byron did, and, like him, "loathe, detest, the mortal made of such quicksilver clay that on his breast no permanent impression can be made" (I do not remember the quotation accurately enough to reduce it to verses), still even the most constant swain will occasionally make an excursion to gaze on other shepherdesses than his own, if it were only to glory in her supremacy over all others.

And perhaps I may have had a lurking idea that my cousin Eleanor might value her newly-found relative none the less for a brief interval of absence. All this on the supposition that she was more to me than any other pretty woman, which, you are aware, I have not yet admitted. But story-readers, as well as story-tellers, are a gossiping generation, and can seldom see a young man and woman in company together, without putting constructions on what they say and do, which perhaps it had never entered into their hearts to conceive. But as my course is a perfectly straightforward one, with no traps and pitfalls set to catch the interest of the reader, it is my duty to remove out of the way all objections that arise as they come along.

But still, as my fortnight's fast was drawing to an end, I began to feel a good wholesome appetite for Wensley again. Not only did I feel the wish growing strong within me to renew my cousinly relations with Woodside, but I longed to see the good Parson once more, and the worthy Jasper, whose sable image formed, as it were, the shadow of that of his master. In my talks with Markham, I told him all that I have told you about these characters in my rural drama, and he expressed a strong wish to be brought face to face with them. Of course I was not slow in asking him to come and pay me a visit. Major Grimes's doors, both of his house and his stable, ever stood open for the welcome of man and beast, and I could warrant him a friendly reception from all the rest. He thanked me, and promised to come at some convenient season before he left New England on his tour through the country.

I was a little surprised at his not being more in a hurry, when I made an accidental discovery in the course of one of our rides. We were discussing the comparative claims of two rival beauties, both of whom we had visited in the course of the afternoon. I do not remember how it came about; but I illustrated some criticism of mine by a reference to Miss Allerton, whose superiority over both the ladies in question I maintained. I averred, that, beautiful as they both were, they had nothing so striking as the effect of Miss Allerton's upward glance, from the contrast between her dark flashing eyes and her "fairly fair" complexion and golden hair.

"It is perfectly unique," I said, "as far as my observation goes. I have seen nothing like it."

"Not so remarkably so," he replied quickly, "as her downward look. Her eyelashes are perfectly preternatural."

"What!" I exclaimed. "Then you have seen her? I had not an idea of that!"

"Why, yes," he answered, a good deal disconcerted, for he had evidently committed himself, very much to his own vexation, — "why, yes. Have I never mentioned it to you before?"

"Mentioned it!" I responded. "To be sure you have not! But where did you meet her? and what do you think of her? and why have you not been up to see her?"

"Why, as to that," he replied, still somewhat confused, "I hardly feel myself sufficiently well acquainted with her to visit her at this distance of time and place. I met her once or twice in Devonshire, when reading there during the long vacation, about three years ago. It was not long before they came to America, I believe."

"But did you not think her splendidly handsome?" I inquired. "You don't mean to say that you have many such women in England, do you? Was not she as uncommon there as here?"

"She was very handsome, certainly," said he with more coolness than suited my own ideas. "But her style is not so rare in England as it is here. Yes," he continued, with an air of deliberation, "I think I may say that I have seen as handsome women as she."

I did not believe him, and put down his affirmation to the credit of his John Bullism, which would not suffer him to admit that anything could be better in this country than he had left at home.

Having talked over the daughter a little more, I tried to get him upon the father, and endeavored to extract from him some further particulars of his history than I had been able to gather from Mr. Bulkley. But, if he knew anything about him, he kept his own counsel; for I got nothing by my cross-examination. He lived like a gentleman, he said, with nothing observable or distinguishing about him. He had himself been brought into contact with him from the circumstance of his being employed by the British Government in the dispensation of the bounties of the Crown to the families of the loyalists. He was the accredited agent through whom the funds of many of those that had suffered in the Revolution reached the beneficiaries, especially those of them who had returned to America, or settled in the Provinces. He possessed the confidence of the ministers, and was eminently fitted for this business by his personal knowledge of almost all those unfortunate exiles, reaching back, in many cases, to the very time of the emigration. Markham's own father having belonged to this same category, he had had some intercourse with him at the agency in London on his part, and in consequence of this had received friendly attentions from him when he came into the neighborhood of Walford Hall on the occasion above recited. All this was natural enough, and I could not gainsay a word of it. Indeed, I believed it was all literally true; but I was by no means so sure that it was quite the whole truth. Markham, too, seemed to be entering into the conspiracy to mystify me about these people, whose affairs were certainly no business of mine. But, then, if people attended only to their own affairs, a stupid world we should have of it.

Nor was this the only share he had in my mystification. Not long afterwards we were just returning from a ride, and were proceeding towards the livery stable which was connected with the Exchange Coffee House, — at that time the chief hostelry that Boston boasted, — just as the New York stage-coach drove up to the door of the hotel. Everybody who visited Boston at that time will remember that the passage-way in front of that house of entertainment was very disproportionately small when compared with its size and pretensions; so much so, that we were interrupted in our career by the sweeping round of the four horses, and had to pull up for a moment. But that moment was sufficient; for just before my eyes, sitting on the coach-box, was the identical interloper whom I had last seen emerging like a water god from the waves of the Quasheen. There could not be a doubt of it. Though I had seen him but for a moment, the circumstances of that sight sufficed to stereotype his looks upon my memory forever. I should have known him if I had met him on the top of Mount Hecla. He looked at me from under his shaggy eyebrows (which, however, did not hinder his being a very well-looking fellow) as if he had seen me somewhere before. But I do not think he recognized me, as he probably took much less notice of me than I did of him.

His scrutiny of my countenance, however, was over, the moment his eyes glanced at my companion. He evidently enough recognized him, and derived no particular satisfaction from the recognition. He was very clearly a man not to be easily taken aback, and one that had a tolerable command of his countenance; but he could not control the expression of surprise and displeasure that was extorted from him by the suddenness of the encounter. Markham's face showed less equivocal marks of dislike, if not of surprise, as became his younger years and less disciplined facial muscles. He muttered an indistinct comment on the occasion, which did not reach farther than my ears; which being the case, and as it involved an adjective or two which might justly grieve godly ears, I shall forbear to put it upon permanent record. He on the coach-box made a kind of a motion, of the nature of a salutation, in the direction of the brim of his hat, which Markham acknowledged by the faintest perceptible swaying of his head, and then, turning away, rode on through the arch that led to the stables.

"That gentleman does n't seem to be fond of you, Markham," said I as naturally as I could. "Who may he be?"

"Oh, he's a countryman of mine," he replied; "that is, he is my countryman and yours too. He's a half Yankee, as well as myself. We are not over fond of one another, as you suspect."

"And his name is Smith, is it not?" I put interrogatively.

"Smith!" he answered. "What do you mean by that? Do you suppose every Englishman is named Smith?"

"Why, it is a tolerably generic name," I answered. "But I had a more specific reason for supposing it to belong to him, for I have been told so by a landlord of his."

"For God's sake, what do you mean, Osborne?" he demanded in strong surprise. "Where have you ever seen him? He surely does n't pass here by that name!"

I then stated that I had met this personage, whoever he might be, in the neighborhood of Wensley, when fishing, not long before, and that I had accidentally learned, from the landlord where he lodged, that he rejoiced in the general appellation I had applied to him. Of course I made no mention of my cousin Eleanor's name in the business, and seemed to know no more of him than I have just related. Why shouldn't I have my little mystery too? And I rather imagined that he would have given all I wanted to know in exchange for what I had to tell. But my lips were sealed, of course, as to all that had passed between them in my presence. And Markham had to spell out the mystery, as well as he could, without my assistance.

"This is very strange!" said Markham, half to himself. "What could he have been lurking about there for, under a *nom de guerre?*" And then, addressing himself to me, he went on, "The man's name is Ferguson; and I am almost as much at a loss as you to account for his changing it without royal license. But Englishmen have a charter to be odd, and possibly this is the form which Mr. Ferguson's oddity takes unto itself. At any rate," he went on, as if talking to himself again, "we will hope there are not many Englishmen like him. He's a black sheep."

He then changed the conversation; and, it being plain he wished to avoid the subject, I could get no more satisfaction from him about it. And, as this was the last time we were to be together previous to my return to Wensley, I had no further opportunity of recurring to it. At parting, however, he promised me, of his own accord, that he would certainly beat up my quarters before very long; until which time I was perforce compelled to adjourn my curiosity. We parted that night; and the next day Whitefoot carried me safely to Parson Bulkley's door, at which we were both of us joyfully received both by master and man.

## CHAPTER IX.

#### WHICH IS EPISODICAL, BUT PROGRESSIVE.

THE attentive reader will not, perhaps, be surprised to hear that the very first event in the Wensley life of Whitefoot was a visit to Woodside, which occurred on the afternoon of the very day succeeding that of his arrival. He was fortunate enough to meet with the approbation of my cousin Eleanor, and also, which was perhaps a more important testimony to his character, with that of my much respected and more experienced cousin, the Colonel. That gallant officer made a close and scientific inspection of his various points with the eye at once of an *amateur* and of a *connoisseur*, and was pleased to pronounce him very well indeed for a horse bred and broken in America. This, I was well aware, was as high praise as an Englishman (for such Colonel Allerton persisted in considering himself, notwithstanding his New England birth and parentage) could be expected to bestow on Bucephalus, or Pegasus himself, were one or both of those celebrated animals trotted out for his opinion. So I accepted it as the seal of my bargain, and felt entitled to brag according to knowledge of his merits whenever Major Grimes and his party saw fit to disparage him as an interloping rival of Turk.

This interested opposition, however, was confined exclusively to the Grimes faction (a pretty large one, by the way); for the Wensleyans in general, outside of the charmed circle described by the Major's toddy stick, were unanimous in giving Whitefoot the preeminence over his Moslem competitor.

And the feeling of triumph was very universal; for I flatter myself I had become by this time rather a favorite in the town, though neither my modesty nor the necessities of my story will allow of my recounting the whereby and wherefore. I say it caused a widespread feeling of satisfaction when the last convincing proof of his excellence was given by Major-General Boardman, an eminent house-carpenter (builder he would be called in these euphuistic days) of Haverford, the capital town of the county, who did Whitefoot the honor to borrow him for the fall muster, selecting him out of all the steeds of the shire as the most worthy to bound beneath his weight (which was considerable) along the arms-presenting line, and to share with him the dangers and glories of that important field day. To be sure, Major Grimes was heard to suggest to some of his faction, that " it was n't likely Mr. Frank Osborne was going to take any hire for his beast;" which, indeed, it was not; nor yet, I should hope, that an officer of such distinction should have been influenced by so sordid a consideration.

It was also unfortunately true that the gallant General gave occasion for disrespectful language on the part of his subordinate officer, by returning his borrowed charger with a piece of the skin (technically called the *bark*) taken off his near hind-leg, occasioned by backing him against the wheel of a gun-carriage. This gave the enemy great cause for triumph; and I was not over well pleased with the circumstance myself. As for Colonel Allerton, who had the natural antipathy of a regular for a citizen soldier, when I told him of the mishap, he was louder and deeper in the expression of his sense of the General's stupidity than even I had been. Indeed, he spoke of it in terms, which, as they might be neither acceptable nor edifying to the serious reader, I shall considerately pretermit. Suffice it to say that they were of a nature, which, had the Colonel been under the General's command, would have justly subjected him to be court-martialled for "unbecoming and disrespectful language towards his superior officer." I, however, regarding the accident as the fortune of war, to which I was myself in some good measure accessory by consenting to expose my white-footed friend to its casualties, possessed my soul in such patience as I could muster, inly resolving that he should be exempt from military duty from that time forward.

I have thrown these particulars together in this place, although thereby I run before the regular course of my history, to which I am in general careful scrupulously to confine myself, in order that the reader might take in at a glance all the bearings of this important affair, and also that it may be cleared out of the way, so as not to interfere with those scenes of intense interest, which, like the rain in the almanac, may be looked for about this time. We will now return to the afternoon when I first submitted my horse to the cousinly inspection above mentioned. The examination over, and Whitefoot consigned to the care of Mr. Jonathan Snell (who was also pleased to vouchsafe his gracious approval of the same), the Colonel retired to his own room, the same described in my third chapter as enjoying the brevet rank of the library; and my cousin Eleanor and I strolled out to enjoy the exquisite summer afternoon just melting into evening.

We took our way towards the avenue of elms which I have already said descended the other side of the little hill on which the house stood. It was as sweet a walk as a pair of lovers (had we only happened to have been such) could have desired. The avenue led nowhere, to be sure, excepting to a rough field, not long cleared, which was skirted by the old wood which gave its name to the place; but the turf was elastic and velvety, from being kept closely mown and well rolled, in the English fashion; and the branches, thick with leaves, and alive with birds, stretched themselves long and wide until they clasped each other over our head. And after descending the first sharp though short descent, assisted by steps cut in the turf, you were hid by a screen of shrubbery from the house, and might have imagined yourself in Arden or the Black Forest, for any signs of human neighborhood that forced themselves on your notice.

As we paced up and down this "dry, smooth-shaven green," my lovely cousin magnetizing me with the gentle weight of her hand on my arm, we launched at once into the animated discourse of friends to the current of whose talk the interposition of a short absence has given at once a greater fulness and a swifter flow. She gave me such bits of gossip as the village had afforded during the two weeks of my absence, of which Petchell, her maid, who had established relations with certain of the inhabitants, was the voucher. Perhaps it was peculiar to this young lady, that she did not dislike to hear tell of the loves and the bickerings, of the history (private and public, civil and ecclesiastical) of the little neighborhood at her door. And why not? Human beings are human still in such an out-of-the-way nook as Wensley; and they are no more in the throngs of Hyde Park or the Boulevards, of St James's or the Tuileries. And one who sympathizes with the joys and sorrows of men and women, and not with the cost or fashion of their clothes or carriages, who finds interest in their characters and fates rather than in their houses and furniture, will find food enough for sadness and for mirth in more unlikely spots than the one which my gentle heroine gladdened by the genial influences of her sweet and kindly presence.

But I was, in virtue of my absence, expected to be the chief talker; and, accordingly, I retailed whatever store of news I had collected in Boston, for her amusement. In those days, the connection of an inland town, like Wensley, with the capital of the State, was hardly so intimate as the connection of that city with the capital of the world is now, so effectually has steam accomplished that annihilation of time and space for which the lovers celebrated in the Bathos prayed. "The Columbian Centinel" afforded the only loophole through which the curious inhabitants peeped, twice a week, at the busy world; and I believe Mr. Bulkley and Colonel Allerton were the only regular subscribers its hearty old editor, Major Ben. Russell, had in the town. The Colonel, to be sure, had the English papers; but they came at long intervals, and with no great regularity.

I told Miss Eleanor all the private history I had learned, the engagements, the marriages, the deaths, the feuds, and the reconciliations, which made up then, as they do now and ever will, the staple of our communications about our acquaintances and friends. Having emptied my budget of everything I had to tell, excepting the things I was thinking most about, we sat down on a rustic bench placed near the head of the avenue, at a point from which the sunset could be commanded, and remained for a while silently gazing at the gorgeous clouds, which the touch of celestial light had transformed from cold masses of vapor into cliffs and billows of gold and violet, as the eye of genius looks on the commonest things of earth, and they glow as with hues caught fresh from heaven.

As we sat watching these glorious apparitions together,—Eleanor, I am afraid, thinking more of them than of me, and I, I am sure, thinking more of her than of them,—she said presently, rather to herself than to me,—

"It is a strange thing that a sight like this, which happens every day, should never look twice alike either to the eyes or to the mind. The feelings it creates, or recalls to the heart, are as varied, though not always as bright, as the hues it leaves on the clouds there."

"True, Cousin Eleanor," I replied. "But all sunsets are not brilliant and bright like this. Some suns go down in clouds and storms, you know, and darkness comes upon us with no glorious prologue like that before our eyes."

"Yes, indeed," she answered, "more than of such as these. The analogy holds good, which poets and moralists have discerned, and which no one can help feeling, between the closing scenes of life and of day. There are few men, as well as few suns, you remember,

   ' whom scenes like these await,
  Who sink unclouded in the gulfs of fate.' "

"That is true again," I returned; "but then it is the very clouds that seek to oppress the sinking sun that make his ending so splendid, when he has the power to overcome them, and make them contribute to his glory."

"And even where clouds and darkness rest upon him when he goes to his rest," she resumed, "we know that he is still the same bright and blessed orb as when he shone at noonday, and that he will be sure to return again as beautiful and beneficent as ever."

"We know that of the sun," I replied; "for we have the experience of hundreds of generations to the fact. But there, I imagine, the analogy ends. The dead never return again, be their setting bright or dark."

Eleanor turned her eyes from the fading sunset, and looked into mine.. "Cousin Frank," said she, "you have thought seriously for so young a man" (she, you will recollect, I judged to be a matter of a twelvemonth or so older than I, and, as such, entitled to talk wisdom to me). "I should think that your day was bright enough to keep the thought of its ending out of your mind."

"You forget, Eleanor," I replied, dropping the usual consanguineous epithet for the first time,— "you forget, that, though my day may be young, it has not been without its morning clouds, neither. It is not altogether a cheerful thing, cousin, to have neither father nor mother, nor brother nor sister. Mine have all sunk into the gulfs of Fate you just spoke of, and left me to live out my day by myself as I may. I was not old enough then to know or to feel my loss; but I am now to do both."

"I had forgotten, dear Cousin Frank," said Eleanor kindly, in reply; "I confess I had, just then. But I should not have done so, for I am too nearly in your condition myself. My father indeed lives; but he is my only blood relation. And my estate is in one thing sadder than yours, for *I* do remember my mother; and the agony her death caused is still fresh in my mind. Perhaps, however," she said with a sigh, as it were to herself again,—"perhaps, however, it saved her from a yet deeper agony, had she"— And she stopped, as if recollecting herself.

"I do not understand your allusion, of course, cousin," I replied. "But I do not accept your philosophy. It is no consolation to me to think my father and mother are spared from possible or certain evils. I wish them to be alive, and live out their days, as Nature meant they should. She never meant that they should leave me, a wailing infant in the cradle, a burden to friends, or a task to hirelings. It was my part to have laid their heads in the grave long years hence, after they had reared, guided, and taught me in my way of life, which I must now enter upon alone. No, no, my cousin: life is a better thing than death, let its circumstances be what they may; unless, indeed," I added quite casually, by way of an exceptive demonstration of a general proposition,—"unless, indeed, it be infamy. Dishonor, indeed"—

I stopped short; for looking at Eleanor, who was earnestly listening to me as I spoke, I saw that something touched her. A sort of spasm seemed to contract her features; her eyes closed; and she bit her under lip so suddenly that the blood actually trickled down her beautiful chin. At the same time she violently but unconsciously clutched my arm. I was greatly alarmed, and exclaimed, —

"Dearest Eleanor, you are very ill. Let me call Petchell. Let me help you into the house, for God's sake!"

"No, no," said she, recovering herself as I spoke. "I am well again. It was a transient pain; but it is gone now," opening her eyes, which looked preternaturally bright, and, contrasting with her pale face and the trickling crimson from her lip, gave her an expression which almost frightened me, it was so unnatural and wild.

"Come," she said presently, — "come, let us take a turn or two. It will make me better."

We rose and walked slowly down the path under the trees. She leaned heavily on my arm; and after a single turn, in which she rather tottered than walked, she said that she must go in; and we approached the turf steps, which, as I have said before, assisted the ascent to the house. Eleanor paused for a moment at the foot; and I, merely to assist her in mounting them, passed my arm round her waist for her more effectual support. We were kinsfolk you know, at least after a sort, and common humanity, as well as cousinly affection, made it imperative upon me to see that she received no detriment while under my charge. At any rate, as she found no fault with the arrangement (I am afraid that she never noticed it), I apprehend that it can be no manner of concern of yours. Perhaps there was no absolute necessity of continuing it after the steps had been scaled, but something must be forgiven to the force of habit (and some habits do not take long to form); and then it must be remembered that the ground still sloped gently upward as you skirted the screen of shrubbery which divided the avenue from the house.

As we labored rather slowly along this " verdurous wall," some one suddenly turned the corner, and advanced towards us. At first I supposed that it must be her father, and was glad he was coming to my help. But, when I raised my eyes to his face, to my great surprise I saw before me Henry Markham, whom I had parted from at the Exchange Coffee House only two or three days before. I don't know how it was; but I was not as glad to see him at that moment as I would have sworn I should have been to meet him in Wensley, when we arranged his visiting me at some time future. It was quite a new revelation to me that he was on such terms with Eleanor as to come to see her without some greater show of ceremony. And, to do him justice, he did not seem to be much better pleased with the particular grouping of the figures before him. Perhaps he thought it *too* particular. I am sure it was not unpicturesque, and, if he did not like it, why, it was the worse for him. As for Miss Eleanor, she seemed to be surprised out of all her late agitation, and stood quite firmly again in the face of this apparition. The blood rushed into her cheeks with the pretty effect I have celebrated when I first introduced her to the reader's acquaintance; and she had a look out of her eyes at this young man, which was not altogether well pleasing in mine. I spoke first.

"Markham," I exclaimed, "you are better than your word! You are upon me before I have had time to tell Miss Allerton that you were coming to Wensley. But you are welcome all the same, and I am right glad to see you."

I am afraid this assurance must be reduced into the category of that description of embroidery about which Mrs. Amelia Opie wrote a story, which was much in vogue about that time (though, as I remember them, her white lies, if they were not black ones, well deserved to be such), as well as the assertion that I had not had time to tell Eleanor that he was coming. I think that I might have found time, if I had been economical of it, to have told her as much as that. But, for some reason or other, I did not like to tell her of the approaching advent of so handsome and taking an Old-World acquaintance of hers. She cast a look, in which there was a good deal of surprise mingled with a little displeasure, as I thought, at my reticence, and then, bowing to Markham, said, —

" I had heard from papa that Mr. Markham was in

the country, but did not expect the pleasure of a visit from him at Wensley."

"I had no intention of intruding myself upon Miss Allerton," said Harry, a little discomposed, but a good deal *miffed;* "but, missing of my friend Osborne at the parsonage (with rather a savage look at my right arm, which was now relieved from its recent duty, and was supporting hers), I took the liberty of walking over here to find him, and at the same time to pay my respects to Colonel and Miss Allerton."

"Papa and I will be always happy to see the friends of Mr. Osborne," Eleanor returned rather stiffly; "and, if you please, we will return into the house, and I will send for him."

It is barely possible that Markham would have dispensed with this last attention; but he could not well refuse it, and so he turned and walked along with us.

"Are you quite well, Miss Allerton?" he presently inquired. "I am afraid you have met with some accident just now," looking at the scarlet stain on her ivory skin. "Have you fallen?"

"A slight accident," she replied, putting her hand to her lip. "Of no consequence at all. A little cold water will put it all to rights again."

There was no time for further speech, for we were now in the parlor. Eleanor, after ringing the bell, and ordering her father to be called, went up stairs to her dressing-room to wash away the bloody witness from her face. My curiosity was well aroused, as may be well supposed, to learn the relations of my new friend and my cousins; but I had no time for inquiry, as the alert step of the Colonel was heard approaching at the same time almost that her light foot was over the other threshold. He entered with his usual open and cordial face of hospitality that ever beamed upon the stranger within his gates. As the shades of evening were beginning to prevail, he had actually grasped the hand of Markham before he saw who he was. When he discerned his visitor's face, the expression of his own changed as suddenly as did that of the landscape under the thunder-cloud to whose good offices I had owed my first introduction to Woodside. The pressure of his hand was checked in mid-grasp, and that of his visitor dropped, after no prolonged salutation. His air was pervaded with a perfectly courteous but thoroughly frigid tone, enough, I am sure, to have turned me into an icicle, had I been the object of it.

I really pitied poor Markham, though I was not regarding him just then with absolute complacency. I saw that more had passed between him and the Allertons in England than he had chosen to intimate to me; and I would have given Whitefoot, and boot besides, to anybody that could tell me how it all was. But there was no apparent danger of my being led into such a rashness. There was no one who could enlighten me on this side the Atlantic. But stop — was there no one? There was Petchell. She must know all about it. But it would be base and ungentlemanlike to pry into the secrets of my hospitable cousins in that kind of way. So it would. But, on the whole, I am rather glad that I had no opportunity for a *tête-à-tête* interview with "Machiavel the waiting-maid," about that time.

The salutations over, as above described, Colonel Allerton waved us to seats, and then took a chair himself. He first made civil inquiries after Markham's family; which being satisfied, he then proceeded, —

"I did not expect the pleasure of seeing you in America when we parted in London."

"I did not then anticipate visiting this country," said Markham. "But circumstances have made it seem important to me to come hither, though I may have over-estimated their urgency."

"Indeed!" replied the Colonel rather dryly, though very politely. "I had no idea that Mr. Henry Markham's affairs were of such pressing moment. I hope they will arrange themselves to his satisfaction."

"I hope, sir," he returned, "that I shall accomplish the purpose of my journey; though it was not undertaken for my own benefit, and I do not expect either gratitude or reward for what I came to attempt."

"That would be a pity," answered Colonel Allerton a little sub-acidulously. "And perhaps it would have been well to have considered how your services were likely to be regarded by your clients before you volunteered them in their cause. Working for others for nothing, and without their desire, is not the way to become lord-chancellor, Mr. Markham. But, then,

I know nothing of the nature of your affairs," he added in a courteous tone.

"I do not defend the wisdom of my conduct," said Markham, in a tone of deeply-mortified feeling; "but I am sure of its motive; and, as I hope for no recompense, I hope I may be forgiven if I have been fool enough to throw away my own time and pains, looking not for my own again."

"That, sir," replied the Colonel with cool politeness, "is a question which you alone can decide, as you alone know what your plans are. But you will pardon me, if, as an old man, I advise you, a very young one, to direct your chief attention in affairs to those with which you are thoroughly acquainted, and in which you have a legitimate call to assist."

Markham was evidently much hurt by the words and manner of his host, though I could see no reason why. Of course I knew that more was meant than met my ear; but that was small comfort to me. He made no reply except a bow, by no means as easy and *dégagé* as those I had seen him make in the drawing-rooms about Boston. But just then Miss Allerton re-appeared, calm and composed as ever, and forthwith rang for lights and tea. The conversation was not very well sustained after this event; the three others being, apparently, thinking of something besides what they were saying, and I as busily engaged in thinking what that something could be. I was rather too fast in saying that Eleanor's manner was as calm and composed as ever. It was plain to me, on the close though guarded observation to which I subjected her, that she was making a strong effort to appear as if it were. But there was a little tremor in the hands as she took her cup of tea, and a careful avoidance of Markham's eye, which soon recovered courage enough to go in search of hers, which I saw plainly enough, and which, though it was none of my business, I did not like at all.

For the first time since I had visited at the Allertons', and often as I had partaken of the fragrant decoction of Cathay in their company, the elements of that most social of meals (some people prefer breakfast; but I am apt to be sulky then) were dispensed from a circumambulatory tray, instead of resting on a solid, steadfast tea-table. It was, in short, what some opprobriously, but justly, style a *lap tea*, — an institution which I detest and execrate. I must confess to a secret sense of exultation when I have seen a clumsy boy upset a cup of tea over the glossy silk of the lady of the house, or drop a slice of bread and butter — "and always on the buttered side" — upon the puffy pile of her Wilton or Axminster carpet. It must have been a "lap tea" at which Belinda assisted on the fatal day of the Rape of the Lock; only it was before dinner, and was coffee, and not tea. For what did the sylphs think it necessary to do?

> "Straight hover round the fair her airy band :
> Some, as she sipped, the fuming liquor fanned ;
> Some o'er her lap their careful plumes displayed,
> Trembling, and conscious of the rich brocade."

Now, there would have been no such need of this anxiety if her (I beg pardon, "*la reine d'Espagne n'a point des jambes*") — if her *lap* had been safely ensconced under the mahogany. What wonder, then, that, while thus engaged, the relentless baron should have reft the envied tress

"From the fair head forever and forever."

I am the more zealous to maintain the integrity of the tea-table, as an occasional slight fit of the gout (entirely hereditary) compels me, though so young a man, to forego prolonged sessions after dinner. But this is aside from the stately march of my narrative.

I drew one inference from this innovation on the customs of Woodside, which was, that, though its character for hospitality was to be maintained, it did not think it necessary to be cordial. So, after the tray had made its third and last round, I ordered my horse, and took my leave. Markham, though he had come on foot, departed with me, and with no entreaties to the contrary to resist. The Colonel and Eleanor bade him good-night very civilly; but they threw even more than their usual cordiality into their manners towards me. I was not flattered by it this time, nor yet was poor Markham; for we both understood it well enough. He walked alongside me, with his hand on the saddle (Whitefoot walked remarkably fast and well), and I accompanied him to Grimes's door.

He said but little, and I not much more, as it was impossible to say what I wanted to. He showed no disposition to make me his confidant; and I was none the nearer plucking out the heart of this mystery, supposing it had one, than when I first suspected its existence. Arrived at the Major's, I resolutely declined Markham's invitation to go in, and the more earnest if less disinterested urgency of the host himself to partake of a mug of flip or a rummer of punch, as a safeguard against the night air. Facing this enemy without either infallible spell against its perils, I put my horse up to his speed, his hoofs marking their course by a continuous line of sparkles, and the bridge returning a hollow roar, heard far through the village, as he galloped over it. A very brief time sufficed to bring us to the parsonage and to Jasper.

The next morning at breakfast, as I was telling Mr. Bulkley the particulars of Markham's visit to Woodside, — only suppressing, as is usually the case with most human communications, what was most characteristically essential to them, and he was listening eagerly to my narration, — Jasper entered with a more important countenance than usual, looking as if he had something to say too. When I had done my story, the Parson turned to Jasper and said, —

"Who was that in the wagon I saw you talking with just now? Anybody to see me?"

"No, sir," replied Jasper; "it was only Jehiel Abbot, from Jericho (meaning, not the ancient city of that name, at which unscrupulous moderns — why, I know not — are apt to wish troublesome things and persons, but a remote school district so christened by common consent). He says there's a scrape up there, sir."

"Scrape! What scrape? What d'ye mean?" interrogated the divine.

"Why, he says, sir," answered Jasper, "that old Captain Hunt swears that his daughter Sukey Ann sha'n't marry Jeremiah Adams nohow. And she's taking on dreadful, he says, sir."

"Not marry Jeremiah!" exclaimed the minister. "What's the meaning of that? Were not the banns stuck up in the meeting-house porch last Sabbath?"

"Yes, sir," responded Jasper. "I saw the folks reading 'em; and I looked over Pete Spicer's shoulder, and they was there, sir."

"Well, then, what's the matter with the Captain?" inquired his master. "What has Jeremiah done?"

"Nothing, sir, has n't Jeremiah," replied the man. "It's Squire Enoch, his father, that the Captain's mad with. It's something about the right to drive his cattle over Hog's Neck down to Rocky Valley to pasture. The Captain fenced in Hog's Neck into his nineteen-acre lot; and the Squire broke the fence down, and said he'd as much right to go over the Neck as the Captain had to go over the road to meeting."

"Oho," said the Parson; "it's the old quarrel about the right of way over Hog's Neck, is it? The land on Hog's Neck," he proceeded, addressing himself to me, and laughing as he spoke, "is worth about three cents an acre, and that of Rocky Valley is worth full three cents less. I thought I had patched up that trouble a long while ago. So it's broken out afresh, you say, Jasper?"

"Worse than ever, sir," Jasper said. "The Captain said he'd shoot the Squire if he touched the fence again; and the Squire told him to fire away, and pulled it down the next morning. Then the Captain swore he'd sue him; and the Squire told him to sue and be"—

"Never mind that part of it," interrupted the minister, laughing. "And the upshot of the matter is, that the match is off between pretty Susey Hunt and Jerry Adams, is it?"

"So the Captain says, and the Squire too; but Jehiel says Jerry says he won't stand it, and he'll marry her whether or no," said Jasper.

"There's a fine fellow!" rejoined the minister, rubbing his hands complacently; for he took the interest of a girl in all the marrying and giving in marriage in Wensley. "He ought to be kicked, though, if he didn't say so. But I must try and hinder any breach of discipline, if I can. Things had better be done decently and in order. So the Captain says he'll sue, does he?"

"He swears he will," replied Jasper; "and Jehiel was to stop at Grimes's and tell the stage to call round this afternoon, as he's going to Lawyer Pratt, at Haverford, about it."

"Merciful goodness!" exclaimed the minister, half in jest, but a full half in earnest. "If he has gone that length, it is time for me to step in, to be sure. Lawyer Pratt in Wensley! That must be hindered at any rate. I can have no such wolf as that among my lambs. Jasper, get my horse ready, and I'll see after it at once."

"Had n't you better take mine, sir?" said I. "He will carry you to the field of action the sooner."

"No, no, I thank you," he replied, shaking his head. "I'll stick to my old friend as long as he lasts; for I'm afraid I should not stick to your new one. I served in the infantry, you know, and was brigade major for only two campaigns. And, by the way, as you will want to see your friend to-day, I'll grant you a furlough from actual service for that time. Bring him to dinner with you, if he will come."

And as soon as he was brought round, the brisk old man mounted his old horse, as if he had been a charger smelling the battle afar off (and perhaps he did), and shambled away upon him in the direction of Jericho. His taking the field thus promptly against the threatened invasion of Lawyer Pratt was, as I had already learned, only a part of the established policy of his realm. He seemed to have erected himself into a high court of justice within its limits, and for many years had judged without appeal in the controversies which would sometimes arise in his parish. Such a thing as a suit at law was unheard of within the memory of the middle-aged section of the Wensleyans.

It is needless to say that such a state of things was unpropitious to the prospects of the noble profession of the law. It was many years since the last suckling practitioner who had ventured to occupy the little square office between the grocer's shop and the meeting-house (built by Mr. Remington, the predecessor of the Allertons at Woodside, away back in the last century, literally before the year one) — it was many years, I say, since Eliphalet W. Peabody, now member of Congress for the twenty-ninth district of Ohio, fled to the western wilderness, as it was then, from before the face of fate, of starvation, and of Parson Bulkley. The office had been for more than a quarter of a century converted (or perverted) into the primary-school-house of the first district, presided over in my time by Miss Lucinda Jane Sparhawk (now Mrs. Judge Wilkinson, of Bytown), who was not a bad-looking girl either.

But I may as well mention, *à propos* to the tender griefs of Jeremiah and Sukey as recounted by Jasper, that there was another troubler of the peace than law, about which the good Parson took an active interest whenever it applied to any of his parishioners; and that was — love. Though a bachelor past hope for many years, he was a great promoter of matrimony. He had a sharp eye for a love affair; and, when he approved of the connection, he was an invaluable auxiliary. Many was the match to which he had smoothed the way, and many was the course of true love of which he had cleared away the impediments that hindered it from running smooth. To look at, he did not seem to be a much properer person to trust a love tale to than Cato himself. But there was nothing stoical about him; and this was so well understood that the young people of the town were as ready to confide their difficulties in this sort to him as to any of their contemporaries. They were sure of a tender and active interest in their affairs which scarcely ever failed to bring them to a happy conclusion, if they deserved such an ending.

In short, he was in himself a parliament of love, as well as a high court of justice, for the domain of Wensley. And he bore his faculties meekly, as well as absolutely, so that no one complained of him, — the very Trajan or Antonine of village despots. I thought I could observe that he had composed a little sort of romance in his own mind, of which Eleanor Allerton and I were chief characters. But I rather felt than saw it, as he abstained from any demonstrative interference or intimation of it with the most scrupulous delicacy. So scrupulous was he, indeed, that I should have found it hard to get an opportunity to tell him what our relations to each other really were. But, if I could, I wonder whether I should have done it. It is odd what satisfaction we find in this world of ours, not only in our own delusions (what should we be without them?), but also in the delusions of others about us.

## CHAPTER X.

### IN WHICH THE CALDRON BEGINS TO SIMMER.

I SPENT the morning with Markham, as the minister had supposed I should; and we made such a *reconnaissance* of the country as the good grace of Black Sally accorded to us. She performed her part of the contract safely and surely, if not with inordinate velocity, and enabled us to respond to the almost parental pride with which the Major seemed to boast of his horses, without more than a simple fracture of the truth. The Major was, of course, a new study to Markham, who had only known the obsequious and deferential landlords of merry England; but he was of a temperament to adapt himself to any concatenation of circumstances which might involve him, and was by no means slack in accepting the platform of social equality which placed the old-fashioned New England host on a level with his guest. Markham was singularly free from the John-Bullism which makes so many of the progeny of that respectable sire appear so very much like *calves* when they find themselves in a new pasture.

To be sure, he was a parcel Yankee; and his mother's milk might yet qualify the elements of which he was kindly mixed. But, as a general thing, your half-breed Englishman is more unpleasantly national than the full-blooded animals themselves, — *Anglis ipsis Anglior*, — and appears to take more than an Englishman's delight in making himself disagreeable. But Markham was none of this sort. He was a cosmopolitan gentleman, and carried with him all over the world that sweetness of temper and sincere wish to make those with whom he found himself happy and on good terms with themselves, which was sure to extract what good there was from whatever men or manners he lighted on, and at the same time to make friends and well-wishers everywhere.

Being such as he was, what could have been the reason of the cold and severely civil treatment he had met with at Woodside, from persons whose characters and manners seemed to be so eminently like his own? I could not make it out at all to my satisfaction. Nor could I well seek satisfaction from Markham himself, unless he led to the subject and volunteered the explanation I desiderated; neither of which things he did during this morning's drive. He was not quite as chatty as he used to be in our rides round Boston; and there was a little shade over his features at first, such as even a passing grief leaves behind it for a season; but it gradually rose from his countenance and dispersed itself, as the shadow of a cloud passes away from the landscape, and he became cheerful, if not mercurial, as usual, long before we betook ourselves to the parsonage in accordance with Mr. Bulkley's invitation.

My account of that excellent man had made Markham intelligently curious to see him; and they came at once into friendly relations with each other. Their points of resemblance and of difference equally fitted them for a close adaptation to one another. Mr. Bulkley was an old man, and Markham a young one. The former had lived for near forty years in the almost eremitic seclusion of Wensley; the latter had spent in the crowds and turmoil of London all the years of his life that had not been passed in the differing but not diverse excitation of a great university. Both were lovers of learning (Markham had graduated with high honors) and of queer books. Markham was vastly more exact in his knowledge of the mechanism of the ancient languages, and more critical in all their ornamentation of metres and quantities, than the imperfect instruction of Mr. Bulkley's youth had made him. But the latter was quite as fully master of the spirit of the greater classics as my younger friend; and he was familiar with a much wider range of authors more talked of than read, including the later Platonists and the mediæval Latinists. Markham, however, was much better versed in contemporary literature than Mr. Bulkley pretended or cared to be,— much better, indeed, than English university men, wranglers, and medallists, who take high honors at Oxford or Cambridge, are apt to be even at this day. Neither of them was a man of surpassing abilities; but they had both of them made the most of what they had, and had them always in order for use. And for "human nature's daily food," I preferred them to most of the great geniuses I have encountered in my walk through Vanity Fair; and I have stumbled, at one time or another, on almost all of special note within the last quarter of a century.

When we were fairly seated at the table, — which Jasper had done his best to set out in honor of the occasion, though he cast rather an evil eye at Markham at first, as "the spawn of an old Tory," as he phrased it, with more of emphasis than elegance, — I asked Mr. Bulkley as to the success of his campaign against Jericho.

"Why, I found it shut up almost as strait as Jericho of old," said he; "but I think the walls will fall down by the time I have compassed it once or twice more, and blown a blast or two on my ram's horn."

"Well, sir," I put in, "and Jasper and I will shout in your cause; for we are all the people you have to help you, I suppose."

"Pray, make me free of your tribe," said Markham, whom I had possessed of the facts of the case.

"With all my heart," answered the Parson; "but I hope you will only have to shout for my victory, and not in my help. I think I have nearly arranged it."

"And how does it stand, sir?" I inquired.

"I'll tell you," he replied. "I found it all as Jasper told us. Squire Adams and Captain Hunt were in high feud, and poor Sue in great affliction, and Jeremiah in a towering passion, and all about a right of way over nothing to nowhere; for that is about the exact value of the matters in dispute."

"Did you tell them so, sir?" I asked.

"Bless you, no, indeed!" he answered. "I made much of it, you may be sure. To make short work of the story, I at last prevailed on Hunt to postpone his visit to Lawyer Pratt, agreeing to get the opinion of Boston counsel as to the right of way over Hog's Neck. And I afterwards got Adams to agree that, if the opinion were against himself, he would give the Rocky Valley pastures to Jeremiah on his marriage to Sukey, if Hunt would concede the right of way to him. So I imagine I shall settle the quarrel without promoting a lawsuit and without damaging a lovesuit. And I am now quite ready for my dinner."

"I am sure you have deserved it, sir," said Markham; "but, if there were many such clergymen as you, I am afraid it would go hard with us lawyers."

"Fear nothing, my young friend," returned the Parson; "there is little danger of the gospel prevailing against the law in your day. The juice of Mother Eve's apple is not worked out of the veins of her children quite yet. And that puts me in mind, Jasper, that you have not brought up the bottled cider."

This oversight was speedily remedied; and frothing cups, such as Phillips, the bard of cider, might have sung, crowned the board. This beverage, of which both the Parson and Jasper were justly proud, as the production of their own orchard and mill, was made from a receipt given to Lieutenant Bulkley by Major Sir John Knatchbull, a baronet of the cider county of Gloucestershire, when he was a prisoner on parole after Burgoyne's surrender. It was produced only on rare occasions, — such as a visit from an Oxonian, who was also the son of an old-world friend from whom he had been separated for such long years by politics and the ocean. A moderate glass of very excellent Madeira, the gift of Lieutenant-Governor Bromfield years ago, concluded the repast. The Parson then lighted his pipe, and Markham and I our cigars; and a fine afternoon of talk we had of it. But that must be passed by in silence; as there is a limit at which a story, like patience, ceases to be a virtue. Before we separated, which was not till after tea and well into the evening, Mr. Bulkley informed us that he should go to Boston the next morning.

"I meant to go the next day," said he, "to see about Dr. Felch's council of dismission; but I prefer putting myself out of my way a little to break this Hog's Neck, inasmuch as they both are a trifle ashamed of giving me the trouble I am to have; and I am confident it will clinch the matter. I think Mr. Hayley must give an opinion which will answer my purpose; and, which is better, he'll ask nothing for it."

Markham, hearing this, declared that he would avail himself of the chance of his company back to town, as he had accomplished his visit to me. I remonstrated against this determination, in which the minister joined me; though, as he said, he was arguing against himself. Markham was firm, however; and the next morning, accordingly, he was in the coach when it came round to the parsonage; and it whirled them both off together, after brief time for leave-taking,— Parson Bulkley declaring that if the proverb were true, that "good company was as good as a coach," certainly good company and a coach too were better still.

Left thus alone, with only the company of Tacitus and Euripides (I do not mention Jasper, as he was engaged in composing some practical Bucolic or Georgic in the fields) to console me, the judicious reader will not be surprised to hear that, after wrestling for a season with these ancient worthies, I closed their "ponderous and marble (covered) jaws," which they had expanded for my torment, and thought that a walk to Woodside would be no more than a proper reward of my diligence. As I passed directly by the post-office in my way thither, I of course looked in to see what was the state of my correspondence. The cross old postmaster, who had held the office since its erection, under Washington, handed me a thick letter, telling me gruffly that there was only a cent to pay, as it was a drop letter, or one put into the office at the town,— the only one, he went on to say, in a tone of injured innocence, that had been put in for more than a year. He guessed it was a love-letter. As I had no reason, that I knew of, for sharing in this conjecture, I opened the envelope as I went along, and, to my surprise, found that it contained a letter addressed to Ann Petchell, my cousin Eleanor's *femme de chambre*. A few lines were written inside the envelope, asking me to do the writer the favor to deliver the enclosure to Ann Petchell herself, as it was a matter of importance to her; but without signature, and in a hand that I did not know. I could not imagine what it meant; and concluded at last that old Kimball, the postmaster, was probably not far wrong, and that the document must be neither more nor less than a love-letter. I was not over well pleased with being made thus the go-between of a waiting maid, and marvelled at the impudence of her correspondent. And it occurred to me further, that if Miss Petchell were involved in an amorous correspondence, such as I supposed this to be, she was not altogether what Eleanor took her for, and perhaps not precisely the person she would choose to have about her if she knew the fact. So I determined that I would let her or her father know the circumstance, before I performed my part of Mercury to Petchell.

I had an opportunity speedily afforded me; for, as I was approaching the gate, which admitted you into the grounds from the high road, I met Colonel Allerton, who was coming down the road from the opposite direction. We turned into the sweep together, and, as we walked along the hard gravel, he said to me, —

"I see you have an unopened letter in your hand. Do not refrain from reading it on my account. You are at the happy age when a letter is a pleasure. Don't delay yours."

"I am much obliged to you, sir," I answered, laughing; "and I should like particularly well to read this particular letter. But, unluckily, it does not belong to me."

"Indeed!" he replied. "Is it for me, or Eleanor?" holding out his hand for it.

"It is for one of your family, sir," said I; "but for neither you nor my cousin Eleanor. It is for Miss Ann Petchell." And I told him the odd way in which it came into my possession.

"Let me see it, if you please," said he. "I see no reason why you should be troubled with her letters. This is odd," he went on to himself, closely scrutinizing the handwriting; "this is very odd indeed. What can it mean?"

We were now at the door; and we forthwith proceeded to his library, where we found Eleanor seated by her father's fire, which a little chilliness and dampness, incident to our hottest summers, made by no means unsatisfactory. While we were exchanging salutations and inquiries the Colonel rang the bell, which was answered by Mrs. Warner, the housekeeper.

"Send Petchell here directly," said he. "I wish to see her."

"Petchell!" said Eleanor, looking at him and then at me in surprise, "Petchell!"

But there was no time for explanation; for the door opened, and that handmaiden entered, courtesyingly and simperingly; but still with a look of some alarm on her features at being so suddenly sent for by the Colonel, who, though a kind and considerate master, was a strict martinet in his family, and the whole *corps domestique* held him in reverential awe.

"Petchell, here's a letter for you," said he, abruptly, holding it out to her.

She courtesied, as she took it, with a glance first at the letter, and then at her young lady, and was about to leave the room.

"Stop, if you please," said the Colonel, in an authoritative tone; "if you have no objection, I wish you to open and read the letter here. I wish to know, if it be not a secret, how you come to be receiving letters from Mr. Ferguson, and why they should come under cover to Mr. Osborne."

Eleanor, on hearing this, gave me a half-reproachful glance, which made me fear that I had made some terrible blunder, though I could not divine what; and Petchell looked as if she should like to tear my eyes out. However, there was no help for her; so she hastened to open the letter, with what show of indifference she could muster. Her fingers trembled, however, in the agitation she obviously felt; and, before she could prevent it, a letter dropped out of her enclosure, and fell on the floor. Colonel Allerton, with the activity of six-and-twenty, instantly picked it up, and, after glancing at the direction, said to Petchell, —

"This is enough. It is all I want of you at present. You may go now."

And she went, apparently nothing loath.

Turning then to Eleanor, he said, handing her the letter, "I did not expect to find you in correspondence with Ferguson, I must confess. And I am still more at a loss to conceive why it should be carried on clandestinely. You did not use to be on such terms with him."

"It is all on his side, papa, now," said Eleanor, paler than ever, but evidently in strong perturbation; "I assure you it is. I have no wish to be on any terms at all with him. Whatever communications he has had with me he has intruded upon me against my will."

"I am sorry," he replied, "that you will still persist in thinking so ill of him. But I cannot imagine why he should annoy you, after what has passed, as you say he has, and still less why he should take this indirect way of doing it. It is not like him."

"Not like him! O papa!" exclaimed Eleanor, lifting up her hands with an expression of impatience and vexation.

"Certainly not," replied her father. "He was always open and candid in his intercourse with us at home; and we are certainly under great obligations to him."

Eleanor made a deprecating gesture of dissent.

"Why," he went on, "you know he told us of the blundering folly of"— he stopped, with a glance at me, and then went on without mentioning any name — "and did his best to counteract it."

I thought that it was about time for me to make a move to retire; as this seemed to be a scene, however interesting, which had better have only the actors for audience. But Eleanor went on without minding me.

"Perhaps we were too hasty in believing him. I thought better, or not so ill, of him at that time; but I would not have believed his story then, had it not been made likely by the circumstances he brought to our knowledge."

"Perhaps, my dear," said the Colonel, very politely, but a trifle provokingly, "you would have been less incredulous had the offender been any one besides Mr. Markham."

If blood was ever eloquent, as we are told it sometimes is, that in Eleanor's cheeks made a very fine speech on this occasion, and one that gave me an odd sensation, which I had never felt before, nor have I since, at least in the same degree. She paused a moment, and then said, very quietly, —

"I think, papa, it would have made no difference. You certainly know that it did not, as it was."

"I beg your pardon, my love," replied her father, caressing her head with his hand. "I was wrong in saying what I did. But you know it provokes me to have you so unjust to Ferguson. He could have none but friendly motives in coming to this country at this time; for his own affairs might have waited a year or two. But he came now that he might be of service possibly to us. And this after what had passed between you."

Eleanor shook her head, as if she received none of this doctrine. The Colonel went on: —

"But how long have you known that he was in America? Knowing your feelings towards him, I did not think it necessary to say anything about it to you."

"I imagine," she replied, "that I knew of it nearly as soon as you, if not sooner. I have known it these six months."

"These six months!" exclaimed her father; "and never mentioned it to me! That is strange. But have you ever seen him?"

"Only once," she answered, looking at me. "It was the day that I sent you word of my getting into the river. I meant that it should bring you home; and I did intend to tell you that it was he that helped me out. But I changed my mind, and Cousin Frank here had to bear all the credit of it."

"I cannot conceive why you should have concealed this from me," he replied, in a tone of some displeasure. "I am not too proud to be grateful for a good office, if you are."

"I could well have dispensed with the service," she replied; "for Cousin Frank here can tell you that the danger was nothing, and that, if it had been anything, he was sufficient to the emergency."

I cordially confirmed her statement in its entirety; for I well remembered wishing the fishing-boots at a considerable distance, and in a much warmer place than the Quasheen, — though that was not very cold that afternoon.

"You see, sir," she proceeded, "that there was no great call for gratitude in the case; and I certainly felt none whatever."

"Eleanor, Eleanor," he repeated, "I do not understand you. You are a changed creature. I cannot make you out this morning."

He rose from the sofa where he was sitting and took a turn or two up and down the room. Then, stopping short before her chair, he said, somewhat sternly, —

"And perhaps you intend to keep me equally in the dark as to the nature of your communications with him. I suppose they must have related to my affairs. They were not likely to have been anything improper for me to know," with a suspicion of a frown on his brow; "but I do not wish to intrude myself into your confidence, nor into that of Mr. Ferguson."

"Dear papa," said Eleanor, earnestly, "do not reproach me so. What real secret can I ever have from you? I may have done wrong in not telling you all about it at once; but I thought I was sparing you from pain, perhaps from danger, by saying nothing for the present. Indeed, I meant to tell you all in time."

"Well, well, my dear," he answered kindly, for, though quick of temper, he was the most placable of men, "I dare say you can explain it all. I have never thought you wrong yet, and I shall be slow to begin now."

The explanation I understood to be adjourned only till I was out of the way; and I was accordingly about to make another demonstration of departure, when Colonel Allerton said, before I could rise, —

"But, Eleanor, you have not read yet the letter of which Osborne here was the courier. I dare say it has nothing in it which he may not see. He ought certainly to be paid postman's wages; and perhaps he will be content to take it out in kind. Had you not better see what it says?"

Eleanor looked up suddenly from the carpet at which she had been gazing, and, glancing first at her father, and next at me, and last of all at the letter, which had lain in her lap all this while, she took it up and opened it. After running her eye over it she handed it to her father, who read it out, to this effect: —

"It is essential that I should have the interview with you I have so long solicited. It cannot be delayed, and it must be had. I have that to say which is of vital importance to you, and — if it be of greater weight with you — to your father. Time presses with me; and the interview I solicit must be at noon this day, or not at all. I will be at the Sachem's Seat at precisely twelve. If you object to coming alone, you can bring your maid with you, or the lad (*lad* indeed!) I saw with you when we met, who I understand is your cousin — if he be discreet."

"I cannot conceive," said the Colonel, studying the note closely, as if to extract its hidden meaning, "what Ferguson can have to say to you about me or yourself that he might not just as well certainly say to me in person. However, my dear, I should not be afraid to make you my plenipotentiary; and I think he would not make this request without some reasonable motive. So you had better get your bonnet, and take Frank's arm, since he is permitted to share in this mystery, and make haste; for," he added, looking at his watch, "it wants but a quarter to the trysting hour."

While Eleanor was gone for this purpose, he went on to me, "So you have seen Mr. Ferguson, it seems."

"Yes, sir," I answered. "I saw him for a moment on the afternoon when he drew my cousin out of the water, as she has told you. Indeed," I added, recollecting myself, "I did see him for a literal moment, when I was in Boston, on the top of the New York coach."

"Ah, yes," he replied; "I knew he had been at the South. I did not know he had returned until this morning. Did not you think him a handsome young fellow?"

Handsome! I thought him as ugly a monster as

I had ever seen. And young! Why, the wretch could not have been less than five and thirty. But seventy and nineteen have different eyes for such things. I did not trust myself to speak, and only made a bow oracularly enigmatical. He went on, without waiting for further answer: —

"You may have inferred from what has passed this morning that there have been some former dealings between him and us. Indeed, I may say to you in confidence, as one of the family (I made a bow here of unequivocal gratitude), that he was an old admirer of hers (old enough, I parenthesized to myself) in England. Had she liked him, I should have been well pleased; for I did. But, as she did not, there was nothing to be said. She has a rooted dislike to him, apparently, which I cannot understand; but, right or wrong, it is something to be considered in the matter of marriage."

"I must say, sir," I put in, "that it seems to me that my Cousin Eleanor is the last person in the world to form an unreasonable prejudice. She is candor and sweetness personified."

"She is a good girl, sir, a good girl," he resumed; "but the best of them take the bit between their teeth sometimes. And then there's nothing to be done but to give them their head. If they're good blood, they'll bring up safe enough when they've had their fling. But here she comes; and it is high time you were off."

We accordingly passed out at what Lord Castlereagh might have called "the back-front" door, which let us out in the direction of the avenue celebrated in the last chapter. We paced again down the length of the walk, and then left it by a path through a belt of trees skirting round the clearing, which connected it with the aboriginal forest, or what remained of it. At no great distance within the wood, but still far enough to be out of the reach of interruption or eavesdropping, was a small opening, of less than a quarter of an acre in extent, either natural or of a very old formation, as there was no trace of stumps or roots among the short, soft grass. It was believed to have been made by the Indians; and a large stone, which had something the look of having been rudely shaped into a sort of chair, was called the Sachem's Seat.

Tradition said that this was the sacred stone on which the great King Miantowusett, so formidable to the Puritans before King Philip's days, used to sit and rule his tribe. I can only say that, if he were of like passions with other men, his majesty must, like many another sovereign, have sat uneasily upon his throne. Eleanor said nothing to me during our walk. To be sure, it was soon over; for we walked fast. But she seemed to be absorbed in the anticipation of what was before her; and the only sign she gave of being conscious of my presence was the way in which she rather grasped than leaned on my arm, as if it were done rather to steady her mind than to support her steps.

When we entered the cleared space we found Ferguson walking up and down its narrow diameter, holding his watch in his hand. When he saw us he returned it to his pocket and saluted us, or rather Eleanor, with a politeness which was rather punctilious than easy. She made as slight an acknowledgment of his bow as could be and be any at all; while I unglued my hat from my head just as much as I thought my share of his courtesy demanded. Eleanor dropped my arm, and advancing by herself, sat down upon the Seat of the Sachem as Portia might have assumed the judgment-seat, had it been hers of right.

I admired the spirit and grace of the movement, while I thought I understood its motive. She was resolved, at at all events, to have the firm support of this seat before she suffered herself to be subjected to the agitation or provocation of what this man had to say. I dropped modestly back towards the alley by which we had come in, and left the stage to the two performers. Ferguson took a stride or two more on the greensward; while Eleanor said, as calmly and coldly as if a statue had spoken, —

"I am here, sir. What may your pleasure be with me?"

"My pleasure is," said he, pausing in his walk and turning towards her, — "my pleasure is to do you good, if you will let me."

She answered only by the haughtiest inclination of her head, which spoke more of scorn than of gratitude.

"You think, perhaps," he went on, eyeing her with no amiable expression of face, — "you think, perhaps, madam, that I offer more than I can perform, when I say I wish to do you good."

"If I can put any faith in the letters with which you have annoyed me for so long," she replied, "I must suppose that you can do me some hurt, though you have not been pleased as yet to indicate how or why."

"And if that be true," he returned, "even in the offensive sense in which you choose to take my wish to serve you, is not the refraining from doing a hurt sometimes a positive good?"

"I did not come here, sir," she replied, "to enter into any discussion with you, or to hold any conversation not essential to the business, whatever it may be, which has made you call me to this place. If you have anything to say to any purpose I will listen to you; otherwise I will return as I came."

"Eleanor — Miss Allerton," he went on, after a pause, in a softened tone, "you know that I have had but one motive in following you to America — but one in seeking you here. I do not pretend to the romantic folly of seeking your happiness apart from mine. I hope to deserve my own by securing yours. Is there no service that can purchase hope? I ask no more as yet."

"I thought, sir," she replied with a coldness which might have frozen quicksilver, — "I thought, sir, that all this was at an end long ago. If I have ever done anything to make you think that fresh importunity would make me think better of what I said when we parted in England, it has been my misfortune, and not my design. I never give hopes, sir, which I do not mean to fulfil."

She made a motion as if about to rise and retire; but Ferguson made a restraining gesture and said, —

"*You* have, indeed, done nothing to give me heart; but perhaps others have. Circumstances may have happened which may alter even your resolution. Your father"—

"My father!" she interrupted. "You do not presume to say that you sought this interview with his knowledge?"

"Oh, no indeed," he replied; "he knows nothing of it. I did not choose he should at present, or I should not have communicated secretly with you, as I have done. You know he would have made me welcome to his house, if I had seen fit to come openly."

She bowed an unwilling sort of assent and said, "What of him, then, sir?"

"He is a gentleman of a distinguished position, of an honorable name, of unblemished honor, of a large estate."

"Well, sir," said Eleanor, somewhat anxiously, "what of it? I believe none of these things have ever been disputed."

"Perhaps not," he answered, fixing his eye, which was generally looking down, on hers, as if by an effort. "Certainly not. But you know that there have been men as happy as he in all these particulars who have lost them all."

"No doubt there have been many," said Eleanor, suppressing an intense interest as well as she might. "But what is that to me or to my father?"

"Suppose his entire estate in England were lost and confiscated."

"Well!" said Eleanor, growing almost breathless as he proceeded.

"Suppose his honor were blasted, his place among men obliterated, and his name infamous."

"Well!"

"Suppose him condemned to drag out his life in poverty and disgrace, an exile from his country, from which he is shut out by the absolute certainty, if he returned, of dying the death of *a forger?*"

"Well!" in a low voice, and pale as ashes.

"And then suppose one, who can bring all this down upon the father, lays his power at the daughter's feet, and seeks, as his chiefest good, to identify himself with the life, honor, and prosperity of the one, and to devote himself to the happiness of the other."

"And this was what you have been hinting to me through the letters you have forced upon me," said Eleanor, her color returning, and her eyes kindling with some strong emotion or other.

"Precisely this," he answered; "though I was not prepared till now — I did not see fit — to tell you the exact truth."

"The exact truth!" she exclaimed in a tone of the most derisive unbelief. "Had you told me all this at first, you would have spared me some anxious fears which your black suggestions conjured up. I thank you for relieving me of them all."

And she rose with a deal of scorn, looking beautiful "in the contempt and anger of her lip," and was moving towards me, when Ferguson laid a detaining hand upon her arm, which she shook off as if it had been some crawling reptile.

"Stay a moment," said he. "I do not blame you for rejecting what I say at the first hearing. It would be strange indeed if you did not. But do you suppose I would commit myself in this way if I had not facts and evidence behind me? I do not ask for my reward till I have established my claim by indisputable proof of the service."

"Service! reward! facts!" ejaculated Eleanor, as if she could not quite put her thoughts in order. But presently she said, very collectedly, "And I can purchase exemption for myself and for my father from all this misery by taking you as my — husband?"

"Not purchase exemption," he replied; "but reward fidelity and devoted service."

"Fidelity!" she exclaimed, starting up from the stone on which she had seated herself again. "And if I reject your offer, you will let it loose upon our heads? Am I to understand that to be the alternative?"

"I believe it to be inevitable as death," said he in

reply. "Your fate and your father's is in your hands. It lies with you to decide whether it shall be life or death, honor or infamy. And you must decide at once."

"It will not take me long," said she, her eyes flashing, and her voice tremulous with anger. "I give no credence to what you say. I believe you capable of any villany, of contriving any plot, to compass any end you have in view. But do you suppose I will believe my father capable of what you charge him with? And even were he"—

"Had you not better wait," interrupted Ferguson, "until you know, whether capable of it or not, what the case against him is?"

"The case!" she exclaimed, stamping her little foot. "I care nothing for your case! You have proved yourself a villain by the proposal you have made me; and I am sure my father would sooner die on — as you say, than suffer me to purchase his life so infamously."

He looked as black as midnight, and scowled at her as he said between his teeth, "You reject my offer, then?"

"Reject it!" she said, with a look of utter loathing. "I spurn it! I trample on it! I spit upon it!"

"Then take the consequences!" he said struggling against a furious passion. "The ruin of your father, which you might have prevented, be on your head! And perhaps," he added, after a pause, in a quieter tone, but one steeped in malignity, — "perhaps the world will believe other rumors touching other persons. I have helped suppress them. Perhaps it will be impossible any longer. Mr. Markham has been seen in this neighborhood, I believe."

Eleanor blushed deeply with just anger at this insolence; and I stepped forward and said, —

"Sir, I accompanied this young lady hither by her request and for her protection. You will repeat your impertinence at your peril!"

"At my peril, you monkey!" he thundered out in a towering passion, which he was glad to vent upon somebody; and he advanced upon me with uplifted hand. I was but a mouthful to him; but I happened to take up, mechanically, as I came out with Eleanor, the cane which I usually carried. It had a blade in it, as college canes were very apt, foolishly enough, to have in those days. I drew it in an instant, and shortening it as he approached, exclaimed,

"Lay a finger upon me, sir, and by ——, it will be the last mischief you will do!"

Perhaps my eye was a little wicked; but at all events, he stayed his hand a moment, while Eleanor screamed aloud and was rushing between us, when we were all brought to our bearings by a quick rustling among the branches behind me, instantly folowed by Colonel Allerton's voice of command.

"What's this?" he said sternly to me. "Put up that gimcrack, sir. What in God's name is the meaning of this disturbance?"— looking first at one and then at the other.

"It means, sir," said I, "as far as I am concerned, that that rascal there (perhaps the noun was qualified by an expletive 'now better far removed') insulted Miss Allerton, and when I interfered he offered to strike me; and I was only giving him to understand that he would n't do it more than once."

"Ferguson! Eleanor!" he said, in a great amazement. "What is the meaning of this? Eleanor, is it true that he insulted you? Frank must be beside himself."

"Insulted me! Yes, indeed, sir," said she, "and you too."

"Me? Impossible!" cried the father. "In what way, pray?"

"Miss Eleanor," Ferguson put in, as if to give her time to reflect and withhold her communication, "regards the renewal of my unfortunate addresses as an insult to her and you. But I hope, sir, you may not regard it so seriously when you know my motives for my presumption."

"Don't believe him, papa!" cried Eleanor. "He is a liar, and the truth is not in him. What do you think," she continued, going up to him, and resting her hand on his shoulder, and looking up into his face, — "what do you think this wretch has been saying about you? — that you had committed some horrid crime, — forgery, I believe, — and that it depends on him to save you or to" — and she burst into tears on his shoulder.

"Yes," said I; "and the price of his silence, of

your life, I believe, was to be Eleanor's hand in marriage."

"Ferguson, are you mad?" said Colonel Allerton to him. "Can you have said these things?"

"Mad!" cried Ferguson, who did seem nearly beside himself with rage and disappointment. "Mad indeed! Well for you if I were! *Can* I have said these things? I have said them, and they are TRUE!"

"True!" exclaimed the Colonel. "Mr. Ferguson, you know such charges as these must be brought to a strict account."

"Strict enough, sir," replied Ferguson with a devilish sneer: "you may be assured of that. But it must be by twelve men, and not by twelve paces. Satisfaction, sir, is the due of a *gentleman*, and not a FELON."

"Scoundrel!" cried the Colonel; and, shaking off Eleanor, he snatched my blade, still unsheathed, and made a step towards the other. Eleanor clung again to his arm, and I stepped between them; while Ferguson said, laughing loudly, —

"Come on, by all means, sir. Add murder to your other crimes. A man can be hanged but once!"

"Tush!" cried Colonel Allerton, tossing down his weapon. — "I meant nothing, Eleanor, my girl. It was an involuntary movement. Let the rascal go. I would n't touch him."

"I humbly thank you, sir," cried Ferguson, taking off his hat, and making a mock bow to the party, with eyes full of hatred and malice; "and, since I have your gracious permission, I *will* go, as I have business elsewhere. Good-morning."

And, turning round, he stooped under the branches of the trees in the side opposite to the entrance on our side, and disappeared. As we stood looking after him, we could hear him crashing his way through the undergrowth and the interlacing boughs of the forest.

## CHAPTER XI.

IN WHICH WILL BE FOUND WHAT CAME NEXT.

WE stood in silence for a moment after Ferguson disappeared under the branches. I scarcely knew which way to look; but, without knowing it, I found myself glancing out of the corner of my eye at Eleanor, who had remained standing during all the last part of this singular scene. She stood gazing earnestly at her father, whose eyes were not yet withdrawn from the place where Ferguson had vanished, with an expression upon his face in which a towering passion seemed to contend with an extreme astonishment. Presently, however, as if controlling himself by a strong effort, he turned to Eleanor, and taking her arm under his, without saying anything, hastily proceeded to the avenue, and thus on to the house. I followed at a proper distance, so that they might have spoken together, had they chosen to do so, without fear of being overheard by me. But they made no use of the opportunity, both appearing to be absorbed in their own thoughts; or, rather, the father seemed plunged in a moody cloud of meditation, while the daughter was anxiously considering him and his conditions. Though she stepped firmly, and kept pace with her father in his hurried walk, I could see that her arm trembled upon his, and that she was trying, as she had opportunity, to get an unsuspected glance at his face.

That I felt a profound curiosity, as well as interest, about what I had seen, need not be said; though I could not help feeling that my presence, although fairly and honestly brought about, might be intrusive and unwelcome. So I was meditating a sudden and secret retreat as soon as we approached the house, thinking, that, as my room might be better than my company, it was very likely my companions would not notice my sudden substitution of the one for the other. Just as they entered the house, however, through which it was necessary for me to pass to make a dignified retreat, Eleanor said a few words to her father, with a glance at me over her shoulder. I pretended to drop my cane, and lingered behind so as to leave them free to say what they liked about me; when Colonel Allerton stopped, and, turning round to me, said, —

"Frank, step into my room, if you can spare the time. I should like to have your advice in a matter of some importance."

I felt greatly flattered, of course, and looked on myself as promoted to be a middle-aged man at a jump, or at least as having received the brevet rank of five and twenty. I passed on through the hall, and went into the library, the father and daughter remaining in conference near the hall-door, while

I seated myself before the fire that was never quenched, and gazed up at the white wig, rubicund face, and wild, protuberant eyes of his late Majesty, who returned my look with a half-frantic expression not altogether out of keeping with the queer doings of the last hour. Presently I heard Eleanor's step ascending the stairs, and immediately afterwards that of her father approaching the door of the library. I rose as he entered; but he made me a sign to take my seat again, and then walked two or three times up and down the room in silent thought. Then seating himself on the sofa, which made an angle of some sort (I never was much of a mathematician) with the fireplace, he turned to me with the cordial, confiding air which marked his manner, whatever might have been the reserve it covered, if Mr. Bulkley's theory was right, and began,—

"Well, Frank, you will have a lively scene to describe in your next letter to the Deipnosophoi. Quite a godsend to your journal, by Jove! You could hardly have hoped for anything so animating in such an out-of-the-way corner of the world as this. I am sure I little thought what was coming when I walked down the avenue to meet you as you came back, and to make Ferguson come along with you."

"I will not deny, sir," I replied, "that I have been deeply interested in what I have seen this morning, and in what has come under my notice before as to this Mr. Ferguson, if that be his name; but I beg to assure you that nothing I have seen or heard will ever be told to any living soul, unless it be the wish of my Cousin Eleanor and yourself that the facts I have been witness to should be truly stated at some future time."

"Thank you, thank you!" he answered. "I believe you to be a discreet lad. And perhaps it may be as well not to make this adventure a topic of gossip just yet. It is quite likely it may become such, however; and in such case I am quite willing to leave your testimony in your own keeping, to be used or withheld at your own discretion. And I am sure Eleanor would feel the same. She has a high opinion of you, Frank, my boy; though the little accident by which you were brought into Parson Bulkley's keeping did not argue vehemently in favor of your prudence and steadiness of character at first."

I blushed to the very soles of my boots to hear this opinion of Eleanor in my favor; though, had I known as much as I do now, (the more's the pity!) I should have known that prudence and discretion are not always the best recommendations of a man to a woman. Luckily for me, however, these virtues have not always been so inconveniently preponderant as to stand materially in my way.

"I am much obliged to my Cousin Eleanor and to you, sir," I said, half laughing, at the conclusion of his speech, "for your good opinion of me. I am sure that I shall always look on the accident you speak of as one of the luckiest things that ever could happen to me; as, without it, I should have never known you, or her, or Mr. Bulkley. I do not pretend to be wise above my fellows; but I have sense enough to know the value of such friends as you all have shown yourselves."

"I thank you for our share of the compliment," said the Colonel, "and the rather, considering the character which you have just heard an older acquaintance than yourself bestow upon me, and the fate he was obliging enough to suggest as my due."

"His may be an older acquaintanceship than mine, sir," I replied; "but I know that mine is the better of the two; for it is enough to make me laugh at any such ebullition of spleen as that."

"I was taken by surprise this morning, myself," he resumed, "and was nearly as much astonished as you could have been at what Ferguson said. I have always thought well of him, and, had Eleanor fancied him, I should have been very well content to have had it a match. But she seems to have known him better than I did. By Jove! these women have an instinct which is a surer protection to them than the knowledge of the world we men brag so much of."

"She certainly had an escape, sir," I interpolated, as he paused; "for he must be a precious scoundrel, besides having a devil of a temper."

"You are right undoubtedly," he went on; "though I was not clear-sighted enough to read him so. I thought him a sincere friend in the vexation in which I was involved through your friend Markham's *étour-*

*derie* ; and I liked him all the better for it, because he was a rejected admirer of Eleanor's. But no doubt, as I always supposed indeed, he hoped thus to recommend himself to her."

He paused, and, as I knew nothing of the circumstances of which he spoke, I had nothing to say, excepting a confused observation to the effect that he would have been a fool, as well as a rogue, if he had failed to do his endeavor in such a cause. But the Colonel did not heed what I stammered out, but went on as if no break had taken place in the chain of his ideas.

"However that may be," he continued, "there is no doubt now as to his villany; and I only wish that I knew the extent of it. Angry as he was, and carried by his passion beyond his self-control, he had some meaning in what he said. It was 'miching malicho,' as Hamlet says, and meant mischief. I dare say he would give his ears (I wish to God they were nailed to the pillory, as they deserve to be!) that he had kept his tongue between his teeth. But, as he was surprised out of what he did not mean to say, I must make my advantage of it. And the first thing I must do is to get back to England as soon as I can to confront his charges; for I have no doubt that he is already on his way thither to make them, whatever they may be."

"To England, dear papa!" said Eleanor, who entered by the door behind him as he was uttering the last sentence; and she laid her hand caressingly on his shoulder. "To England! And why to England?"

"Because, my love," he replied, taking her hand in his as he spoke, — "because it is there I must be hanged, if Mr. Ferguson be a true prophet. I really don't recollect having done anything worthy of death since I came to America. Ferguson is not a fool; and he did not talk in the way he did, though he was in a passion, without some vicious meaning or other. He has some design, and it must be put into execution in England; and there I must be to counteract it."

She passed round the corner of the sofa where he sat, still holding his hand, and seated herself by his side.

"No, no, dear papa!" she said, in a voice full of tender emotion: "do not put yourself within the reach of that villain. You do not know his ability in wickedness. You will find it more than a match for your innocence and the simple honesty of your way of dealing. Pray, do not go! Stay here with me!"

"What! my dear," he said to her half reproachfully, but all tenderly, "you surely would not have me stay here, and admit by default whatever slanders he may have concocted? That is not like my Eleanor. For my own part, I had rather mount the drop at Newgate next Monday morning than live under such an imputation. I will at least show my own confidence in my innocence, whatever happens. But you shall remain here until the whole thing is settled."

"I remain here!" she exclaimed, her eyes filling with tears, which she hastily brushed off her long lashes before they fell, — " I remain here, papa, while you go to difficulty, if not to danger! That would be like me, indeed! You know that I was not thinking of myself. But I have a dread of this man's power of mischief which I cannot help. He has haunted me for more than two years; and I am afraid of him, I confess. If we are beyond his reach here, for God's sake, sir, let us stay here till he is out of our way."

" For more than two years, Eleanor!" said her father in a tone of surprise. "What do you mean, my dear? How comes it that I have never heard of this before?"

Eleanor blushed deeply, and, looking divinely downwards, said, after a moment's pause, "I could not tell you, papa: indeed I could not. I could not trust you; for the man"— She paused a moment, and then added, as if with pain and difficulty, "The man insulted me. And"—

" Insulted you!" exclaimed her father, starting up, with a deeper imprecation than I had ever heard come from his polished lips. "Why did you not tell me of this on the instant? But it is not too late to overtake him yet." And he had his hand upon the bell-pull, when Eleanor seized his arm, exclaiming, —

" Dearest papa, this man is not worth your anger: he is beneath your resentment. What, what, are you going to do?"

"Do!" he exclaimed. "I am going to order my horse and be after him. I can be in Boston as soon as he."

"And what then, papa?" Eleanor persisted, still holding on to his arm.

"Leave that to me, my dear. I will find a way to chastise him for his insolence. Have no fears on that score," said the veteran; and he glanced significantly at me.

"Ah, dear papa!" expostulated Eleanor, in a tone that might have disarmed Sir Lucius O'Trigger himself, "surely you would not put your life on a level with that wretch's, if that is what you mean; for you can hardly hope to inflict any chastisement in any other way. And now you wonder that I did not tell you all this two years ago. You have a pretty way, have n't you, of coaxing my confidence? Come, now, sit down by me again, and ask Cousin Frank there, if he does not think you a choleric, testy, foolish old gentleman."

Bluebeard could not have withstood such entreaties and the blandishments that accompanied them; and Colonel Allerton did sit down again, evidently growing cooler and cooler, and said, "Well, and what does Cousin Frank think on the subject?"

"I think, sir," I replied, "that you do well to be angry for such a cause; and I can find no fault with your wish for satisfaction, if it were a case in which it could be had. But, putting aside the question of whether this man is entitled to be treated like a gentleman, I suppose he could use this accusation, whatever it is, as he has already suggested this morning, as a reason for refusing to meet you, if he chose. And besides, sir, you will remember this is not Old England; and the ordeal by combat is not one our Puritan notions accord with."

"Very true, very true, Frank," he said, quite calmed down again. "I was an old fool to have thought of such a thing. And then he might say that I wanted to rid myself of my accuser in this extra-judicial way. So go on, my love, and tell me how he has continued to annoy you since" — And his eyes flashed again, and his hand clinched, at the thought he did not utter.

"He hinted to me before we left England," she resumed, "substantially what he said to-day, — that he had your honor, if not your life, in his hands. And he made me believe that he actually prevented your arrest, when we were on the eve of sailing, by putting the officers on a wrong scent."

"And why did you not tell me all this, my child?" said her father.

"Perhaps I was wrong, papa," she answered; "but I did what seemed to me for the best. I knew you well enough to know that nothing would prevent you from staying, and facing any hazard if you knew of it; and I was weak enough to wish you safe on this side the water. I knew that the perplexity into which Mr. Markham's imprudence had thrown you was capable of being put into a bad shape; and I was sure that this man was capable of twisting it into any shape that suited him best. So I let things take their course. But, if I have done wrong, I have been fully punished; for I have suffered tortures of mind the last two years." And she closed her eyes, and pressed her hand to her forehead, as if in severe bodily pain.

"My poor Eleanor," said her father, tenderly taking her hand, "you would have done better to have told me all this. I could have convinced you that his assertion about the arrest must have been a lie, and that so his others most likely were."

"Could you, indeed, sir?" said Eleanor. "He told it to me connected with so many circumstances which I knew to be true, and actually pointing out the officer, that I thought that was certain, if nothing else."

"Had you been acquainted with affairs, my dear," he returned, "you would have known that an arrest of such a character could not be initiated without a degree of notoriety which would have followed us here, and that the subsequent legal measures could not be done in a corner. But no matter for that now. Let me know what you have had to do with Ferguson since then."

"He wrote to me several times from England, proposing to renew his addresses to me, and on that condition to hush up the 'ugly business,' as he called it. — The next time I knew anything of him was when we saw him together at the river," she said, addressing herself to me. And then, after briefly reciting the adventure to her father, she proceeded, "One other letter, under cover to Petchell (as, indeed, all his letters were sent), came while Cousin Frank was in Boston. It was postmarked 'Washington.' But I was on the lookout for this; and as soon as it arrived, without opening the outer sheet, I sent it back to him at Boston, where I knew he would be béfore leaving the country."

"And that was the reason, no doubt," said her father, "why he enclosed the letter of this morning to Frank here. He thought it would be more sure of being opened, if it came through him; though, to be sure, it might have met with no better luck than its precursors, had it not been for Frank and me."

"It certainly would not," she replied. "But I am very glad now it happened so, though I was not very well pleased with it at first, as you may have surmised," turning to me (she was quite right — I had so); "for I am now rid of the first secret I ever kept from you, papa; and it shall be the last, I promise you."

And she put her arms round his neck, and kissed him twice. Great Heavens! why was not I sixty-five years old and a papa? Sir Walter Scott somewhere feelingly complains of the affliction caused "to us male creatures" by the sight of the caresses which the ladies are so fond of wasting in such unnecessary profusion upon one another. I am not sure that it is any better to see them thrown away upon heavy fathers and stupid brothers. However, it is a part of the discipline of this mortal life; and I had to submit to it in this instance, as in a many since. Colonel Allerton presently resumed:—

"But still, darling, I am not clear that I ought not to return to England to show that I am not keeping out of the way of his accusations. What think you, Frank?"

Eleanor gave me an imploring look; and, as I certainly had no wish to give an answer that should send them out of the country, I replied,—

"I cannot give you any opinion, sir, on the subject. I do not know enough about it to have formed one."

"Is that so?" he replied. "I have been talking to you all this while under the belief that Eleanor had made you her confidant, and told you all about our affairs."

I assured him that I had not been thus happy. And Eleanor, while she confirmed my statement, was good enough to say that she had determined to do so at the very first opportunity that offered itself.

"I did so long for a friend to talk with about these things, which I could not tell whether I ought to keep to myself or not! I was so in want of advice and comfort!" she said, and sighed.

Oh, why had she not yielded to this impulse? I do not know how I might have answered as a friend and comforter, but I am sure I should have done my best; and at any rate it would certainly have been a very great comfort to me.

"You would have done right," replied her father. "Frank is entitled to our thanks and our confidence; for he has shown himself truly discreet and friendly, as I understand it, and he shall have both." I bowed, and he continued, "In fact, there is not much to tell you. Just as I retired from the army, now more than twenty years since, old Vinal Grayson, who had been the agent for the loyalists ever since the year '80, died; and, as it was important that the post should be held by some person having some knowledge of the Colonies and the people claiming relief from time to time, I was persuaded by Lord Hobart, then colonial secretary, to act in that capacity, though much against my will. For, though a limitation of time was prescribed in the bill for the compensation of the loyalists, still the government was very liberal and considerate in the admission of claims in cases of special hardship which might be strictly barred by lapse of time."

"The British Government stood handsomely by those who stood by them, I have always heard," said I.

"You have heard the truth," he replied. "Of course it was impossible to satisfy the demands of all that made them; nor could the real losses we sustained be made good. But the successive ministries all behaved as well as they could, I believe. But this liberality exposed the government to the danger — which, indeed, is incident to all systems of compensations and pensions — of fictitious and forged claims. This could hardly be avoided with the greatest diligence, especially as many of the pensioners had returned to this country, and the distances over which they were scattered made it very hard to keep a strict eye upon them all."

"That is plain enough," said I. "I should think it must have been out of the question."

"We did our best," he went on. "But it was hard to guard against all the devices of the enemy. Some three years ago, or thereabouts, I was strongly suspicious that an extensive fraud had been carried on for some time. In the course of my investigations I had consulted with this Ferguson, as I had done frequently before, regarding him as a shrewd legal adviser, and as one particularly well qualified to act as such from his own connection with the loyalists. Young Markham, too, who was frequently at my offices in London with his father, and who was just then about to be entered at the Inner Temple, was also taken into confidence, and employed in a subordinate capacity from time to time."

"What was the nature of the fraud you suspected?" I asked.

"It was a claim purporting to be of one Michael St. John," he replied, "for a large seizure of specie and goods which he was transferring from New Jersey to New York, at the beginning of the Revolution, for protection from the British troops, and taken by the rebels. With interest upon interest, it was made to amount to near fifty thousand pounds. It seemed so well supported by vouchers and affidavits, and the case as stated appeared so hard a one, that Mr. Perceval (for it happened during his short rule) consented to allow the man a pension of five hundred pounds a year for his life, provided Mr. Jackson, then minister at Washington, should certify to the necessary facts. This was done; and, as soon as the certificate arrived in due form, it was all settled, as I supposed; and all I had to do was to remit the money to New York every year on receiving the regular evidence that the man was alive."

"And how long did this go on, sir?" I inquired.

"For eight or nine years," he answered. "And it would never have been suspected that there was anything amiss, had I not had occasion to look into some American despatches in the foreign office on another matter relating to my department; and, to my surprise, I found no record, at the time the certificate of the identity of St. John was sent over, of any such transaction. Mr. Jackson was dead, and his secretary at one of the Northern courts, and there was no immediate way of sifting it. I looked farther back, and found several other cases of like nature (of less amount, but very considerable in the aggregate), all of which were payable to the same agent in New York who held St. John's power of attorney."

"And what did you do then, sir?" I asked, naturally interested in the story.

"I at once sent for Ferguson," he answered, "who seemed as much perplexed and amazed as I was;

and he advised me to say nothing, for the present, to the colonial secretary, but to lay a trap for the rogue at New York, so as to get his testimony as to the origin of the business."

"And you did so, I suppose?" I suggested.

"Yes, I am sorry to say I did. It was the grand mistake I made. I ought to have reported the whole thing at once; for, when it transpired in that quarter, — as it very soon did, through Markham's imprudence or ill luck, — it had an ugly look."

"And how was that, sir?" I inquired of him.

"Why," said he, "Markham had a brother who was a clerk in the colonial office; and he happened to be there one morning when the secretary came through the room where he was. He remembered that Markham had been sent to him by me on business once or twice, and called him into his private room to ask him some questions on a matter to come before Parliament that day, that he supposed he might know about. I can't tell you how the cross-purposes occurred; but Markham, supposing he was speaking of this matter, of which his own thoughts were full, made answers which aroused the curiosity of the minister, and he did not release him till he had learned all he had to tell."

"That was unlucky, certainly," said I. "But it was rather poor Markham's misfortune than his fault."

"So I have tried to persuade papa," Eleanor put in, blushing, and looking down; "but he" —

"Ah! but you forget, my dear, that, although he was taken by surprise at first, he admitted that he went on deliberately afterwards in his account of the matter, thinking, forsooth, that it was best for all parties! He think, indeed!"

"But perhaps he was right, papa," said Eleanor, growing a little warmer as she went on. "You say that you were mistaken in not doing this very thing at first: why, then, are you so very severe on poor Mr. Markham?"

"He and I were very different people, my dear," he replied; "and the conduct which might have been wise in me was uncalled for and impertinent in him. And that is harder to forgive than an intentional injury, of which I have never suspected him. Had he held his tongue, we should have been at Walford to-day, instead of Wensley."

I really could not find it in my heart to bear him malice for that; though I did not think Miss Eleanor had any occasion to blush so when she named him. I only said, however, "And what was the upshot, sir?"

"Why, the upshot was, as you might suppose, that the minister was high, and I was as high as he. He spoke of the whole business in a way that I could not stand, sir, and I threw up the office on the spot. His lordship made no objections to receiving my resignation, and soon afterwards appointed this very Ferguson my successor."

"Ferguson!" I exclaimed.

"Oh, yes!" he replied; "and a very proper appointment it seemed to me then." Eleanor lifted up her eyes and hands as a slight protest. "Well, there was no reason I knew of why it was not, my dear; and I made no quarrel with Ferguson on that score."

"But how was this connected with your coming to America, sir, if I may ask?" said I.

"Very naturally," he answered. "As these frauds had occurred during my incumbency, I felt myself bound to do my best to get to the bottom of them, and to bring the perpetrators to justice. It was due to the government and to my own character; and the most direct way seemed to be to look into them in person and on the spot. And so I came over; and, as this foolish girl would not be left behind, I had to bring her with me."

"And what success have you had, sir?" I inquired.

"Indifferent enough," was his reply. "The conspirators on this side the water must have had timely notice of the discovery: for I have got no trace of them yet, and I fear I never shall now. But I had resolved never to go home until I had cleared this mystery up; and nothing but some imputation on my honor and character, such as Ferguson threw out to-day, would shake my resolution."

"Perhaps, sir," I suggested, "what he said was a mere burst of spite and vexation; for I must say that my cousin's reception and treatment of him were not of a gratifying description. Will it not be time enough to decide and to act, after you have some definite information as to what he means to do and say? Possibly you may never hear from him again."

"I do not think that at all likely," he rejoined. "But, as you say, perhaps there is no hurry about it. At any rate, I will be ruled by a girl and boy to the extent of taking time to consider before I do anything further."

And Eleanor thanked him again in the manner heretofore protested against by Sir Walter Scott and myself. I added, when this was over,—

"And I wish, sir, you would take the boy's advice in another particular."

"Ah! and what is that?" said he, smiling graciously.

"I wish you would take Mr. Bulkley into your counsels. He is odd, but kind, and a genuine friend to this house, if faith may be given to his words behind your backs. And he is shrewd and wise in his generation, and as true as Toledo steel; and I know that your confidence would be very gratifying to him."

"Oh, I have the highest value for the good Parson," he replied good-naturedly, "and would trust him with my soul, body, and estate. I do not imagine he can do much for us; but, if you should like to take him into counsel, I have no objection. — Have you, Eleanor?"

"No, indeed, papa!" she replied; "and I think he is a very knowing old man. Perhaps, as Cousin Frank says, he may make some useful suggestion. At any rate, he will be a kind and good friend; and surely we have no superfluity of such."

"You may tell him what you think best of our affairs, then," the Colonel said, in conclusion, "whenever he comes home, and say I should like to talk matters over with him. And now, come, take Eleanor into the dining-room; for you must be ready for your dinner by this time."

And so, in truth, I found myself, as soon as I could descend to consider the matter; and, as the hour when poor Jasper had spread his table for me was long past, I made no resistance to this hospitable suggestion. I don't know whether I ought to put it on record or not; but the fact is, that, notwithstanding the agitations of one kind and another we had undergone, we gave all the evidence good appetites could imply of good consciences. During dinner we talked on indifferent subjects; and the servant who waited on us could not have suspected from our ways that anything out of the common course had occurred that morning. Such are the funny conditions of the human microcosm. After dinner, I returned to the parsonage, and applied myself to my classics with what appetite I might.

## CHAPTER XII.

#### FRIENDS IN COUNCIL.

BY the encouragement of Colonel Allerton and Eleanor I was almost daily at Woodside until the return of the good Parson, which was delayed several days beyond the time he had fixed for it. And, so curious is the mechanism of humanity, it seemed to me that I had never seen them so much at their ease as since the adventure of the Sachem's Seat. Eleanor, particularly, seemed as if she had thrown a load from off her heart; and its shadow, which used too often to steal over her features, had disappeared with it. There was certainly a little flush of excitement often on her cheek; but the air of abstraction and revery was gone entirely. Her manners to her father were more caressing and tender than ever, and to me as open and affectionate as a friend could desire. Colonel Allerton retained his old calmness of exterior, and looked, as he said he was, as if he were waiting for the next move. Eleanor spoke freely to me of the relief she felt at having this mystery, which had been haunting her for so long, take a definite shape, so that she knew what it was she had to fear, and at the restoration of entire confidence between her father and herself. I had a full intellectual sense of the rascality of Ferguson; but I could not but feel that he had done me the best of service by putting me into these confidential relations with the people I valued the most on earth.

Things went on thus for some days, until the minister at last returned. I was standing ready to assist him in alighting from the coach, which arrived just before tea-time. I noticed that he did not seem so cheery and lightsome of mood as he usually was; but I attributed it entirely to the fatigue of the journey, which even he might feel more than he would choose to admit at seventy years. At tea I asked him as to the issue of his onslaught on the Hog's Neck; and he told me, that Mr. Hayley had given him in writing just such an opinion as he expected, and which he was sure he could use to restore peace within the walls of Jericho. But, still, he did not treat the matter in the jocose and airy strain with which he was wont to encounter such oddities of adventure. Indeed, he did not seem to be thinking about it even while giving me this account of his success. I thought, too, that I could observe him regarding me, when he thought I was not noticing him, with an air of deep sympathy and commiseration. In short, he had a good deal the air and manner of one of those fearful friends who have some piece of bad news for you which they keep back in order to prepare you for the shock, but which they can't help from peeping out from the corners of their eyes and mouth, and which frightens you ten times more than the baldest and rudest display of the facts would do.

"———— Ye gods, avert
Such plagues from righteous men!"

When Jasper had withdrawn the tea-things and gone about his business to some other part of the domain, I said to Mr. Bulkley,—

"My dear sir, you do not seem yourself this evening. You are not usually so done up by a journey of twenty odd miles, are you? You have heard some bad news I am afraid, sir."

"Bad news!" he repeated. "Why so? why should you think I had heard bad news? I have heard none that affects myself or you particularly." And I could see that he was eying me with the look of a tender-hearted surgeon (if such an anomaly exist) just before cutting off the pet leg of his intimate friend.

"Perhaps, then, it relates to the Allertons," I suggested. "I don't know who else there is that we have any common interest in."

"The Allertons!" he replied, still looking kindly but mournfully at me. "And why should you think of them and bad news together? Have you any reason to suppose that any such may be likely to be heard of them?"

"Perhaps I have, sir," I answered; "and I will not imitate their reserve, of which I have heard you complain, if you will be as open with me."

"I have little to tell, my dear boy," said he, with strong marks of surprise and interest in his face; "and that is merely the gossip of Boston, which may have no foundation whatever. So, pray, tell me what it is you mean."

Thus urged, I proceeded to tell him all that I have already told the world in the foregoing pages, and especially the final explosion, not forgetting the permission they had given me to take him into the secret and the request of Colonel Allerton for his counsel.

"The secret!" said the minister, after he had listened with the most earnest attention to all that I had to say. "I am afraid that there is no longer any secret to be admitted into. This business was the talk of Boston this morning. I do not mean that all the details you have given were blown; but there was a vague rumor that Colonel Allerton had fled his country for some great crime which had only been recently discovered. As to my advice and assistance, if I can afford any, God knows all I have is at their service. But, Frank, you seem to have been taken into their confidence in a remarkable sort of way. I should have been most glad to have known it before this mischief developed itself."

I assured him that my being admitted into their counsels had been owing to inexorable circumstances, and that I had received no more confidence from them than had been extorted by the necessities of the case. He shook his head and said, sadly, after a short pause, —

"I am an old fool, I suppose. But I had been building a castle in the air for you and Eleanor, I confess; and I was made unhappy, I admit, by the thought that this scandal would probably blow it sky high. I never made a match for myself; but I have always been making matches — planning them, that is — for other people. To be sure, I have been oftener disappointed than not in my schemes."

"This scandal, sir," I replied, determined to keep a good face, though I caught my breath a little as I spoke, — "this scandal would have nothing to do with your castle; for I am afraid that I am not the man Eleanor has chosen to inhabit it with her. But had it been otherwise, and should even this slander be proved to be truth, I should have scorned myself if I permitted the fault of a father to influence my feelings or my conduct towards such a daughter, had I any species of claim upon her, which I certainly have not."

"You are right, Osborne," he replied, still looking sadly and kindly at me, which I pretended not to observe, — "you are right, and speak as a man of honor and just feelings should. But suppose we walk up to Woodside at once. We shall find them just done tea."

Of course I made no objection to this proposal; and we were soon on our way thither, only making a forced halt at the post-office, where the Parson was intercepted by Major Grimes, Deacon Holt, and several of the other dignitaries of the village, and compelled to disburse the latest news from town. He then received, in his turn, their contributions as to the condition of the parish, particularly as to health and sickness; for I believe I have forgotten to tell, among other particularities of Wensley, that the Parson was not only its lawyer, but its doctor to boot. Whether it was owing to his skill in medicine (for he had dabbled a little in that as in almost everything else) or to his very moderate exhibitions of the same, Wensley was always in a state of rude health truly disheartening to any young and enterprising practitioner; so that the few that had ever pitched their tents there had soon struck them again and departed for more hopeful fields of labor.

Jasper was Mr. Bulkley's main assistant in his medical practice; for he had learned to breathe a vein during the war, with perfect accuracy, when in attendance for a while on the hospital department; and, as phlebotomy was still a main arm of the war service against disease at that time, he was an invaluable auxiliary. In cases of a critical character, to be sure, he would call in the famous Dr. Whittredge, of Sandover, who was his ancient friend and willing adviser, and almost as great an oddity as himself. When I was last in Wensley there were more doctors' signs even than meeting-houses, regular and irregular, allopathic, homœopathic, hydropathic, botanic: all systems had their zealous professors, ready to dispense life and health to all who had the faith and knowledge to come to them. I wonder whether Wensley is better in body and soul now than it was when Priest Bulkley lorded it there, with gentlest despotism, in things temporal and eternal?

We were most kindly received on presenting ourselves at Woodside, and the good Parson cordially thanked for the promptitude of his visit. If there were any embarrassment on either side at the meeting, it was on ours. Colonel Allerton and Eleanor possessed their souls in the same calm and imperturbable equanimity which generally marked their manners, and which I alone had been permitted to see disturbed. We talked over the Ferguson business with perfect openness, and discussed its various bearings freely, or rather the elders did; for Eleanor and I were only listeners, for the most part.

They did show some sensibility, indeed, when Mr. Bulkley told them that their affairs were the town gossip in Boston that day; for who can know that their conduct is the theme of common talk and vulgar discussion, however blameless they may know themselves to be, without a feeling of wounded pride and a bitter sense of injustice — to feel that, at that very moment of time, hundreds of strangers, or, which is worse, professing friends, are engaged in exclaiming, wondering, and conjecturing about your affairs, and in tearing your character to shreds, extenuating nothing, and setting down everything, if not in malice, at least with a good nature, which is an excellent imitation of it? However, they swallowed the momentary pang, and the conversation proceeded.

"The essential thing to be done," said Mr. Bulkley, "seems to be to discover the agent who was employed to receive the moneys in New York. Have you no clew to him?"

"None whatever," replied Colonel Allerton. "I made it my first business to inquire him out; but he had disappeared past recovery. He had no domicile, apparently, there, but came to the city as the remittances were expected."

"That is strange," said the Parson. "But does it not occur to you as possible that some trace might be got of him by the way of this St. John you speak of — the man in whose name the pension stood? Of course he is probably dead; but there must have been such a man, I take it, and somebody must remember him."

"I don't know that," replied the Colonel. "I could hear nothing of him in all the inquiries I could make after him. Did you ever hear of such a person?"

"No," said the minister; "I never did. But, then, I have no acquaintance in the Jerseys; nor do I know anybody that has. But stop a minute," he continued, putting his finger to his forehead; "I'm not so sure of that. There's my Jasper; he's a Jerseyman. It's barely possible he may remember such a person; for he never forgets any one, and especially a Tory," laughing as he spoke.

"It is not at all likely," replied the Colonel, "that he should have put his rebel memory to so good a use as this, especially as it would be to oblige another Tory; but it can do no harm to ask him the question."

"Another thing," said Mr. Bulkley. "Has it ever suggested itself to you that this Ferguson may have had some cognizance of this matter? He seems rascal enough for it."

"I certainly never thought anything of the sort," returned the Colonel, "until the other day. Since then, I confess, it has occurred to me; but I have no ground of suspicion except my ill opinion of him."

"But what are his connections in this country?" asked the minister. "You said, I think, that he was of Tory blood. That may give us some inkling to guide us."

"His family were from the Middle States somewhere," answered the other; "though I believe his mother was from New England. But she died before I knew anything about them. His father was Colonel Robert Ferguson, who died in Jamaica about the year five. I knew him there ten years before."

The minister's countenance fell. After a brief pause he asked, in a constrained voice,—

"He was receiver-general there, was he not?"

"Receiver or registrar general, or something of the sort," replied the Colonel, little thinking how rude a wound he was giving his old friend.

I comprehended the whole in a moment. It flashed into my mind at the same moment it did into Mr. Bulkley's that this Ferguson must be the son of the fair, the frail, the unworthy Julia Mansfield, his first and only love, whose unworthiness he had mourned more bitterly than her scorn or her death. This man was the inheritor of her blood — her representative!

Mr. Bulkley sat in silence for a few minutes as if to recover from the shock, as I saw. Our companions did not remark it; for, though they had heard the story of the good Parson's cross in love, they had paid no particular attention to the names of the parties and had probably forgotten them entirely. Presently he rose and took leave, saying he would come again the next day and talk over the matter further.

"And if you will give me leave," said the Colonel, as we were leaving the house, "I will walk down to the parsonage to breakfast to-morrow and hear what Jasper has to say on the St. John matter, if the day be fine."

Of course this suggestion met with a cordial acquiescence; and Mr. Bulkley and I passed out into the night. It was cold for the season; but the chill air seemed to refresh him. He drew a long breath and set off rapidly towards home. Then he slackened his pace and then quickened it again, as if unconscious of what he did. I felt his arm tremble upon mine, and knew that deep feelings and strong passions agitated his aged bosom. I reverenced his sorrows and paid them the homage of perfect silence. His was a heart that never could grow old; and out of its warm recesses what were the images that glided forth and walked with him through that glimmering night? What eye but his could see the phantom in all the loveliness, and innocence, and gayety of fifty years ago evoked by the necromancy of a chance word that stirred his being to its depths? What visions of youth, and love, and hope waited upon her! What memories of disappointment, of despair, of grief, harder to bear than either, followed after her! Who but he could tell?

I could not tell what was the procession of shadows that passed before him as we walked side by side; but I felt that it was sweeping by, and I religiously forbore to disturb it by a loud breath. I had no sense of the fifty years that separated us. Something there was (I wonder what it could have been?) that *contemporized* us, to use a word of Sir Thomas Browne's coinage. The sympathy I felt with him was that of youth with youth, and not of youth with age. He felt, too, that I understood him, though no words had passed between us; and his grateful pressure of my hand, as we stood on the door-stone, told me so and thanked me for it. He took the candle from Jasper, who opened the door for us, and went directly into his bedroom, and we saw him no more that night; though the great Bible lay open on his study table, with the lights, all ready for prayers.

Jasper looked at me as I went in and took up one of the candles, and said, shaking his head, "Somebody's been a-talking to him about that Tory Mansfield girl?"

I nodded acquiescence; and he went on: "I knowed it as soon as I see him. It's been just so this forty odd year that I've lived with him. Ah! Master Frank," he continued, in a truculent tone, "a woman's bad enough, anyhow; but a woman that's a Tory too is the devil!"

With this apothegm he made me his military salute and left me to my meditations. And he had certainly given me a text for them too. I could not help feeling, as I lay in bed thinking the day over, that I knew an individual of the kind, and with the specific difference he had thus denounced, whom yet I could not consent to refer to the order in the spiritual hierarchy to which he had reduced all such in a lump. While still engaged in these commentaries I fell asleep.

The Colonel was as good as his word the next morning, and arrived before Jasper had laid the table for breakfast. Mr. Bulkley and I were walking up and down the gravel walk which bisected the garden, enjoying the clear light and bracing breath of a fine October morning, when he passed through the house and joined us. He seemed not quite as well at ease as he had done the evening before; and, after salutations had been exchanged, he said, —

"My walk has been productive of more enlightenment as to the state of my affairs than I had expected when I proposed coming here."

Of course we both of us begged to know from what direction this illumination had come.

"By a natural way enough," he replied. "As I was passing the post-office, old Kimball came running after me with a letter, which he said had fallen aside yesterday afternoon when Snell went for the letters. It is from the British Minister at Washington."

We neither of us knew precisely what to say; and so prudently waited till he was ready to proceed, which he presently did.

"It is a private and friendly, not an official letter. He is my very old friend, and, as such, wishes to give me all the help he possibly can. But, as it might be misrepresented, perhaps it is better that the circumstance should not be mentioned."

We assented, and he gave Mr. Bulkley the letter, who read it out as we walked. It was friendly in its tone, but diplomatic in its terms, and gave no more information than was necessary for his object. Beginning with expressions of regret at what he had to tell, his excellency informed Colonel Allerton that charges and evidence had been forwarded to England by the packet of the sixth which might give rise to a criminal prosecution against him, but which he, the Minister, was sure Colonel Allerton was fully prepared to meet and explain. He thought it not improper, considering their ancient friendship, to state to him these facts, in order that Colonel Allerton might take such measures for his exculpation as the case demanded. And he felt it the more incumbent upon him, as a personal friend, to give him timely notice, inasmuch as Colonel Allerton must be aware that his property in England would be taken possession of by the government, to await the final issue of the affair.

"It's very odd, by Jove!" said he, when the reading of the letter was done, "that I had never thought of that before. But of course it is a fact; and I must reduce my establishment within the limits of my American property, which, unless your general court sees fit to let go its gripe on the Clarke estate, is little enough. But, luckily, I have just received the balance of my half-yearly settlement with my agent at home; so that I am not absolutely without the means of carrying on the war for a while."

Our consideration on this point was presently interrupted by Jasper, who appeared to announce breakfast. While we were engaged in discussing the admirable results of his morning's labors (and he had an artist's pleasure in making the work of art before us as perfect as possible) Mr. Bulkley said to him, —

"Jasper, in what part of New Jersey did Colonel Cuyler live?"

"Up north, sir," he replied, "among the mountains, on Marking's Kill, three or four miles west of Williamsboro', near the Pennsylvany line."

"Very good," responded the minister. "And did you ever happen to know a man in Jersey named

Saint John — Michael Saint John ? " giving out the name of the evangelist with emphatic distinctness, and laying particular stress on the title which Christendom in general agree to prefix to it, (though he never used it in his public services, regarding it as a rag of Romanism,) so as to impress the name strongly on Jasper's mind and to recall the man if possible.

Jasper took time to consider, during which we hung upon his lips in anxious expectation; but he shook his head and said, —

"No, sir; I never knew any such man there, nor nowhere."

All our countenances fell a little at this, as we had all entertained a faint hope that we might get some glimpse of light from our dark friend. Even Colonel Allerton looked rather disappointed; though he affirmed that he had reckoned nothing on this most remote and unlikely possibility. So we presently resumed our conversation and pursued it as if this interruption had not taken place, and went over again the Saint John mystery, as men will talk over a hopeless business, as if discussion gave relief, if not hope. We none of us minded Jasper's presence; both because we knew that he might be trusted with an absolute confidence, and because there seemed no particular reason for making any more of a mystery of the matter than it was in its own essence. After breakfast Colonel Allerton took his leave and proceeded towards the village, leaving the minister and me to our morning tasks.

We had not been long engaged upon them when Jasper came into the room from the garden, whither he had repaired after disposing of his breakfast things, and said to Mr. Bulkley, —

"I beg your pardon, sir; but I have just been thinking that I used to know another man in Jarsey that you were talking of this morning."

"Another man!" said the Parson, rubbing his forehead. "I don't remember. Whom do you mean?"

"Why, I used to know a Mr. *Sinjin* there before the war. I don't know whether you care about him, sir."

"Bless your soul!" cried the Parson, jumping up. "And was his name Michael?"

"I believe it was, sir," replied Jasper; "though I'm not sure of that. But there was a Mr. Sinjin lived the other side of the Kill, about two miles off. My master had n't much to do with him latterly; for he was a bloody Tory, and went down to York before we went to the wars."

"It must be he! it must be he!" exclaimed the minister, making the historian Tacitus describe a somerset in the air quite out of keeping with his usually staid and saturnine temperament; and then, clapping his hands, added, "It must be the very man, Osborne, must n't it?"

I assented to the probability.

"Do you know anything of him since then, Jasper?" he continued.

"No, sir," Jasper answered. "I have never heard of him or about him for better than forty year."

"Never mind, never mind," the sanguine Parson proceeded. "We have found the first track; and it will be hard if we don't follow it up. You could direct us to the very place, I suppose, could n't you?"

"Lord bless you, yes, sir," answered Jasper. "I could find my way there in the dark if you'll put me down at Williamsboro'."

"To be sure you could!" said the minister; "to be sure you could! This comes of the English habit of eating up proper names. The Colonel shall not hear the last of it soon, I promise you. *Sinjin*, indeed!"

"Perhaps, sir," I suggested, "he may have something to say to you; for, if you had given the name as he did, Jasper would have known what you meant. He was the judge of how the name was to be pronounced, you see, after all."

"Ah, but you see the man was a Tory," said the minister, in high spirits; "so it's no wonder he did n't know how his own name should be pronounced, is it, Jasper?"

"He *was* a Tory," answered Jasper, simply, as if that was the gist of the matter, as he left the room.

## CHAPTER XIII.

#### IN WHICH GREAT PROGRESS IS MADE.

I SUGGESTED to Mr. Bulkley that it would be well to lose no time in apprising Colonel Allerton of what Jasper had said. He assented to the general proposition, but added, —

"It will be soon enough after dinner. This is news that will keep cold. And as our studies have been somewhat interrupted of late, I think we will hold by them this morning, if you please."

Of course I had to comply, whether I pleased or not; and we resumed our lecture, though to what degree of edification I do not think I can precisely testify at this distance of time. The morning was over, however, at last, and dinner was despatched, and a proper interval allowed for the difference of dinner-time at Woodside. Then the Parson told me I had better proceed on my errand by myself, as he must make a journey to Jericho to settle the rights and wrongs of the Hog's Neck. So I set off alone, not unwillingly. On arriving at Woodside I entered the hall-door, which was standing hospitably open, it being a fine day, though well on in October, without giving any warning of my presence. My habits of intimacy at the house also authorized me to enter the parlor where Eleanor usually sat without ceremony.

The room was never very light, owing to the shadow of the piazza and the climbing and drooping plants that festooned it; and on that afternoon the curtain of the second window to your right was let down to keep out the blaze of the westering sun. As I entered I saw, as I thought, Eleanor and her father seated at the very end of the room in earnest conversation — so earnest indeed, that they did not at once notice my approach. I advanced hastily, full of my news, when the pair rose in evident haste and embarrassment on perceiving me. I had my message on my lips, when, my eyes turning from Eleanor to her companion, I was astonished at seeing that it was not her father, but Mr. Harry Markham. My own confusion eclipsed theirs when I perceived this conjunction, which my heart misgave me boded me no good.

The feeling that mine was a most unwelcome intrusion crimsoned my cheeks for a second; but a bitterer pang soon drove the blood back to my heart. A flash of light seemed to search the closest coverts of my being, and I saw myself as I never did before. I had never said, even in my secret thoughts, "I love Eleanor Allerton!" till now that I felt that she was lost to me forever. It seemed as if years had passed over my heart since I entered the house a few moments before. I was a youth no longer. The passions of a man burned fiercely in my heart, and the simplici-

## IN WHICH GREAT PROGRESS IS MADE. 233

ties and follies of boyhood shrivelled and vanished in the flame.

I was conscious that my agitation of mind was written in my face. I felt that my knees trembled and my throat was parched; and I waited a moment till I was sure of commanding my voice before I spoke. But I was master enough of myself to see that I was not the only embarrassed one of the party. Whether it were the sight of my emotion, or the conflict of strong feelings of her own, the alternations of Eleanor's countenance (and its expression changed continually) had a painful, suffering air as she looked at me, which I thought I could read plainly enough.

"She is sorry for me — poor foolish lad!" I said bitterly to myself; and I felt as if I could eat my heart with rage that she should know that I was to be pitied.

"And does *he*, too, extend his tender compassion to me?" I continued, within my teeth.

I could not tell; but I thought, on thinking it over afterwards (I could only see and feel then), that his thoughts were not on me. Why should they be? He was not a demonstrative person at any time, and his face was not a book easy to be read. But it did not express a mind at ease. A mind at ease! Disturbed, perhaps, at the very height of his dream of joy, and hardly knowing whether it were a dream or a reality, how could it be at ease? It must be so. And I — I had discerned where my life of life was garnered up, just as it was scattered to the winds. It was a cruel moment for me — a moment into which an eternity was crushed together.

As soon as I could somewhat command my voice I stammered out, in a huskyish tone, "I — I beg pardon; but — but I had a message for your father; and — and I thought I should find him here. Is he in his library?" And I made towards the door by which I had entered.

Eleanor advanced towards me and said, not without agitation of look and voice, "Stay here, Cousin Frank; I will call him. He will be glad to see you; and we will hear your message together, if there be no objection."

And she disappeared through the arched doorway which led into her father's room. Left alone with Markham, he came up to me and offered me his hand, which I could not refuse; and we exchanged a few sentences of mutual inquiry, though I have no recollection of what it was now, if I had any perception of it at the time. I stood in a whirl of thoughts and emotions which I could not analyze. I could not reason; I could only feel that the lamp of my life was trampled out just as I discerned the shrine before which it burned, and that I was doubly orphaned from that hour forward.

I had not long to wait however; for, as we were talking, I heard the quick step of Colonel Allerton moving about in his room; and almost immediately he entered, alert and erect as ever, followed by Eleanor. After giving me a friendly greeting he said, —

## IN WHICH GREAT PROGRESS IS MADE. 235

"And so you have a message for me, Eleanor says. And what has the good Parson to say now? You need n't mind Markham here. He knows all that we do." And he gave him an open, cordial, friendly look, very different from the frigid politeness of his address when I saw them last together, but which stung me to the heart. What could be the meaning of it? Was there to be a mystery always brooding over this house?

I told my story as collectedly as I could, but with very little of the animated interest which I had brought with it from the parsonage, but which I had laid down at the threshold of that room. Luckily it was not a very complicated narrative, or I should have bungled it; for I was thinking but little of what I was saying. My statement, however, greatly interested Colonel Allerton; and he succeeded in making the other two talk it over with him as a circumstance which might possibly grow to some importance in their affairs. I took no part in the conversation, and found it hard to express the interest I ought to feel, and really did at bottom, when any of them addressed themselves to me. I could see that Eleanor was privily observing me, which did not assist me in concentrating my ideas; but Markham was clearly so full of what concerned himself and his friends, for such they now plainly were, that he had no thought to bestow on me. Colonel Allerton, however, was more observing; and after the matter had been discussed and put in all probable points of view, and not much more remained to be said, he turned to me and said,—

"But what ails you, Frank, my boy? You are not like yourself this afternoon. Are not you ill?"

I confessed to a headache, (though I apprehend that the seat of the disease was not the *head*,) and rose to depart, to cover myself from further observation.

"Nay, but stay and spend the rest of the afternoon with us," the Colonel hospitably urged. "You have not seen Markham this long time; and I prescribe his good company and Eleanor's as excellent for a headache. I have tried half the mixture," he continued, looking at Eleanor, "often myself, and have always found it a sovereign remedy."

I tried to laugh; and I thought, though I did not say so, that the remedy was like to be worse than the disease. So I resolutely excused myself, alleging that Mr. Bulkley would expect me and that I must go.

"Then come again this evening," persisted the Colonel; "and be sure and bring him with you. I want to hear his opinion about it."

I was going to decline again on my own account; but, looking at Eleanor, I saw her eyes fixed on me, while her lips expressed rather than uttered,—

"Do come!"

So I half muttered and half bowed an assent and hurried away. Still, as I walked homewards I again resolved that I would not return to Woodside again while Markham was there. I could not endure it.

## IN WHICH GREAT PROGRESS IS MADE. 237

It was plain, that, however it had been brought about, the displeasure which Colonel Allerton had felt towards him, and in which his daughter had certainly appeared to share in a lesser measure, was now removed. He was there apparently on familiar and intimate terms. Could it be possible that the change in their circumstances had bent the proud spirits of the father and daughter, and made them willing to accept addresses for her now which they had spurned in more prosperous days? That his name had been connected with hers, that there had been a closeness of connection and intimacy between them enough to excite remark and gossip, I knew from Ferguson's insolence, which compelled my interference, at the Sachem's Seat. I had observed, too, her embarrassment on more than one occasion when he had been spoken of, and her attempts at a partial defence of him from the strictures of her father.

I soon rejected all that was unworthy of Eleanor and her father in these surmises. I blushed that I had ever entertained them. It lowered me in my own eyes. But still, the main result of my conference with myself on the subject was the same. Everything confirmed it. His coming to America at this time; his reserve on my first acquaintance as to his relations with her; the particularity of these relations at some former time, proved by the very coldness and distance of his treatment at his first visit as well as by what Ferguson had said; her own looks and language when he was in question; this sudden change of demeanor towards him; the earnest *tête-à-tête* I had interrupted, — all, all proved beyond a peradventure that whatever had parted them was removed, — that Markham was the favored, the accepted lover of Eleanor Allerton.

Well, suppose he was. Was it anything to me? Could she ever be anything to me more than the kindest of sisters and friends? I cursed the idea of sisterhood and friendship. An hour before, I should have blessed them. The scales had fallen from my eyes, and I saw that they were not what I wanted. I cursed the hour that brought me to Wensley; and the next moment I cursed myself for the thought, and could have wept to think of never having known, though but to lose her forever. In short, I was furiously in love and furiously jealous, and was guilty of as many follies as my predecessors and successors in that category. Follies are they? Perhaps they are; but there is a good deal of what passes current for wisdom that one would exchange for them if one could — ay, and give boot into the bargain.

I had some time to torment myself with these thoughts and imaginations before the Parson returned. But at last he arrived, chuckling over the success of his mission, which, it seemed, had resulted in the renewal of the family compact between the two dynasties, to be consolidated by the marriage of Jerry and Sukey and confirmed by the sacrifice of the Hog's Neck. Mr. Bulkley was so full of his story that he did not remark the slight attention I gave to it, though it was garnished by many of his best imitations and attended by a running accompaniment of his merriest laugh. At last, however, when he was entirely done, and had wiped the tears from his eyes, which always waited on his best laughs, — tears like those of Matthew, "of one worn out with mirth and laughter," — he suddenly seemed to catch sight of my face as of some new thing.

"Bless me, Osborne!" he exclaimed. "What is the matter with you? Has anything happened at Woodside? Nothing wrong there, I hope."

"Everything is wrong there for me, sir," I replied, bitterly; and then, yielding to an impulse which seemed to urge me on whether I would or no, I told him the whole history of the afternoon, of the revelation which it had made to me of myself, and of the cruel despair in which it had left me. I have said before that the minister was a chosen confidant of love troubles within his own jurisdiction; and I now felt the influence upon my own mind which made him such. I do not think that there was another human being to whom I could have made that confession. But there was a sweetness and sympathy of soul about that blessed old man that invited and drew forth perfect confidence. I never could have said the same thing to any of the Deipnosophoi. No, indeed. The sense of the ridicule which is so often, though so cruelly, made to wait on a hopeless passion, bad enough in itself, heaven knows, would have sealed my lips upon the rack. But such an idea could not be associated with that of my dear old friend. Were there many such priests as he, I should accept the sacrament of confession. He listened to my story with the tenderest interest and tried to give me what comfort he could. But I thought I could discern, under all the consolation and encouragement he gave me, that he was of my opinion in the matter. Indeed, he gave me no direct encouragement; only he soothed my irritation of spirit so wisely, and showed me how I might have been too hasty in my conclusions, after all, that it had the effect of comforting me.

At tea-time I could hardly help laughing through all my distress to see how the good old man pressed upon me the best of everything on the table, and made Jasper bring out his choicest stores, reserved for solemn occasions. If the very best tea in the house, and preserves, and marmalade, and diet bread (as sponge-cake used to be called in those days) were a specific for a wounded spirit, mine would have been whole on the instant. I did my best, however, to satisfy his kind intentions; and soon after he had released me from my endeavors, which hardly came up to his wishes, I reminded him that Colonel Allerton wished to see him at Woodside. I was still inclined to remain at home; but he would not hear of it, and insisted on my accompanying him.

We arrived before the Woodside party had risen from their tea table. And here I saw again that the relations of the parties around it were changed since I last assisted with them at that evening sacrifice. Here was no *lap tea*, but a well-spread, sociable board, around which the three sat as friends, with every appearance of entire cordiality. I was sorry I had agreed to come. But it was too late then; and I took my share of the welcome extended to us with the best grace I could assume. I could feel with "the sixth sense of love" that Eleanor's eyes were often fixed upon me with a melancholy earnestness when I was looking another way; but they were dropped or withdrawn before mine could meet them. I despised myself for being the object of her pity; and I could see that Mr. Bulkley was covertly watching us; and this did not assist in the preservation of my equanimity.

We soon adjourned to the Colonel's room, where his wood fire gave out a cheerful, crackling, dancing light, in which we sat and talked over what was most in our minds, (or rather in theirs,) and never thought of ringing for candles till it was nearly time to break up the session. I did not attend much to what was going forward; but I could perceive that the talk was chiefly on the possibility of making some use of the glimmer of light Jasper had thrown upon our darkness, and whether it might not show us a way out of our perplexities. After a brown study of some duration, during which I sat with my eyes fixed on the blazing logs and listening rather to the spattering hiss with which the sap exuded from them upon the hearth than to the discussions going on around them, I was aroused from it by hearing the minister say, —

"An excellent plan, indeed! And I'll tell you what — Osborne shall go with you. He is entitled to have a run for a week or two; and I'll be answerable for him to the authorities at Cambridge."

"With all my heart," replied Markham; for it appeared that the remark was addressed to him; "it is just what I should have proposed myself if the plan went forward. What say you, Osborne? Will you go with me?"

"Yes — certainly; that is," I stammered out rather uncertainly, "if I can be of any use — if Mr. Bulkley thinks best."

"Oh, I do think it best, by all means," the minister replied; "so consider that as a settled thing."

As I thought I might as well know what the settled thing was of which it seemed I was to be a component part, I rallied my thoughts and tried to fix them on what was going on; and before we parted I had gathered that Mr. Bulkley had inspired the Colonel with a portion of his own confident belief that Jasper's information might be followed up to some good result; and they had agreed that Jasper had better be sent to the spot with some judicious person, who might pursue the game which he might by possibility set on foot. Markham at once volunteered to be the judicious person aforesaid, and offered to set off on the shortest notice; and it was as an amendment to this suggestion that the minister moved that my name, too, should be put into the commission. As soon as I understood how it was I fell in with the plan with a feverish eagerness; for I was just in the state of mind when motion and change of place are hungered and thirsted after. I felt a burning, longing wish to be anywhere away from Wensley, and was comforted to hear that we should set out the following day.

It soon grew to be time to go; and we took leave at the same time — Mr. Bulkley, Markham, and I — and walked to the turning to Grimes's together. I took a hasty leave of Eleanor and her father, and resolutely pushed out of the room first, so as to give Markham a moment with her without the Parson and me as spectators, which I considered (and do still consider) a handsome thing on my part. But he followed very soon after us, which might have surprised me had I not reflected, that he would probably walk up the next morning to renew the "sweet sorrow" of farewell. This hypothesis did not tend to concentrate my thoughts on what was passing between my companions; and I am not sure whether it was during this walk, that the Parson extracted from Markham the secret of his altered relations with Woodside, or whether it was during the next day's journey to Boston. But the facts were briefly these.

Markham's brother, the clerk in the colonial office, had just written to him, that it had transpired in the office that it was Ferguson himself who had given Lord Bathurst the hint touching the trouble in Colonel Allerton's department, which had induced his lordship to enter upon the cross-examination the result of which had drawn down Colonel Allerton's displeasure on poor Markham's head; and Ferguson it was that had persuaded Markham that it was best for all concerned that the facts should be made known to the secretary, though it was done so skilfully, that he could deny it with a good face if laid to his charge; and Markham now remembered, that it was Ferguson that contrived the accident which took him to the colonial office that particular morning. Having received this intelligence, and hearing of the rumors about Colonel Allerton before they had got wind fully, he sent it at once to Wensley with all these explanations. He at once received a cordial invitation to repeat his visit, which he lost no time in doing, and had a very different reception from the one he had before, — the Allertons looking upon him as the innocent instrument of the same man who had wound his toils about themselves. They acquitted him of all blame, even for indiscretion, and felt the desire natural to generous minds to make more than amends to one whom they had treated with injustice. So he said to us. "Amends with a vengeance!" said I to myself.

The next morning we were unable to take the

Haverford coach, as we had to apprise Jasper of his unexpected expedition, and to make all our preparations. Jasper entered into the plan very readily, only doubting how his master would get on by himself. But when he found that this difficulty had been provided against by the Allertons insisting upon his becoming their guest during the absence of the grand vizier (or *wuzeer*, as they ridiculously spell it now) on foreign service, his scruples were at once at an end, and he lost no time in putting the house in order for so extraordinary an event. As we wished to make what despatch we could, we resolved not to wait for the Pentland coach, which came along towards night, but to put Black Sally into the Major's covered wagon, and get over the ground before night. When we had come to this conclusion Mr. Bulkley suddenly expressed his determination to accompany us as far as Boston. He should like the excursion, he said; and he thought he could manage to drive Sally back again by himself the next day or the day after. Of course we were glad enough to have his society — at least I was; for I did not care for a *tête-à-tête* journey with Markham after all that had passed. And I shrewdly suspect that it was the feeling that this was the case, that induced him to volunteer his company.

We arrived before dark, and, after putting our horse up at the Exchange Coffee House stables, and bespeaking our passage by the Providence coach for the next morning, I proceeded at once to Mr. Moulton's, accompanied by Mr. Bulkley, to obtain his permission for the expedition. There was no great difficulty in procuring this on the representations of the good minister, for whom my guardian had conceived a warm regard. I did not pay much attention to the reasons he urged in my favor; but I well understood in my secret soul, that the real ones which induced him to make the original suggestion were not so much the expectation of good to the Allertons as of good to myself, which might accrue from this diversion of thought and passion. However, the consent was granted, and Mr. Bulkley prevailed upon to be Mr. Moulton's guest for the night. Markham did not come, though I had invited him. He is writing to Eleanor, said I to myself; and the glass of wine I had at my lips (though it was the famous old Suffolk Madeira) almost choked me at the thought.

The next morning came in due season. Who does not remember, that is old enough, the morning of a journey to New York in those days before railways? I had slept but little during the night; and was just fairly asleep, about four in the morning, when a thundering knock at the hall-door and a violent ring at the bell announced that the coach would soon come lumbering along. Then the dressing in the dark, the half-awake, slipshod servants, making a pretence of getting you some breakfast, which was always just too late; the dressing-gowned and slippered friends (Mr. Moulton and the Parson in my case) stumbling out upon you to see you off in spite of your entreaties overnight, that they would do no such thing. Then the long, hot or cold, dusty or muddy, never pleasant journey to Providence. And then the old Fulton steamer. How we used to admire her! What a marvel of speed and comfort that ill-contrived old hulk seemed to our innocent minds, not as yet sophisticate with the later luxuries of locomotion! To be sure, it was better than the week's hard coaching, which was necessary to bring the two cities together before her time. And New York itself, — Newest York now, — how changed since that my first visit! Her very *caravanserais* have fled, like the sojourners of a day. Where is Bunker's? Echo, if she could make herself heard above the roar of traffic, might answer, if she had nothing better to say, *Where?* And where is the City Hotel? Oh, Chester Jennings, art thou indeed forever fled? And the Park Theatre too? But I forbear.

We hurried through New York and put ourselves on the road to Williamsboro' with all the speed we could command in those more deliberate days. But it took us nearly two days, as the roads were bad, and the wagons, bearing the local rank of coaches, yet worse. But here Jasper made our fatigues less with the stories he had to tell, suggested by almost every point of our route; for he was now among familiar scenes. There, a mile or two on this side of Hackensack, he had first smelt gunpowder, one cold autumnal night, in a slight affair of outposts.

Farther on, it was coming out of that house that he had first seen General Washington. And at Morristown, where we spent the night, he showed us, not only the head-quarters of the commander-in-chief, but the very baker's shop over which he himself had been billeted. And it happened, oddly enough, that the business was still carried on by the baker's son, a boy at that time, but who perfectly remembered the sable guest of his father. The next day we got more and more, as we advanced into his own country, and he had a history for almost every house we passed. It seemed to have been a region fertile in Tories; for his narratives were mostly of that tribe, which was to him as that of Barabbas. We arrived at Williamsboro' too late to push on to the scene of our inquiries that night.

The next morning we took an open wagon and pair and proceeded onward. Jasper's interest in all the scenes about him now grew intense. He had not seen them for nearly fifty years; and he seemed to remember them and to cling to their memory with the strong local attachment of his race. We sympathized so strongly with his feelings, that, though in impatient haste ourselves, we proposed a stop at the house of the Cuyler family, where he was born. But here he was doomed to disappointment. The house was there, to be sure; but it was degraded into a mere farm-house, and not a well-appointed one neither. It had a decayed, tumble-down look; and the out-buildings and fences were sadly out of repair.

A shrewish-looking woman, not over clean, sharply asked our business; and her inquiry was enforced by half a dozen hungry, snarling curs, who opened mouth upon us in full cry; while a swarm of dirty children clustered about the door, staring over one another's heads at the rare spectacle of strangers. She did not seem particularly well satisfied with the account we had to give of ourselves; and, though she called off the dogs and did not order us to leave the premises, she kept a suspicious eye upon us as we looked about them.

But there was not much to detain us. The only thing that recalled the former state of the Cuylers was the old chariot of the family, which stood rotting to pieces in a dilapidated coach-house with one door off its hinges, and which, if not a habitation for dragons and owls, was clearly one for cats and chickens — a litter of kittens garrisoning the inside; while the outworks bore unmistakable evidence of being a roosting place for poultry. There had plainly not been energy enough to clear away this old piece of lumber, as it must have seemed to the occupants. The woman of the house rather apologized for its toleration by saying that the children liked to play in it. But she had no knowledge of its former owners. She came from Pennsylvania, she said, and had never heard of the Cuylers. The very name of the family seemed to have died out even upon their ancestral acres. We left the place almost as sad as Jasper himself.

We hastened on, and, crossing the Kill, soon arrived at the house where the Michael St. John, the unconscious cause of so much trouble to us all, had lived. Jasper led us directly to its door, as he had said he could, without inquiry or hesitation. And here we received a very different welcome from our last from John McCormick, its present owner. He was a hale, middle-aged man, of a cheerful and intelligent countenance, and well disposed to give us what information and assistance he could. It did not seem to be much, however. St. John had never returned to that part of the country, the father of McCormick having bought the farm of the State, by which it had been confiscated; and he knew nothing of the particulars of his fate. This seemed to be death to our hopes. We looked with blank disappointment in one another's faces; and Mr. McCormick went on:—

"There has been inquiry made about this St. John before; and if my father and I had not possessed this farm for more than forty years, I should think there was some design upon it."

"And, pray, when and by whom was there ever inquiry made about him?" asked Markham, with the air of a man catching at a straw.

"It was ten or a dozen years ago," McCormick replied. "There was a man came from York way who hunted up everything that could be found out about him from town records, parish registers, and what not. He didn't make much noise about it; but, as I thought it might concern my title-deeds, I kept an eye on him and found out what he was at."

"And do you know his name?" asked Markham, eagerly.

"His name? Yes," he answered. "Let me see. Yes, his name was Abrahams; he was a sort of Jew lawyer, I believe."

Markham and I looked at each other. It was the name of the agent in New York who used to draw the pensions.

"Abrahams!" said Markham. "And do you know anything further about him, or where we should be likely to find out where he is?"

But he knew nothing on the subject; and we were in the dumps again. We liked the appearance and frankness of McCormick so much, that, after a consultation of looks between Markham and me, he briefly stated to him our case and how important it was to us that this man should be found, he being unquestionably the accessory to the fraud on this side the water. He could give us no clew to what we wanted; and we talked over the matter in a spirit of despair. Presently Jasper said, —

"You say he was a Jew, sir?" McCormick assented. "And his name was Abrahams? I wonder if he could be the son of Aaron Abrahams, who was a commissary in the year seventy-seven?"

"His name was Aaron, I remember," said McCormick; and so did we.

"Did you know him?" said I.

"Know him!" repeated Jasper. "I guess I had reason to know him. I know he almost starved us; and would quite, had not a lot of our men threatened to burn his house down about his ears for him. They tried to do it, too. Ben Simpkins was hanged for it, poor fellow!"

"Then you know where he lived?" asked Markham and I in a breath.

"I guess I do," he answered, laughing. "I mounted guard there for a month after poor Ben was hanged. And I lived well, too, I tell ye; for they was awfully frightened."

"And where was it?" we all asked at once.

"It was down Monmouth way," said Jasper, "not far from Horseshoe Inlet, near where the Falmouth was wrecked. It was an awful wrecking-place, and old Abrahams's house was full of cabin furniture and things. Folks said he had got rich by wrecking. He was rich, any way. But I don't believe such riches is any good to people."

We looked at one another again and with more hopeful faces. To be sure, it was not much to hope about; but it was better than nothing. Jasper seemed really to be our guardian angel; though poor Tom might have called him a black one. We held a consultation over this hint, and resolved, as we did not know what better to do, that we would follow it up and see whether we could get any trace of Abrahams in that neighborhood. It was the faintest of possibilities; but, as we had been disappointed in our discoveries at this place, we were impatient to be trying after them in some other. I felt relief only in motion, and was in haste to be off.

McCormick pressed us to stay until after dinner; in which case he agreed to accompany us, with a reasonable compensation for his time, the rather as the heaviest of the harvesting was now over. Markham had made this proposition to him when it first occurred to us to continue our search, inasmuch as it would be convenient, if not essential, to have some one of the party able to identify Abrahams if he could be overtaken. So we yielded to his hospitable urgency and partook of a plentiful Jersey farmer's dinner, presided over by his eldest unmarried daughter, a fine girl of eighteen, his wife having been dead for several years. He was urgent, furthermore, that we should spend the night there and commence our journey fresh in the morning. But we would not hearken to this proposal; and, according to our first plan, we set off about two in the afternoon, our host with Markham in his own wagon and pair of stout black horses, and Jasper and I in the one we had brought from Morristown — having first sent information of our intentions to the owner, so that we need not have the hue-and-cry after us as horse-thieves.

In this order we traversed nearly the entire length of the State. It took us nearly three days to accomplish it. I had purposely chosen Jasper as my companion, because I could talk with him or be silent as I pleased. I was moody enough for the first part of the way;

but, when we got upon the line of operations of the campaigns of '76 and '77, I could not help being diverted from the gloomy train of my own thoughts by the lively reminiscences of my companion. He was familiar with the whole of the ground; and it was like having been part of those movements one's self to hear his account of them. It was the little personal details proper to himself that gave this De-Focish air of reality to his narrations.

When we were passing over the battle-field of Monmouth, for instance, — "It was about here," said he, "that I was coming up with the reserve when General Washington came riding back from the front, where he had been on a lookout. It was an awful hot day; and he pulled up by me and says, says he, 'Jasper,' says he (for he had seen me often with Colonel Cuyler when he was alive, and had slept under the same tent with me, bless you, the night before we got to Morristown), 'Jasper,' says he, 'what have you got in your canteen?' 'Rum and water, sir,' says I. 'Very good,' says he; 'let me have some.' I took it off and reached it to him. 'Take a drink first yourself,' says he (that, you know, was because somebody had tried to poison him just before). So I took a pull; and so did he, a good one too, after me; and then we went into action."

Farther on towards the sea-coast, too, his knowledge continued fresh; for he had been stationed in that quarter to keep the Tories in order during the spring of '77, after the successes at Trenton and

## IN WHICH GREAT PROGRESS IS MADE. 255

Princeton (in both of which he partook) had induced Sir William Howe to evacuate the Jerseys. Towards night on the third day we reached a shabby little village, or rather hamlet, not far from the shore, called Sinkers — a place of a very evil reputation as the head-quarters of wreckers of the worst description, who in those days, not to say in these, too, infested that "shipwrecked coast." At the wretched tavern which dispensed their daily rum to these worthy citizens, and at which we were compelled to put up, we directed Jasper to try and find out what he could about this tribe of Abrahams without exciting notice. This he easily did while busy about the horses in the stable; and he soon came to us with the unexpected intelligence that the commissary was yet living at his old house, though much reduced from his former flagitious prosperity, as Jasper had esteemed it.

Encouraged beyond our hopes by this news, we sent him forward that night to reconnoitre his old ground and find how matters stood. When he returned he reported that he had attempted an entrance, but had been repulsed by the very commissary whom he had helped to guard in former days. He could not, or would not, remember any such service; and refused to acknowledge any gratitude for it or to admit him to whom he owed it into his house.

"There was sickness there," he said; "he could not come in. There was a tavern at Sinkers; he might go there." The noise of this discussion brought up the effective reserve of Mrs. Abrahams, an aged matron among the daughters of Israel, who opened a fire of flying artillery upon him, which soon made him beat a retreat. " What business had he to come there at that time of night disturbing them, and they with a son at the point of death in the house ? If he did n't take himself off they 'd let fly the blunderbuss at him for a black rascal as he was." And much more of the same sort.

So Jasper did take himself off, and reported progress as above. Matters seemed now to be in the train we had long wished for. We considered what step to take next, and agreed that the time had come for the interposition of the civil arm if we could get hold of it. We were for looking up the nearest magistrate; but McCormick dissuaded us, on the ground that it would be better to procure one from a little farther off the coast. So we gladly assented to his proposal that he should mount one of his horses and ride back to Monmouth and apply to " an honest lawyer," as he termed him, whom he had had dealings with, to come over and help us. The next morning early he accordingly appeared with this phenomenon, Mr. Sturdevant by name, and an officer, in case of need. About ten o'clock we proceeded to the scene of action. We left the large covered wagon at the foot of the steep, sandy hill, just on the other side of which Abrahams's house stood, and walked up it, both for the sake of speed and secrecy. Jasper was to bring it slowly after us.

## IN WHICH GREAT PROGRESS IS MADE. 257

Arrived at the door of the house, it was some minutes before we could effect an entrance. We were aware that we were reconnoitred; and it was not until we made an assault on the door that threatened to bring it down that it was at length opened by old Abrahams himself. He would fain have held parley with us; but we pushed by him into the room at our right, of which the door was open, and which proved to be the kitchen, but yet the apartment usually occupied by the family. Here we made a stop, and the old man had time to ask us our business. To this, under the circumstances, not unreasonable request, Mr. Sturdevant stated that our business was with his son Aaron, whom we knew to be in the house. He denied the fact, and fortified his denial by a volley of imprecations more appropriate to the character of a Christian than of a Jew.

Mr. Sturdevant intimated to him that he had the necessary process and officer, and should proceed at once to satisfy himself by a search of the premises. Old Abrahams seemed greatly alarmed at this information; and, changing his tone, begged to know why it was that this perquisition was set on foot. He was informed that it was on a charge of being concerned as principal or accessory in an important forgery. This naturally enough increased the old man's distress; but he still persisted in maintaining that his son was not there, but with less voluble assurance. At this point the wife, the very heroine who had routed Jasper and put him to flight, came in by a door opening into the kitchen, and said, disregarding the signals telegraphed to her by her husband, —

"And what do you want here? What business have you to disturb an honest man's house in this way? Are you the gang of that black rascal that tried to break in here last night? Don't you know that there's a sick man in the house? Get off with you, or you'll be the death of my poor son. He's been plagued enough already this morning, poor fellow, and you'll finish him!"

This is a very faint copy of the tirade with which she favored us, and which seemed to produce more effect on her husband than on us. He stamped with his feeble foot, and clinched his fist impotently, more at her than at us, but said nothing.

"We must see your son, ma'am," said Mr. Sturdevant, kindly, but firmly.

"You shall do no such thing," the dame responded as resolutely, setting her back against the door.

"It must be done, ma'am," he continued, in the same tone; "but it shall be done as quietly and with as little disturbance to him as possible."

He then gently removed her, though she struggled violently and made a resistance which saved the credit of her courage and spirit, although she had to yield to a superior force. We pushed through a narrow passage, at the end of which was a door opening into a bed-chamber, where lay the

## IN WHICH GREAT PROGRESS IS MADE. 259

man we were in search of, propped by pillows, and testifying by his looks to the truth of what we had heard as to his condition. As soon as we had looked at him, our eyes all involuntarily turned upon McCormick, who signified by a nod and look that he was the man we were after.

Having received this confirmation, Mr. Sturdevant approached the bedside of the sick man to open his business. Just at this moment we heard a loud noise, in which Jasper's tones were distinguishable, as if there were some difficulty on his line of march. At Markham's request, McCormick went out to see what the matter was, while we remained to see the main play played out. Mr. Sturdevant had not advanced very far in his cautious statement of the reason of our being there, when we heard loud voices and footsteps approaching the house. Jasper's and McCormick's voices were soon heard in the kitchen; and Markham and I forthwith went thither to see what had happened. Jasper we found sitting on a rush-bottomed chair, with one arm over the back, looking very faint, while a stream of blood was dribbling down from the ends of his fingers upon the floor. But this spectacle did not hold us long when we looked at the third person of the party.

"Ferguson!" exclaimed Markham.

I was too much amazed to say anything.

"Yes, sir, Ferguson!" the other repeated fiercely. "And I should like to know whether it was you that set this black ruffian upon me as I was peaceably upon the highway."

Markham and I looked at each other, not knowing exactly what to say, when the magistrate came out of the sick-chamber, and we briefly explained the facts. He turned to McCormick, who only said that he had found Jasper and this man struggling together on the ground, the former wounded and bleeding, and had merely interposed and brought them both along to the house; which he was quite competent to do, though Ferguson was a strong man. We all now turned to Jasper, who said, rather feebly,—

"First tie a handkerchief tight round my arm, just below the shoulder." This was done at once. "Now, Master Frank," he went on, "put your walking-stick through the bandage and give it a hard turn, and hold it so." I did as I was directed; and this extemporized *tourniquet*, which Jasper had learned in the hospital, stopped the bleeding. A small exhibition of brandy, of which medicine McCormick happened accidentally to have a moderate supply about him for emergencies, restored poor Jasper to the speaking point.

The amount of his information was, that as he was slowly coming down the sandy hill, having stopped for some time on the top to rest the horses, he saw a window of the Jew's house open, and a man jump out of it and hurry up the hill towards himself. It immediately occurred to him that this must be the very man we were after; and, accordingly, he appointed himself to the service of cutting off his retreat. This he found to be one of no little difficulty and of some danger, inasmuch as his antagonist drew a knife after they had closed, and stabbed him in the arm; and, had not McCormick come to his assistance, the enemy would have made good his escape.

"Well, gentlemen," said Ferguson, "this is all true enough; but what objection have you to make to what I did? I merely defended myself when attacked, without provocation, on the highway."

But Mr. Sturdevant intimated that his sudden exit from Abrahams's window, taken in connection with the known circumstances of the case, would justify his detention for further inquiry.

"Very well, sir," said Ferguson; "you know that you act at your own peril; and you may be assured I shall exact all the redress I can get."

Mr. Sturdevant merely bowed his acquiescence, and said, "But you also know, sir, that I must have your person searched. Anything not bearing upon this case will be immediately returned to you." And he called the officer from the bed-chamber.

At this announcement Ferguson turned pale as death, and, hastily putting his hand in his pocket, drew out a crumpled packet of papers and threw them on the fire. Luckily it was an economical household, and the fire was but newly kindled. Ferguson sprung forward to strike them into the coals with the heel of his boot, but was held back by McCormick; while I snatched them, only a little singed from the flames. This authorized more emphatically his being taken into custody, which was formally done. But the papers did not afford us much light at the first glance, as they were written in cipher, and were Sanscrit to us. After a brief consultation aside, Mr. Sturdevant returned alone to the sick Jew's chamber, taking the manuscripts with him. We remained busy in taking care of poor Jasper, who seemed very weak, and in keeping guard over Ferguson. But his spirit seemed to have deserted him. He appeared as one stunned, and sat in gloomy silence at the table, leaning his head on both his hands. Markham and I exchanged looks of congratulation — believing, though we did not know how, that a way of deliverance was opened before us.

It was long before Sturdevant returned to us, so long that we had despatched McCormick for a surgeon, who had dressed Jasper's arm and departed before the magistrate appeared. But we had not waited in vain. I have not time to go into the detail of all the particulars; for it is high time that the thread, too long spun out, of this narrative should be snipped off. But of course everybody whose memory (Heaven pity them!) can extend back thirty years will remember all about the story, which made a nine days' wonder in this country, and a week's even in England. Any one that will take the trouble to consult a file of the London Times of that date will find all the documents, letters, and affidavits, with the official exoneration of Colonel Allerton, at full length. As near as I remember them, — for my mind was not entirely engrossed by them even at the time, — they were substantially these : —

Ferguson, from his knowledge of that department and of the parties likely to obtain relief from the government, had planned this St. John forgery, and several other lesser ones, and had found an apt instrument in Mr. Aaron Abrahams. This gentleman had transacted the American part of the business more to the satisfaction of his employer than his own, inasmuch as he did not think he was allowed his full share of the booty. The communications between them were carried on in cipher after the very beginning, which was arranged when Ferguson was in New York on a former visit undertaken for the purpose. After the suspicions of Colonel Allerton had been excited, Abrahams, who had received instant notice of them from Ferguson, took himself out of the way until the storm should blow over — this being undoubtedly Ferguson's object when he advised a delay in communicating the facts to the secretary. So effectually had Abrahams done this, that Ferguson himself had great difficulty in tracing him; for he seems to have had no great confidence in his English confederate; and it was not until his illness took him back to his father's house that he fairly came up with him.

The object he had to gain was twofold : first to

arrange Abrahams's testimony so that it should throw the whole blame on Colonel Allerton; and, secondly, to get possession of the letters in cipher, which contained his instructions to his agent during the whole transaction. In these laudable pursuits he had been engaged for a day or two at such times as he could have access to the sick man, and in these he was busy when our opportune arrival interrupted him; and he had succeeded so far as to induce Abrahams to produce the letters (which he always kept with him) on some pretence, but with the unquestionable purpose of getting possession of them by force or fraud. When the alarm was given of our arrival, and he actually saw Markham and me, he snatched the documents and made his escape as described by Jasper.

The principal difficulty Mr. Sturdevant had to contend with on the part of the excellent invalid was to persuade him on which side his interest lay. But it being made clear that whatever hope of favor or reward the case admitted of lay with us, he ingenuously stated the whole matter, and gave the key to the cipher, which made it perfectly clear as to where the guilt rested. This he was the more willing to do from his discontent with his principal, nothing allayed by this last operation of his which plainly was intended to leave him without proof of any connection between them.

Before we left the house Markham and I had the satisfaction of shaking hands upon the entire success of our expedition; and our satisfaction was increased by knowing that the relief of our friends had been greatly hastened by it. Although it was Mr. Sturdevant's opinion and our own that such a web of fraud and perjury could not have stood the test of an English investigation, still it was much better to avoid it with all its gossipings, and scandals, and lifelong suspicions. Ferguson was committed to the county jail to await the decision of the higher authorities as to the jurisdiction to which his crime belonged; while an officer was put into the Jew's house to keep guard over Abrahams. We returned to the inn, taking with us poor Jasper, who was not fit to be removed farther for a few days.

My mind being now at liberty to dwell on my own affairs without distraction, I was half frantic at this delay, and felt that I must know how matters stood between Eleanor Allerton and Markham or die. Sometimes I hoped that things were not advanced as far between them as I had feared. He certainly did not seem inordinately happy; but then he was parted from Eleanor. Then again I was quite sure that he had had no letter from her. To be sure, it was hard to hit us, as we always were on the wing; but I think I could not have pardoned Eleanor, were she my lady-love, had she not contrived to do it.

The suspense was intolerable. I was haunted by a thousand insane imaginings. I was afraid I should be taken ill, too; perhaps I should die, and never see her again. And it was Markham himself that relieved me from my distress at last. He it was that proposed that I should be the messenger of our glad tidings. He wished to wait on the spot until the whole business in regard to Ferguson was settled. "Is this a happy lover?" said I to myself; and I felt a foolish sort of comfort as I said it. The only difficulty was about poor Jasper; and this was settled by McCormick agreeing to stay with him till he was able to travel, and then to see him to New York, and, if necessary, to Wensley.

Things being thus arranged, I did not suffer the grass to grow under my feet. I set out at daybreak the next morning, and got on to New York as fast as men and horses, urged by money, and, I am afraid, by Newark whips, could take me in those days. But I did not reach the city till the next day. Fortunately, the Fulton sailed that evening; and I was at Providence about three o'clock the next afternoon. I would not wait till the stage coaches could describe the two sides of the triangle, but pushed on over the base line, which I had just mathematics enough to know must be less than the sum of the other two. I spared neither money, pains, nor horse flesh, and hurried on across the country to Wensley. I had to stop over night at Wexboro'; but, early the next day, I was on my hot way again. I came in sight of Wensley about eleven o'clock in the morning of a delicious Indian-summer day. The haze, that was not a haze, gave a dreamy beauty to tree, and hill, and stream. At the gate I leaped out of the open wagon which had brought me my last stage and hastened up the sweep. I entered the house. I passed on to Eleanor's parlor. I opened the door. She was sitting at the farther window, and alone. When she saw me she started up and exclaimed only,—

"Frank!"

"Eleanor—dear Eleanor," said I, "all is well! Everything is cleared up, and all is safe!"

I had nearly crossed the room before I had finished my sentence. She gave me a look never to be forgotten; and, coming forward a step or two to meet me, fell upon my neck and burst into tears. Aha! it was not Fairy's neck this time. It was my turn now. And *these* were tears of joy.

Presently I led her to the sofa, and, still holding her hand, (she let me, by Heaven!) told her as briefly as I could the whole story. When this was done, and we paused a moment from the subject, I looked into her eyes (how could I have ever thought them hard to read?) and said,—

"Eleanor, then it was not Markham, after all?"

"No," she replied, her lip quivering and her eyelids drooping under my gaze; "no, Frank, it was not Markham."

Ah, Sir Walter Scott, Sir Walter Scott, it was well for your peace of mind that you were not within eyeshot just then!

## CHAPTER XIV.

#### BEING THE CONCLUSION OF THE WHOLE MATTER.

THERE is really no occasion for this chapter. The little more I have to say could be stitched on to the last one just as well as not. But, then, I do think that chapter ends well; and, moreover, I would not have this story of mine rounded by a *thirteenth* chapter. No, indeed; I would as soon have had thirteen guests round my wedding supper table. So we will have chapter fourteen as *L' Envoi*, if only for luck.

Well, well, it seemed a good while before that marriage supper was spread. But it came at last. And it has been a good while longer since, only it has not seemed so. Not that we had any very cruel opposition to encounter. Had I been writing a novel I should have been a dunce to have allowed Eleanor to have had so good-natured a papa. But I cannot help the fact; and in real life such characters are not uncommon, and by no means unpleasant, if uninteresting. Colonel Allerton only laughed at us, and refused to recognize any engagement for a year or two, thinking that it was only right a boy and girl of nineteen (for I found that I had imagined Eleanor older than she was, as boys are apt to do in such cases, and that I was, in fact, just eleven days her elder) should have a full opportunity to change their minds. But as he allowed us perfect freedom of intercourse personally and by letter, we consoled ourselves by resolving to show him that we could not change our minds. At any rate, we did not.

Mr. Bulkley was, of course, the first person out of that family to whom I communicated all the good news I had to tell, withholding nothing. The whole story gave him the extremest pleasure, but none so exquisite as the part which told that I was the accepted lover of Eleanor. His joy was not profuse of words; but it glistened in his eye, and seemed to pervade his whole nature and to glow in his whole life. I believe he loved us both dearly, and rejoiced from his heart that we loved each other. And then a constitutional match-maker feels an artist's pride in the match he has planned and helped to make.

I thought he would be more distressed than he seemed to be at Jasper's mishap. But he treated it very slightly. He seemed still to hold to General Wolfe's doctrine, that it was the business of a soldier to die; and, of course, that includes being wounded. Only he was glad that he had done his duty and been mentioned with distinction in the despatches. This was also very much Jasper's own opinion, when he arrived soon after in the company rather than in the care of the good McCormick, who came on with him to see the Allertons, at their earnest request and at their charges. Major Grimes told me Jasper said "that a fellow that made a campaign in the Jarseys must be willing to run the risk of being stuck by a Tory." As the story was told to me, the future state of the Tory was somewhat distinctly intimated. But, as Jasper had lived so many years in a minister's service, I cannot but hope that the qualifying participle was an interpolation of the gallant narrator.

The remainder of my exile from college soon passed away, and I returned thither with much more reluctance than I had left it; and I returned much older in heart and mind. I was a boy then; I felt that I was a man now. My pursuits were modified by the change in my feelings; and if I did not absolutely forsake the Deipnosophoi (which would have been ungrateful in view of my obligations to them), at least their ritual services absorbed a very small part of my thoughts or my time. Encouraged by the hope of showing myself worthy of the love of Eleanor and of the good opinion of her father and Mr. Bulkley, I gave myself to study as I had never done before; and I believe that, when I came to take my degree, I neither disgraced myself nor disappointed them.

Within a year after my graduation, having then attained my majority, Mr. Bulkley joined Eleanor and me in holy wedlock at Wensley. It was an occasion of mixed joy and sorrow, of smiles and tears, as all such momentous crises must be to those that reflect and feel. The greatest grief that clouded that happy hour was the thought that it foreshadowed the sad hour of separation from Mr. Bulkley and Wensley; for almost immediately after our marriage, we accompanied Colonel Allerton back to England, where we lived until his death, which occurred about three years afterwards. There our friendly relations were renewed with Markham, who had returned home almost immediately after the events of the last chapter and succeeded to the office left vacant by the dismission of Ferguson, which he held until it expired, not long since, with the gradual extinction of the unfortunate class it regarded. I never knew what passed between Eleanor and him at the time of his visit at Woodside. I never asked her, and she never told me.

After the death of her father, Eleanor and I returned to America and lived a year or two at Wensley. But the climate of New England did not agree with her health; and we removed to Pennsylvania, where we live to this day. Our house stands finely on a spur of one of the Appalachians, just where the mountain range begins to melt into the champaign country below. Behind us the mountains stand in everlasting yet ever-changing beauty; while, before the rushing river foams and flows through a delicious country of meadows, pastures, cornfields, and woodlands, dotted with cattle and sprinkled with villages, until it is lost to sight in the blue distance. It is situated in the township of St. Philipsburgh and the county of Monongahela, about three miles off the state road from Harrodstown to Foxley, to the west. There we have lived for many years and have had — but as Miss Martha Buskbody said to Mr. Peter Pattieson, when he was about to make a minute statement of the felicities of the married life of Henry Morton and Edith Bellenden, "It is unnecessary to be particular concerning our matrimonial comforts."

As long as Mr. Bulkley lived we never failed to pay him a visit of two or three months every summer, and for that purpose retained Woodside until after his death. This took place about twelve years from the time of our marriage, at the age, as the inscription on the monument erected by the Wensley Sewing Circle informs us, of eighty-four years, seven months, and five days. It was, as he had always wished it should be, instantaneous. I chanced to be in New York when it happened; so that I was able to reach Wensley in time to lay his head in the Minister's Tomb. Eleanor mourned him as another father, and I as the only one I had known. He left a moderate property, as he had had a captain's pay for several years under the last pension act. This he left to the town, the income to be paid to Jasper during his life. His books he bequeathed to me; also his sword and firelock, which, as I write, are crossed over the fireplace of my library as they were over his. His cocked hat, wig, and goldheaded cane I bought at the executor's sale at a moderate figure, and still preserve them with filial reverence.

Jasper survived his master nearly ten years, and

was a good deal past ninety when he died. He was
"a prosperous gentleman" in his last days; for,
besides Mr. Bulkley's bequest, he had savings of his
own, as he was a pensioner under the first act, and
received his ninety dollars a year till his death. He
suffered me to give him the use of a cottage near the
borders of a pretty little wooded lake, which is
known as Jasp's Pond to this day. I was never in
Boston without going to see him; and, though I was
at home when he died, I honored his memory with
a marble headstone, according to a promise made
to him during life, and which seemed to reconcile
him more than anything to the idea of dying. The
Minister's Tomb is in the north-east corner of the
burying-ground, and Jasper lies buried a little to the
west and south of it. You would know the place by
a fine larch which grows near it.

I have been so busy with the memories I most love
that I had almost forgotten to tell what became of
Ferguson. After the first joy of the discovery of his
villany was over, I could see plainly that the minister
was depressed by the idea of his undergoing any
shameful punishment. I mentioned this to Colonel
Allerton; and he, too, felt no disposition to pursue
him to extremities. This he intimated to Mr. Sturdevant, who informed him that he should promote his
wishes the more readily from the great doubt he entertained whether Ferguson could be prosecuted to conviction. He could not be sent to England for trial;
and it was more than doubtful whether the original

instigation of the crime, when in this country, could be proved, after the death of Abrahams, which soon followed the scenes at his bedside. So he was discharged from custody by the consent of all parties. His spirit was thoroughly broken, however, as may be inferred from this fact. When the negotiations relating to his release were going on, Mr. Sturdevant received from Boston an anonymous letter, containing a draft for five hundred dollars, to be given to the prisoner on his discharge. This he must have supposed to have come from Colonel Allerton, the man he had tried to ruin; and yet he took it. *We* knew that it was an offering to the memory of Julia Mansfield. Ferguson went to South America, where the revolutions were then raging, and nothing definite was ever heard of him. If the rumors which reached us were true, his life and death were miserable enough.

And now I do wish to Heaven that I had the least spice of invention in my whole composition. I always thought that these facts, simple and natural as they are, were capable of artistic treatment in proper hands. And here I have bungled the whole thing, because all I could do was to tell them in the order in which they occurred. I had not the least intention of saying anything about myself or my concerns, except with respect to Parson Bulkley and Jasper, when I began. And yet I have told you this long story, of which, after all, I seem to have blundered into being the hero much against my will.

But I could not help myself; I could not arrange and improve my incidents. All that I can claim is the humble virtue of strict and literal fidelity in my narrative of facts. I believe the faculty of imagination was left out when I was put together.

Then, again, I wonder whether this *is* "A STORY WITHOUT A MORAL" or not. I am sure I did not mean that it should have any. I have been taken in so often by false pretences, and found that I had bought a tract against Catholicism or against Protestantism, in favor of free trade or of protection, of high church or low church, when I thought I had been buying a novel, that I was determined, when asked by my intrepid publishers to furnish something for their press, that it should be something not in the remotest degree edifying or instructive. I don't know how I have succeeded; but I have done my best. I was horribly afraid, however, when I first saw the name in print, that it might turn out, after all, a "MORAL WITHOUT A STORY." But I don't think it has. The only moral I can discern in it is, that, if a young gentleman gets into a row and is sent away from college, he will be rewarded with the most charming of young women as a wife. But I really think this is too violent a generalization; and I would earnestly entreat the academic youth of America not to act upon it as a settled principle. If my story have any moral, it is because one is the inevitable attendant upon all the events of human life. I will only say, at parting, that I shall be amply rewarded for my pains in telling it if I have succeeded in exciting for a brief moment in the minds of my readers a portion of the interest and pleasure which is ever renewed in my own breast by the name of WENSLEY.

# MOUNT VERNEY.

# MOUNT VERNEY;

## OR, AN INCIDENT OF INSURRECTION.[1]

> "Rise like lions after slumber,
> In unconquerable number !
> Shake to earth your chains, like dew
> Which in sleep had fallen on you!
> Ye are many ! they are few !" — SHELLEY.

IT was towards the close of an April day (how different from those he had left behind him!) in the year 1773, that a gentleman of some political prominence in the town of Boston found himself riding up the approach to Mount Verney, — an estate lying in one of the midland counties of South Carolina. The visit of Mr. Langdon (by which name it is our sovereign pleasure that our traveller shall be known) to the Southern Colonies was partly of a personal, and partly of a political nature. His physicians had doomed him to expiate his intemperate excesses of study and professional application by some months

---

[1] I had my grandfather, Josiah Quincy, jun., in mind, as the *motive* of the description of Mr. Langdon. This story has a groundwork of historical truth. There was such an insurrection in 1739, in South Carolina.

of exile from New England; and the stirring character of public affairs at that time induced him to select the more important of the Southern provinces as his place of banishment. The signs of an approaching collision with the mother-country were too plain to be mistaken; and Massachusetts Bay, as the ringleader of the gathering revolt, was naturally anxious to know to what extent the other Colonies were ripe for the conflict, and how far she might rely upon them for assistance in the last appeal.

It is no part of my purpose to give any particulars of his success or ill success in his demi-public capacity. I will only say, that though his mission looked towards "Disunion," and even towards the possible contingency of "cutting their masters' throats," his reception and treatment were very different from that extended a year or two since by the same sovereignty, to an accredited ambassador of Massachusetts, who visited it for the purpose of instituting a suit-at-law, before the tribunals of the nation, to settle a question of personal liberty. Nor will I embrace the opportunity, though a tempting one, to remark upon the folly of the Northern provinces, even at that early day, in reaching after the broken reed of Southern alliance, which has from that time to this only pierced the hand that leaned upon it for support. My only object in giving these particulars is to satisfy the constitutional craving of my countrymen, which would not be content without a sufficient explanation of the circumstance of my traveller being in the avenue to Mount Verney on the day and year I have indicated.

There he was, however, and, as he walked his tired horse along the picturesque road that wound its way up the side of the gentle hill upon which the house stood, he could not help contrasting the scene and the climate with what his native land was affording at that moment. Though it was early in April, the luxuriance of the vegetation put to shame the leafiest summer of his colder clime. The sides of the hill he was ascending were hung with tufted woods of the tenderest green, stretching far away upon the plain. Though the primeval forest was in some sort cleared from the hillside by which the planter's mansion-house was approached, still there were left clumps of forest-trees and thickets of flowering shrubs, with here and there a single tree of colossal dimensions, which threw sharply defined shadows upon the brightest and freshest of greenswards as the sun hastened to his setting. Delicious perfumes, wafted from a thousand blossoming trees and shrubs, and myriads of birds of strange plumage and new song, and the balmy sweetness of an atmosphere which it was luxury to inhale, made the traveller feel that he was indeed transported leagues away from his bleak native coast, and borne nearer to the sun.

Following the windings of the road along the park-like slope of the hill, Mr. Langdon at length drew rein before the chief entrance of the mansion. It was a building of no particular pretensions to architectural beauty, excepting such as it might derive from its adaptation to the climate. Deep piazzas, their slender pillars garlanded with creeping plants of an ever-changing variety of flower and fragrance, lent to the lofty hall and spacious apartments a shade and coolness deeply delicious. The rankness of the vegetation gave to the grounds in which it stood a somewhat untrimmed and neglected aspect; yet the place had a distinguished air and a look of tropical elegance. It seemed to be an abode where the mere pleasure of animal existence, and the delights which dwell in the senses, might be enjoyed in their highest poignancy.

The rare event of a visitor at Mount Verney was soon made known by the clamorous uproar of an infinity of dogs of every degree, and by a bustle, scarcely more intelligent, of troops of curious negroes jostling one another in their anxiety to see, under the pretence of serving, the new arrival. The master of the house, to the monotony of whose life any interruption would have been a relief, hastened out to welcome his guest with hospitable earnestness. He had heard that Mr. Langdon was in Charleston, and had written to him to beg him to take Mount Verney in his way. His prominence among the disaffected of the Colony, his intelligence, and his wealth, made Mr. Langdon think it worth his while to accept the invitation, although it took him somewhat out of his way. Mr. Verney ushered him into the house, and heaped upon him every hospitable attention.

Mr. Verney was a bachelor of some forty years,

"or by 'r lady" inclining to five and forty. He lived alone with his slaves, without the solace or the care of female society. Like most men of such habits of life, he had an older look than belonged to his years, and there was, besides, that indefinable air about him, which gives one an instinctive consciousness that he who wears it is not a happy man, that melancholy and depression are his abiding guests. But, though these fiends might not be far remote, they were certainly exorcised for a season by the magic of exciting and intelligent companionship. He was all animation and festivity of spirits under the stimulus of the congenial society of a man fresh from the world of life and action. He was full of questioning curiosity about that world from which he chose to live remote, and seemed to relish the rare luxury of conversation with all the keenness which long abstinence could give.

The evening wore away in various talk, for which their common friends at Charleston, the newest gossip of the town, and the latest public news, afforded topics enough and to spare. Supper-time came, and they were ushered by a sable seneschal into the dining-room, the size of which was curiously disproportioned to the number of the party. The appointments of the table indicated the wealth of the host in the affluence of plate and china they displayed. The viands were rather barbaric in their profusion, perhaps, than *recherché* in their preparation; but they were none the less welcome to a hungry traveller.

This repast, in those days and latitudes, was the principal meal of the day. The chase and other sylvan sports, which formed the chief business of the planters, furnished their tables with every variety of game. The yet unexhausted soil yielded, almost without labor, the choicest vegetables and fruits. The " murdered land " had not as yet begun to haunt its assassins with the spectres of poverty and want. Those were the golden days of Carolina.

The repast was accompanied and succeeded by flowing cups. The cellar of Mount Verney was bid to yield up its most treasured stores in honor of this hospitable occasion. Punch, too, the most seductive and deceitful of beverages, was there in a brimming bowl of the daintiest of china, — a libation with which that generation welcomed, speeded, and crowned the business of every day. Neither the health nor the habits, however, of Mr. Langdon permitting the indulgence which was the approved custom of that day, the circulation of the bottle and the bowl was made to give place to animated discourse, which was prolonged late into the night.

As the large hours began to melt into the smaller ones, they gradually concentrated their discourse on the serious temper of the times and the portentous events which seemed impending. The probabilities of an actual contest with England, and its chances, if it could not be avoided, were fully discussed. The weight of the several Colonies in the scale of battle, should battle come, was considered and calculated, —

which could be relied upon as firm in the faith, which were wavering, which strong, and which weak, in the prospect of the coming struggle. Mr. Verney did not hesitate to indicate the radical weakness of the Southern Colonies.

"Our slaves," said he, "will be a continual drag upon us. The British will forever have an army of observation, and of occupation too, if opportunity serves, in the very heart of our country, cantoned about in all of our houses, and quartered upon our estates."

"You do not think, then, that the slaves are to be depended upon, in case of an invasion?"

"Depended upon! Were slaves ever, since history was, to be depended upon when they had a chance to be even with their masters? Yes, they may be depended upon for our deadliest and bloodiest enemies."

"I cannot but think," replied Mr. Langdon, "that you do not take sufficiently into consideration the force of long habits of obedience, and the personal affection of the slaves for their masters."

"Their personal affection for their masters! My dear sir, had you lived your life among slaves, as I have done, you would know what reliance to put on that head! God knows that I have had an experience against which no theory and no philosophy can stand." And as he spoke a deep shade of melancholy clouded his features.

After a pause Mr. Langdon proceeded, "What

you say is an argument fatal to the defence of your slavery. It shows it to be incompatible with the existence, or at least the safety, of any commonwealth where it is permitted."

"To be sure it is!" replied Mr. Verney. "None but a fool or a villain would attempt to defend it on its merits. But what are we to do? We have the wolf by the ears, and we can neither keep him, nor let him go."

"It is hard to say, indeed," said Mr. Langdon. "But could you not first tame your wolf, and then let him go? A wolf may be tamed: a negro may be civilized. Educate your slaves, prepare them for freedom, and then there can be no danger in giving it to them. Does not a wise foresight point this out as the only feasible precaution against consequences terrible to think of?"

"My friend," replied his host, in a voice agitated by strong emotion, "you talk of you know not what. Relax your hold upon the wolf, as you must if you would tame him, and he will bury his fangs in your vitals for your pains. No, no! such an attempt would be full of ruin. My whole life has been but too bitter a commentary on your philosophy. God forbid that the curse of an unreasoning philanthropy be visited upon other innocent heads!"

Mr. Langdon saw that his new friend was deeply moved by some uncontrollable emotion. He knew nothing of his history, and consequently could not divine its cause. He felt a strong curiosity to know what it was; but politeness, and a sense of what was due to the evident mental sufferings of his host, forbade any expression of it. He accordingly waited in silence.

After a short pause, Mr. Verney recovered his equanimity, and, turning to his guest, said, "But I ought to apologize for keeping a tired traveller so long from his rest. Shall I show you your chamber?"

Mr. Langdon assented, and, following his host, was ushered into his apartment.

. . . . . . .

The room into which Mr. Verney conducted his guest was on the same floor with the dining-room and parlors, as they were called in those days, before drawing-rooms. It had the look of having been intended, and of having been formerly used, for the reception of company. The furniture, though evidently of an age anterior to that of the inhabited part of the house, was of a style and description better befitting what our ancestors used to call a "day-room" than a bed-chamber. The height and size of the room, however, made it a very fit place for the invocation of slumber in the climate of Carolina. A journey of thirty or forty miles on horseback gave it a very inviting air to the tired traveller, and he thought he had seldom seen a more tempting object than the ample and luxurious bed, to be ascended only by a pair of steps, which reared itself in one corner, as if the appointed altar of Morpheus himself.

Mr. Verney shook hands with his guest at the

door, and, wishing him a good-night, left him to his repose. Mr. Langdon was too tired and sleepy to take much notice of anything the room contained, excepting his couch; but he could not help observing, as he was undressing, two large portraits, nearly full-lengths, of the size of life, which occupied corresponding panels on the side of the room opposite to the bed. The one nearest the bed was of a gentleman in the dress of the days of Queen Anne, or of George the First, his dark intelligent face looking out from the fullest of full-bottomed wigs; and the other, of a lady in a fancy dress, which made it more uncertain as to the age in which so charming a shepherdess had predominated over the two sheep which seemed to make up her flock. Mr. Langdon took but a hurried glance at them as they looked down upon him from their elaborately carved frames of tarnished gold. He bestowed one wondering thought upon them as he climbed up to his repose, marvelling that two old family portraits of the apparent consequence of these pictures, were suffered to hang neglected in a place where they must be so little seen. But sleep soon banished all thought of his neighbor's affairs, or of his own, from his mind.

It was broad day the next morning when he awoke (for early rising was not one of the vices of Mount Verney), and, when he looked at the pictures again in the light of the sun, he felt yet more surprised than he had done the night before, to think that they should be relegated to a remote bed-chamber. He was no connoisseur, as he had had few opportunities of seeing good pictures; but a correct natural taste, assisted by personal intimacy with Copley (then in the prime of his genius), and familiarity with his works, made him sensible that they were paintings of no common merit. Especially in the picture of the gentleman did he think he perceived the hand of a master. Upon taking a more minute survey of his apartment, his surprise was yet further increased by the discovery of a picture opposite to these, of three beautiful children — two boys and a girl; the boys, apparently, from seven to ten years old, drawing the little girl, of four or five, in a garden carriage, or rather the elder drawing, and the younger pushing it from behind — in all the glee and romping spirits of childhood. There was a quaintness about the look of the children, dressed, according to the fashion of that day, in the costume of men in miniature, that struck Mr. Langdon, whose passion was children, even more than the elder portraits.

After breakfast, by Mr. Verney's invitation, he rode with him the rounds of his extensive plantation. He inspected the fields of rice and of indigo, on which depended the profits of the proprietor, and surveyed the plantations of Indian corn, yams, sweet-potatoes, and other esculent vegetables for the support of the negroes and the supply of the great house. He visited "the quarter" where the slaves lived, and saw how slavery looked in the shape of womanhood, of worn-out old age, and of childhood, more hopeless and melancholy than old age itself. Although the arrangements for the slaves were as good, or better, than he had seen on the other plantations he had visited, still there was that about the home that was no home, — sordid, cheerless, melancholy, — of the negroes, that struck a deeper horror of the system through the veins of the stranger than all the burning toils of the field. The gardens and grounds about the house were viewed the last. At each stage of their excursion, the economy of a great plantation was explained and illustrated by Mr. Verney, whose strong native sense, joined to his long experience, eminently qualified him for such a lecture.

The ride occupied the chief of the morning, and dinner was announced soon after their return home. As they were sitting over their wine, after dinner, it was next to impossible that they should talk of anything but slaves and slavery. Mr. Langdon had a natural abhorrence of the system, which was not at all diminished by what his own eyes had seen of it. His zeal for liberty was a principle universal in its nature and in its application, and he was deeply sensible of the disgraceful inconsistency of a contest for freedom carried on by the masters of slaves, and trembled lest this element might prove fatal to the whole movement. Mr. Verney assented to all his general principles, and had nothing to say against his deductions from them.

"What you say, my friend, is all unquestionably

true. But here are we, and there are the slaves, and what are we to do?"

"I will tell you what you may *not* do, if you really wish to be rid of this horrid curse, and that is — *nothing*. You are in the mire, I admit; but you can only get out of it by putting your shoulder to the wheel, and, the sooner you begin, the better for you."

"It is easier to say that something must be done than to say what that something should be. We find ourselves bound up with the blacks in this infernal spell, and how to break it passes my art, I must confess."

"Were it not," replied Mr. Langdon, with some hesitation, "that the suggestion last night seemed to give you pain, I should insist on what I then said, that you cannot expect your slaves ever to be in a condition to receive their liberty, unless you begin to put them in a condition to receive it. Pardon me," he continued, seeing a cloud again begin to brood over the brow of his friend, — "pardon me, if there be anything painful or improper in what I have said; for you must know that I can have no design to give you pain."

"There can be nothing improper," Mr. Verney replied, "in so natural a suggestion as yours; but I will not affect to deny that it is painful, deeply painful, to me. If I have reason to know anything on earth, it surely is the fallacy of your proposition. It does indeed touch me nearly."

Observing Mr. Langdon looked concerned and interested, he proceeded, —

"I see that you are curious to know what all this means, and, having raised your curiosity, it is no more than right that I should gratify it, though it be a task that I would willingly decline."

Then, silencing with a hasty gesture a polite attempt on the part of his guest to waive the subject, he added, —

"Nay, what I have to tell is no secret: it is part of the history of the Colony. And it is a weakness in me to shrink from what I am liable to hear of, and do actually hear of, from almost everyone (but that is not a great many) that comes to see me. Did you observe anything in particular in your bedchamber last night or this morning?"

"You can hardly think me so blind," replied Mr. Langdon, hoping that here was an opportunity of saving his host from an unpleasant personal narrative, "as not to have observed and admired the admirable family pictures that hang there. I only wondered at their being there instead of here or in the hall. By whom, pray, were they painted?"

"They are what I meant," said Mr. Verney, with a forced calmness eloquent of deep emotion. "They are all that remain to me of my house, once an honored one in two countries, — my father, my mother, my brothers, and my sister, all united in one horrible destruction, and I left alone, of the happiest of households, the last of my name and race. You can hardly wonder, my friend, that I do not choose to have such mementos always before my eyes. You will wonder the less when I shall have told you of their fate."

. . . . . . . .

I shall give the substance of Mr. Verney's narrative, as it remains among the papers of his guest, in my own words, for the sake of the succinctness and brevity which the inexorable limits of this volume demand. I believe that I have omitted nothing material to the story, though I have left out many conversational digressions, and explanations of the way in which the narrator obtained his knowledge of incidents which did not come under his personal observation. I only hope, that, in laboring to be brief, I may not become obscure.

Colonel Verney, the father of our acquaintance, was the grandson of the first emigrant of the family to the New World. His grandfather was a French Huguenot, of a noble family, who was one of the multitudes dragooned out of his native country after the revocation of the Edict of Nantes. The Vicomte du Verneuil and his ancestors had always been among the pillars of the Protestant faith in France. Their blood had helped swell the orgies of the feast of St. Bartholomew, and had been poured out on almost every battlefield during the long wars of religious ascendency. For the century, nearly, that the Edict of Nantes remained in force, they were always active in the intestine broils which disturbed the reign of

Louis XIII. and the minority of his successor, and in the later intrigues which gave to religious bigotry the air of statesmanship, in the act which expelled half a million of the best subjects of France from her soil. The representative of this turbulent house, therefore, had no claim for exemption, had he wished it, from the common fate of his faith.

M. du Verneuil first took refuge in England. He was kindly received, as were all his unfortunate countrymen who escaped thither. But his very superiority in point of rank made his position more irksome to him than the humbler artisans, who easily obtained employment, and melted into the mass of the laboring population, found theirs to be. He had brought away with him a remnant of his property, which, though relatively large, was very inadequate to support him and his family in the style they deemed essential to their dignity. He was soon obliged to cast about for some mode of living which would save his pride and his dwindling estate at the same time.

About this period, public attention in England was strongly directed towards the proprietary Colony of Carolina. The noble proprietaries were endeavoring to revive on those distant shores the decaying feudality of the Old World. They had called philosophy to their aid, and, in making John Locke the Lycurgus of their infant realm, the fantastic spirit of Shaftesbury thought they had imitated the wisdom of the ancients, who made their philosophers their lawgivers. But the experiment redounded as little to the credit of philosophy, as the incorporation of negro slavery with the institutions he ordained did to the honor of the philosopher. But at the first establishment of the constitutions of Carolina, their defects were not developed, and their fanciful structure attracted more general attention, doubtless, than a more rational plan would have done. But there was one great want yet to be supplied. Palatines, landgraves, and caciques, chancellors, chamberlains, and admirals, there were good store; but the proprietaries sadly lacked common people over whom these dignitaries were to predominate. Accordingly, they did their best to promote emigration by every means in their power.

The tide of industrious and worthy emigrants which now flowed from France came very opportunely for them, and they endeavored, with success, to direct it in part towards their new Colony. The names of many of the principal families in Carolina — Manigault, Petigru, Legare, Gaillard, DeSaussure — still bear witness to that great emigration to her shores, as the names of Bethune, Revere, Deblois, Amory, Bowdoin, Faneuil, and many others, testify to our own share in it. M. du Verneuil, as a man of some property, was a very desirable recruit. His attention was drawn to this Eldorado of the West by the Earl of Berkeley, and all its real and imaginary advantages set forth in golden phrase. It seemed to be what he wanted, and he was easily persuaded to embark himself, and all the fortunes of his house, in the hazardous adventure. He set sail for the New World, and arrived with his wife and only child, a youth of about sixteen, at Charleston, in November, 1686. It need hardly be said that his golden expectations were disappointed. He found a scene as different from that whence he came, as can well be imagined. But with the elasticity of spirit, and power of adaptation, of his nation, he soon conformed himself to his new circumstances, and became one of the most prominent men in the rising Commonwealth. Madame de Verneuil died soon after their arrival in the Colony, having sunk under the strange hardships and discomforts of her new lot; but his son, the grandfather of Mr. Langdon's host, took kindly to his adopted country, and throve apace in it. He married early, and established himself, after his father's death, at Mount Verney, then on the frontiers of the province. His name, the pronunciation of which had long been an offence to English tongues, was finally corrupted, and Anglicized into Verney,—a change to which he readily consented. As the Colony flourished, he grew rich, and increased in goods, and like a patriarch, as he was, he had gold and silver, men-servants and maid-servants, and much cattle.

His contentment with his lot, however, did not blind him to the disadvantages of his position for the education of children. He accordingly sent his only son at an early age to England, to receive his education there. As his body-servant, and in some sort his companion, he sent with him a young slave, who had had charge of him from his earliest years. Arnold, for so the slave was named, from his original master, was not many years older than young Verney; but he had shown a discretion and considerateness so much beyond his years, and evinced so genuine and tender an affection for his young charge, that Mr. Verney was perfectly content still to intrust the care of his personal safety and comfort to him. Arnold, as well as his young master, looked forward with delight to the new and strange scenes in store for them, and he felt a sense of trust and responsibility which raised him sensibly in his own estimation.

To England they went early in the last century. Young Verney, still accompanied by Arnold, proceeded from Eton to Oxford, and from Oxford to the Inns of Court. Wherever he went, Arnold was still a prime favorite both with his master and his young companions. His imperturbable good humor and lightness of heart were a continual letter of recommendation, while his sterling excellences of character won for him genuine respect. He availed himself of such snatches of instruction as he could seize by the way, with such success, that it was a common saying among Verney's companions, that Arnold knew more than his master. However this might be, he was singularly well instructed for one in his condition of life, and might have passed muster very creditably among persons of much higher pretensions than he. In his zeal for knowledge, he was encouraged and assisted by his young master, who seemed to feel as if all the intelligence of his sable satellite was but the reflected radiance of his own.

At length the time of return arrived, and somewhere about 1720, Verney, accompanied by Arnold, sailed for home. It was a great change for Verney — that from the crowds and gayeties of London to the solitude and monotony of his father's plantation. But it was a yet greater change for poor Arnold, who found himself transported from a land of freedom to a land of slaves. The kindness with which he had been uniformly treated, and the circumstance that in England he was rather better treated than worse, on account of his color, had almost made him forget that he was a slave. His return to Carolina was to him almost like a reduction from absolute freedom to hopeless slavery. His eyes had been opened, and he saw his own condition, and that of his race, in all its horrors. The abominations, the cruelties, the debasement, which necessarily attend upon slavery, shocked him as they never could have done, had he remained always surrounded by them. The thought that he, too, was one of the victims appointed by an inexorable fate to this dreadful destiny, filled him with anguish and despair which could not be uttered.

Gloom and despondency settled down upon his soul. The change which had come over him was obvious to all, and the old planter easily divined the cause.

"You have spoiled that boy, Jack," said he to his son: "you have made him above his business. You had better let Jones put him into the field for a while. There's nothing like hard work and flogging to take the sulks out of a nigger."

His son, however, refused to take this humane advice, and still kept Arnold about his person, as his body-servant, contenting himself with forbidding him the use of books and writing-materials. He prided himself much upon his sagacity in devising this notable remedy, when it appeared at last to be crowned with success. After a long period of depression and melancholy, the cloud seemed suddenly to pass off from Arnold's countenance, and the weight to be removed from his heart. He addressed himself to his duties with all his former assiduity, if not with all his old gayety of spirit. Had his master been an acute physiognomist, he would have seen that the look out of his eye, the air of his head, the carriage of his body, were all different from what they were of old. But he only observed that he was cured of the sulks, and congratulated himself on his wise prescription of abstinence from books and pen and ink.

But this change had deeper springs than the philosophy of Verney dreamt of. It proceeded from the reception of a great idea, the adoption of an absorbing and abiding purpose for which to live. While he was plunged in the depths of his despondency, —

despairing for himself and his race,—a thought flashed into his darkened mind, and illuminated its gloomiest recesses.

"Why," thought he, "are my people and myself slaves? Why do we remain slaves? Is there, indeed, no remedy? Is it a necessity, that when we outnumber our tyrants four to one, and every one of us is a match for four of them in strength,—is it a necessity that we remain slaves forever?"

The thought nerved his mind anew. His gloom passed away. He saw clearly the relative strength of the masters and slaves. He remembered that the Spaniards were at hand in Florida, ever ready to sow dissension in the Colony, and to breed discontents among the slaves. He felt that a blow might be struck, which would give all the broad lands of Carolina to those hands that extorted wealth from them for others. He felt that a mind only was wanting to watch and guide events in order to conduct such a revolution to a triumphant issue. He was proudly conscious that his was a mind capable of this great task. He looked upon the advantages of education he had enjoyed as something providential, and designed for a mighty end. He saw himself the appointed leader of his people in their exodus out of the land of bondage. In his excitement of thought, he saw the whole process of deliverance pass, as it were, before his eyes, and he beheld his nation free and happy in the homes they had wrested from their oppressors. He accepted this natural operation of the mind as a prophetic intimation of duty and revelation of success. His destiny was fixed. He devoted himself to the rescue of his miserable race. A deep calm brooded over his soul. He was conscious to himself that he was equal to the work he had undertaken, and he was at peace. And he had yet another seal of his fitness for his mission, — he was willing to wait.

Long years he waited; but the purpose of his soul was fixed. The deliverance of his race became the absorbing, the overwhelming passion of his being. The degradation in which he saw them plunged, the vices which were forced upon them, the barbarities which they endured, made his life bitter to him, and his only relief was in the distant hope of rescue and retribution. His character was obviously changed; but, under the quiet gravity with which he performed his offices about his master's person, nothing was suspected to lurk, except the desperate contentment of a hopeless slave.

As time passed away, the usual changes which it works were wrought in the condition of Colonel Verney; for such was the rank which Arnold's master held in the colonial establishment. Death, marriage, and birth had bereaved and blessed him, according to the common lot of man. He succeeded his father in the possession of Mount Verney, he won the chiefest of Carolinian beauties to share it with him, and he was girt with growing infancy, the charm of the present moment and the hope of future years. His political position was eminent and influential.

His plantation was a mine of still increasing wealth. He seemed to have nothing left to desire.

The public duties of Colonel Verney took him regularly every winter to Charleston, and frequently to various and distant parts of the Colony. On all these expeditions he was attended by Arnold as his body-servant. The opportunities which were thus given to the restless observation of the slave to discern the strength or the weakness of the different portions of the province, and to select the disaffected spirits among the servile population on whose co-operation he could rely, were faithfully improved. His manner of life, too, was eminently favorable for watching the signs of the times, and for seizing the moment which they should pronounce auspicious. He bided his time in patience, well aware of the momentous issues of the enterprise he revolved in his mind, and determined not to endanger its success by any premature or ill-considered action.

Nearly twenty years had thus glided away since Arnold first accepted what he considered a call to be the deliverer of his people, and the favorable moment had not yet appeared. At last the conjunction of events seemed to portend the hour at hand. The relations between England and Spain became every day more and more disturbed. The aggressions of Spain upon English commerce and English rights were the favorite topics of one of the mightiest oppositions that an English minister ever had to encounter. Sir Robert Walpole lingered out with difficulty his wise and pacific policy, with continually dwindling majorities, against such antagonists as the elder Pitt, Pulteney, Wyndham, and Lyttelton in the Commons, and Bathurst, Carteret, and Chesterfield in the Lords. But the public mind of England was at fever-heat, burning for a Spanish war. It was obvious that the only chance of the pilot at the helm of state to retain his hold upon it was to shape his course with the tide, whose current was too mighty for him to resist. A Spanish war was inevitable.

The relations of the Colonies of Carolina and of Florida were among the vexed questions which were to be adjusted by the sword. The Colonies, in those days, were ever the pawns of the royal chess-players of Europe, — the first to be moved, and the first to suffer, as the "unequal game" of war proceeded. The Spanish governor of Florida, Don Manuel de Monteano, was a man that well understood the nature of the move required of him. His theatre was a narrow one; but he was an actor that gave dignity to the boards he trod, and he was resolved to grace his narrow stage with action worthy of the widest scene. Long before affairs were ripe for war, he had been busy in forecasting preparation for it. His emissaries had been dispersed, in various disguises, over Carolina. The relative strength of the whites and blacks, the false security of the former, and the necessary disaffection of the latter, were well known to him. He had that greatest of gifts in the craft of government, — a wise choice of instruments with which to work.

His most confidential agent was one Da Costa, a Jew of Portuguese extraction, who fixed his head-quarters in Charleston, where he lived unsuspected, as a pawnbroker, and dealer in small wares. The character of his traffic was such as brought him without suspicion into constant communication with the slaves, and gave him opportunities of judging which were the fittest tools for his purposes. He was too keen an observer not to single out Arnold, at almost his first casual interview with him, as the man of men for whom he had been long in search. A short acquaintance made them thoroughly understand each other, and they became of one mind and of one heart in the work that lay before them. They digested their plans; they assigned to each other and to the few confederates they could trust the parts they were to play. A general insurrection was to be sustained by a Spanish invasion. The freedom of the slaves was to be guaranteed, and the Colony was to be governed by the blacks, as a dependency of Spain. It was a good plot, well conceived and well arranged, and there seemed to be no reason why it should not succeed.

A part of Arnold's business was the encouragement of an extensive system of evasion into Florida by the slaves. This was done to such an extent that one entire regiment of escaped slaves was mustered into the service of his Catholic Majesty, armed, equipped, and paid on the same footing with the rest of the Spanish army, and officered by the picked men of their own number. The colonelcy of this regiment was offered to Arnold; but he justly considered that the post of danger and of honor in such a perilous enterprise as this was in the heart of the insurrection, and not at the head of the invasion. So he voluntarily remained a slave, — though escape was easy, and though freedom, distinction, rank, and equal society were within his grasp, — that he might be a more faithful and effectual servant of his injured race.

Notwithstanding, however, the intimate relations of Arnold with Da Costa, he was far from giving him his entire confidence. He had no faith in the abstract zeal of the Spaniards for human rights, and he believed that their real purpose was only to substitute Spanish for English masters. He foresaw that his end could only be achieved by another servile war, under much less favorable circumstances, following upon the one impending, unless he could guard against this danger. He meditated the subject long and deeply; and his conclusion was one that startled and dismayed himself. He could discern but one way of permanent peace and safety for the blacks; and that was the utter extermination of the whites.

He could not escape from the terrible presence of this dreadful necessity. His heart died within him when it first stood revealed to his sight. It haunted him by day and by night. It was almost enough to stagger his resolution, and make him abandon his design with horror. The images of his master, the companion of his youth and the unalterably kind friend of his manhood; of his mistress, the beautiful, the gentle, and the good; of the generous Arthur; of the frolic, mischief-loving Edward, his especial pet; of the little Alice, — of all of whom he was ever the chosen playfellow and bosom friend — these phantoms made him quail for a moment as they rose before his mental sight in that fearful midnight when this ghastly idea first startled him with its apparition. He had neither wife nor child. All his affections centred with passionate intenseness in his master and his children. They were all he had to love. Was this terrible blood-offering required at his hands? His own life he was ready to pour out. He foreboded that he should not survive the coming struggle. But must he sacrifice lives infinitely dearer to him than his own? He flung himself in an agony of despair upon his face, and wept long and bitterly.

But presently a wail was borne upon the air through the open casement, distant, but fearfully distinct. It was the chosen hour for punishment. He started to his feet. It was a woman's voice, shrill and shrieking, that reached his ear from the remote "quarter." It sounded like the "exceeding bitter cry" of his race, whose wrongs he had forgotten, reproaching him for his weakness. He thought of their blood and tears crying to Heaven for vengeance: a vision of chains and whips and brand-ing-irons, and an endless procession of enslaved generations, rushed upon his soul. Was this great deliverance to be wrought without the dearest sacrifice? Was it to be purchased without a price? He would not shrink from his part of it, dreadful as it might be. But God grant that he might not survive the victory it was to buy!

This necessity was felt by all the blacks who were admitted into his confidence. It was agreed upon that the massacre should be universal, and the future exclusion of the white race from the province the condition of its submission to the Spanish power.

Everything was ready. England and Spain were at war. The Spanish auxiliaries were at hand. The day approached — it arrived. It was a Sunday, and one of the loveliest of autumnal days. Arnold repaired early to the slave-quarter, and harangued the slaves upon a case of surpassing cruelty they had witnessed the night before. A tumult of excitement was gathered around him. The alarm spread. Jones, the iron-haired, iron-featured, and iron-hearted overseer, approached, with two assistants, to suppress the disturbance. Seeing Arnold, whom he hated because beyond his usual authority, he rode up to him with savage glee and uplifted whip. In a moment he was stretched lifeless on the ground. His assistants met with the same fate in the twinkling of an eye.

The taste of blood and of revenge had been given, and Arnold knew that the appetite would grow with "what it fed on." He mounted the overseer's horse, and, sending messengers to the neighboring plantations, led the crowd of slaves towards the great house. As they rounded the offices, and came in sight of the house, Colonel Verney was seen hastily approaching them. His commanding figure and military bearing, acting upon their habit of subordination, checked the progress of the slaves, and they stood indecisively looking at him and at each other. Arnold saw that this was the moment on which all would depend. He rode in front of the confused crowd.

"Why, Arnold!" exclaimed his master, "what is all this? How came you on Jones's horse? and what means this disturbance?"

"It means, sir," answered Arnold, — "it means liberty to slaves, and death to tyrants!"

"Tyrants, you rascal!" replied Colonel Verney. "Dismount this instant, and I will soon thrash this insolence out of you."

Arnold dismounted, and approached his master with a firm step, while the gaping crowd stood awaiting the issue. As soon as he was within reach, Colonel Verney lifted his cane, and aimed a blow at his slave's head. Arnold closed with him. In an instant he had wrested the cane from his master's hand. A slight motion made the scabbard fly far off upon the lawn; the blade which it had concealed glittered in the air for a moment, and in the next it was buried deep in the heart he loved most on earth.

"Ungrateful slave!" exclaimed the dying man as he fell heavily to the ground.

"No," replied Arnold, more to himself than to his master. "A *slave* cannot be *ungrateful*."

I state facts: I do not propose examples. As an historian I tell the doom which slavery once brought upon its victim tyrants. As an abolitionist I show the only method by which such horrors may be averted. But let no one who boasts of blood shed in the battles of freedom affect a horror at such scenes as I have described. If ever blood was spilt righteously for the vindication of rights or the redress of wrongs, that which has flowed in servile insurrection is the most hallowed of all. And let no one whose classic enthusiasm kindles at the story of a Brutus or a Timoleon, whose love of country and of freedom was too mighty for the ties of sonship or brotherhood to hold them back from imagined duty, brand as foul and unnatural murder the sacrificial act of Arnold the slave.

The blow was decisive: it turned the tide of feeling at once. The negroes rushed forward with shouts of triumph, over the dead body of their master, towards the house. Arnold checked them, and found them willing to listen to his directions. He hastily told them that they must make all speed towards Stono, a small settlement about five miles off, where there was a warehouse full of arms and ammunition. Ten were detailed for the bloody business to be despatched at Mount Verney, under command of the only confederate Arnold had on the plantation, — one whom he could rely upon to see that there was no superfluous cruelty committed. All the rest, following Arnold, who had remounted his horse, hurried in the direction he had indicated.

As they hastened along the high road, they were continually re-enforced by parties from the neighboring plantations, so that, by the time they reached Stono, they were four or five hundred strong. The little settlement was soon carried and sacked, every white put to death, and a large supply of muskets and cartridges secured. Arnold now called a halt and reduced his promiscuous multitude to something like order. The guns and ammunition he distributed, as far as they would go, among those of his followers on whom he could most depend. The rest were armed with axes, scythes, clubs, or whatever other weapons their hands could find. A quantity of white cloth furnished them with banners. Drums and fifes were also in the warehouse, and musicians are never wanting where Africans are to be found. Arnold knew human nature too well not to avail himself of these appliances. So they took up their march towards Jacksonburgh, with drums beating and banners flying, in some show of military order.

Long before this, the tragedy was over at Mount Verney. The party to whom it was confided did their work quickly and thoroughly. I will not harrow up the hearts of my readers, nor my own, by the details which my materials afford. Humanity naturally revolts at the horrors of slavery, whether they are administered by the masters or by the slaves, according as the one or the other have the power in their hands. It is enough to say that Mr. Langdon's host, then a child of six years old, was the only white left alive in the house. And his escape was owing to the affection and presence of mind of his nurse, who by affecting zeal in the work, and pretending to despatch this part of it herself, managed to deceive the destroyers until they had left the bloody scene, and hastened after the main body of the insurgents. The terror of the child might well extend its influences over the whole of life. The ghastly spectacles which blasted his infant sight when he was released from his hiding-place changed the current and the complexion of his being. He was thenceforth what these cruel calamities had made him. Such a cloud passes not away with the morning of life, but sheds its baleful shadow over its noontide and its evening hours.

Meantime the insurgent force moved successfully on towards their destination. They destroyed every house on their way, and put every white person they met to death. Unfortunately for them, they found abundance of liquor in the houses they sacked. Their chief in vain urged upon them the necessity of entire sobriety for their safety and success. The temptation was too strong to be resisted, and Arnold saw with dismay an element of failure developing itself, on which he had not counted. He hurried them on, in hopes of engaging them in some active service before they became unfit for it. Presently a small party of gentlemen were seen riding rapidly towards them.

They stopped suddenly on perceiving the strange sight before them, and anxiously reconnoitred the armed mass. Arnold at once recognized in the chief of the party Governor Bull, with whose person he was familiar. The Governor saw the whole truth in a moment, and, wheeling about, galloped off with his companions in the opposite direction. Arnold, who had retained his horse for such an emergency as this, pursued them at full speed, accompanied by a few other mounted slaves. They fired upon the flying horsemen, but without effect, and were soon obliged to give over the pursuit, as the Governor and his company were much better mounted than they. Here was another untoward occurrence, ominous of ill success.

A large congregation was assembled at the little village of Wiltown, in the Presbyterian church, to hear the famous Mr. Archibald Stobo preach. The preacher was in the midst of his sermon, when a sudden noise of horses' hoofs drew the attention of the audience from him. They looked towards the door, and to their surprise they saw Governor Bull enter. They rose to receive him, and Mr. Stobo paused in his discourse. Acknowledging their civility with a slight wave of the hand, his Excellency exclaimed, standing at the door of the church, "Gentlemen, a large body of insurgent negroes is close at hand. They have fire-arms, and it looks like a serious matter. Make a stand against them here, while I ride on to Jacksonburgh for re-enforcements."

In another moment he was off; but the scene of confusion that he left behind him passes description. The men sprung to their arms, which they were required by law to carry with them to church, and issued forth upon the green. The screaming women and children were left within its walls for protection. Captain Bee, the principal gentleman of the neighborhood, assumed the command, and led the small force out of the village towards Stono. His own house stood on an eminence about half a mile off, and the first thing he saw was that it was in the possession of the insurgents. They had evidently got at his wine-cellar, and showed unquestionable marks of intoxication. A negro on horseback was busy among them, riding from group to group with earnest gestures of exhortation.

It was none other than Arnold, who found his forces becoming more and more untractable and insubordinate at the very time when order and discipline were needed the most. He in vain endeavored to prevail upon them to move upon the enemy. Presently the enemy moved upon them. Captain Bee led his men rapidly along the road, and, guided by his knowledge of the country, posted them so as to command the insurgents on the lawn, while they were sheltered by the trees that skirted it. Arnold saw their danger, and ordered the small body of sober men that obeyed his directions to fire upon the enemy in their covert. As soon as their fire was thus drawn, Bee and his men issued from their cover, and, passing by Arnold and his few without notice, poured a volley with deadly effect into the drunken and dancing crowd on the lawn. The panic was instantaneous and complete. They dispersed in every direction, throwing away their arms as they fled.

Arnold now drew off his command to a thicket that bounded the lawn on one side, and bade them sell their lives as dearly as they could. The numbers were now more equal, and the conflict was long and desperate. At last, on the road from Wiltown, a re-enforcement was seen approaching, which the Governor was leading to the battlefield. Seeing his chance of maintaining his ground gone, Arnold rushed out at the head of his surviving friends, to cut their way through the enemy's ranks, before the succors arrived; but it was too late. A body of horsemen galloped upon the ground. The negroes, with Arnold at their head, fought desperately, but in vain. He was cut down, and as he fell, a dozen sabres were uplifted to make his fate certain. But Governor Bull dashed into the circle, exclaiming,—

"Stop, gentlemen! This fellow must not die yet. He knows things which we must know first."

He was taken from beneath the horses' feet, and carried to the town, where his wounds, which were not dangerous, were dressed. This done, he was thrust into a den of torment, called a slave-prison, belonging to a private person, to spend the night. And what a night it was!

The next morning he was brought out and examined; but no word of knowledge could they extract from him. He acknowledged and justified his own part in this rising; but he utterly refused to implicate any others, or to give any information as to the extent of the conspiracy. He was tied up and flogged (for the first time in his life) until he fainted from loss of blood; but no syllable of information, or cry of pain, could be extorted from him. This ordeal was repeated for three days, with fresh inventions of torture; but all in vain. His firmness was unshaken. Then they spoke of pardon and favor as the reward of frankness. But the only reply they could obtain was a bitter laugh, which mocked the delusive offer of the cruelest torture of all. At last, wearied with their vain attempts, and fearing lest he might die of exhaustion, they dragged him to a tree in the public square, and hanged him like a dog.

He died; but his memory, spectre-like, long haunted the Province. His talents and his endurance, which his examination and torture had displayed, alarmed the planters even more than the bloody effects of the insurrection. At the very next session of the colonial Legislature (1740), the instruction of slaves was made a highly penal offence. The alarm was universal. Every man feared lest he might have an Arnold on his estate.

And there was reason for their fears. Notwithstanding the cruel examples which were made of the captive insurgents, the spirit of Arnold seemed to walk in the Province. Partial insurrections, the fruit of his labors, were frequent for several years after his death, and it was not till after the peace with Spain that the Colony regained its former tranquillity.

. . . . .

"Was I not right," said Mr. Verney, with a mournful smile, when he had finished the narrative of which this is an imperfect sketch, " was I not right in saying that I had had an experience that refuted your theory of educating slaves for freedom ?"

Mr. Langdon could make no reply to such a question after such a story. He wrung his friend's hand in silence. He had nothing to say; for philosophy had not as yet taught men by examples, that the safe, sufficient, and only possible preparation for freedom is EMANCIPATION.

The next morning he took leave of Mr. Verney, and pursued his journey homeward, a sadder if not a wiser man. He hated slavery more than ever for this dreadful picture of its works. But, while his heart bled for the blight which it had shed upon the life of Verney, he could not disguise from himself, standing as he did on the brink of a civil war for liberty, that his deepest sympathies were with Arnold.

When the Revolution broke out, Mr. Verney joined the army, and rose to the rank of lieutenant-colonel in the line. He fought in many of its battles with the desperation of a man for whom life has no charm, and death no terrors. But he survived all the great battles in which he had a part, to fall at length in a partisan expedition on which he had volunteered, when on a leave of absence, in his native State.

As he died without children or kindred, his estate escheated to the sovereign people. It has passed through many hands, and has been racked and "murdered," like many another. I am told by one who lately visited its neighborhood, that it is now a barren sandhill, its house in ruins, its trees cut down, its fields a desolation. The pictures which elicited this story alone remain to recall it. But it is only for their merit as pictures that they are valued; the portrait of Colonel Verney being, perhaps, the only original Kneller (except one of Jeremiah Dummer, in Boston) in the country. They are preserved in a public collection in Charleston, and admired by multitudes, as works of art. But their history is fading from memory, and it is only to a few old men whose daily life is in the past, that they recall the pride, the sorrows, and the ruin of MOUNT VERNEY.

# WHO PAID FOR THE PRIMA DONNA?

# WHO PAID FOR THE PRIMA DONNA?

## I.

"IF anything could make a man forgive himself for being sixty years old," said the Consul, holding up his wineglass between his eye and the setting sun, — for it was summer-time, — "it would be that he can remember Malibran in her divine sixteenity at the Park Theatre, thirty odd years ago. Egad, sir, one couldn't help making great allowances for *Don Giovanni*, after seeing her in *Zerlina*. She was beyond imagination *piquante* and delicious."

The Consul, as my readers may have partly inferred, was not a Roman Consul, nor yet a French one. He had had the honor of representing this great republic at one of the Hanse towns, I forget which, in President Monroe's time. I don't recollect how long he held the office; but it was long enough to make the title stick to him for the rest of his life with the tenacity of a militia colonelcy or village diaconate. The country people round about used to call him "the *Counsel*," which, I believe, — for I am not very fresh from my schoolbooks, — was etymologically correct enough, however orthoepically erroneous. He had not limited his European life, however, within the precinct of his Hanseatic consulship, but had dispersed himself very promiscuously over the Continent, and had seen many cities, and the manners of many men and of some women, — singing-women, I mean, — in their public character; for the Consul, correct of life as of ear, never sought to undeify his divinities by pursuing them from the heaven of the stage to the purgatorial intermediacy of the *coulisses*, still less to the lower depth of disenchantment into which too many of them sunk in their private life.

"Yes, sir," he went on, "I have seen and heard them all, — Catalani, Pasta, Pezzaroni, Grisi, and all the rest of them, even Sonntag, though not in her very best estate; but I give you my word there is none that has taken lodgings here," tapping his forehead, "so permanently as the Signorina Garcia, or that I can see and hear so distinctly when I am in the mood of it by myself. *Rosina, Desdemona, Cinderella*, and, as I said just now, *Zerlina* — she is as fresh in them all to my mind's eye and ear as if the Park Theatre had not given way to a cursed shoeshop, and I had been hearing her there only last night. Let's drink her memory," the Consul added, half in mirth and half in melancholy, — a mood to which he was not unused, and which did not ill become him.

Now, no intelligent person who knew the excellence of the Consul's wine could refuse to pay this posthumous honor to the harmonious shade of the lost Muse. The Consul was an old-fashioned man in his tastes, to be sure, and held to the old religion of Madeira, which divided the faith of our fathers with the Cambridge Platform, and had never given in to the later heresies which have crept into the communion of good-fellowship from the south of France and the Rhine.

"A glass of champagne," he would say, "is all well enough at the end of dinner, just to take the grease out of one's throat, and get the palate ready for the more serious vintages ordained for the solemn and deliberate drinking by which man justifies his creation; but Madeira, sir, Madeira is the only stand-by that never fails a man, and can always be depended upon as something sure and steadfast."

I confess to having fallen away myself from the gracious doctrine and works to which he had held so fast; but I am no bigot, — which, for a heretic, is something remarkable, — and had no scruple about uniting with him in the service he proposed, without demur or protestation as to form or substance. Indeed, he disarmed fanaticism by the curious care he bestowed on making his works conformable to the faith that was in him; for partly by inheritance, and partly by industrious pains, his old house was undermined by a cellar of wine such as is seldom seen in these days of modern degeneracy. He is the last gentleman that I know of, of that old school that used to import their own wine and lay it down annually themselves, their bins forming a kind of vinous calendar suggestive of great events. Their degenerate sons are content to be furnished, as they want it, from the dubious stores of the vintner, by retail.

"I suppose it was her youth and beauty, sir," I suggested, "that made her so rememberable to you. You know she was barely turned seventeen when she sung in this country."

"Partly that, no doubt," replied the Consul, "but not altogether, nor chiefly. No, sir, it was her genius which made her beauty so glorious. She was wonderfully handsome, though. 'She was a phantom of delight,' as that Lake fellow says," — it was thus profanely that the Consul designated the poet Wordsworth, whom he could not abide, — "and the best thing he ever said, by Jove!"

"And did you never see her again?" I inquired.

"Once only," he answered, "eight or nine years afterwards, a year or two before she died. It was at Venice, and in *Norma*. She was different, and yet not changed for the worse. There was an indescribable look of sadness out of her eyes, that touched one oddly, and fixed itself in the memory. But she was something apart and by herself, and stamped herself on one's mind as Rachel did in *Camille* or *Phèdre*. It was true genius, and no imitation, that made both of them what they were. But she actually had the physical beauty which Rachel only compelled you to think she had, by the force of her genius and consummate dramatic skill, while she was on the scene before you."

"But do you rank Malibran with Rachel as a dramatic artist?" I asked.

"I cannot tell," he answered. "But if she had not the studied perfection of Rachel,— which was always the same, and could not be altered without harm,— she had at least a capacity of impulsive self-adaptation about her which made her for the time the character she personated,— not always the same, but such as the woman she represented might have been in the shifting phases of the passion that possessed her. And to think that she died at eight and twenty! What might not ten years more have made her!"

"It is odd," I observed, "that her fame should be forever connected with the name she got by her first unlucky marriage in New York; for it was unlucky enough, I believe — was it not?"

"You may say that," responded the Consul, "without fear of denial or qualification. It was disgraceful in its beginning and in its ending. It was a swindle on a large scale; and poor Maria Garcia was the one who suffered the most by the operation."

"I have always heard," said I, "that old Garcia was cheated out of the price for which he had sold his daughter, and that M. Malibran got his wife on false pretences."

"Not altogether so," returned the Consul. "I happen to know all about that matter from the best authority. She was obtained on false pretences, to be sure; but it was not Garcia that suffered by them.

M. Malibran, moreover, never paid the price agreed upon, and yet Garcia got it, for all that."

"Indeed!" I exclaimed. "It must have been a neat operation. I cannot exactly see how the thing was done; but I have no doubt a tale hangs thereby, and a good one. Is it tellable?"

"I see no reason why not," said the Consul. "The sufferer made no secret of it, and I know of no reason why I should. Mynheer Van Holland told me the story himself, in Amsterdam, in the year '35."

"And who was he?" I inquired, "and what had he to do with it?"

"I'll tell you," responded the Consul, filling his glass, and passing the bottle, "if you will have the goodness to shut the window behind you, and ring for candles; for it gets chilly here among the mountains as soon as the sun is down."

I beg your pardon — did you make a remark? Oh, *what mountains!* — You must really pardon me; I cannot give you such a clew as that to the identity of my dear Consul, just now, for excellent and sufficient reasons. But, if you have paid your money for the sight of this Number, you may take your choice of all the mountain-ranges on the continent, from the Rocky to the White, and settle him just where you like. Only you must leave a gap to the westward, through which the river — also anonymous for the present distress — breaks its way, and which gives him half an hour's more sunshine than he would otherwise be entitled to, and slope the fields down to its margin near a mile off, with their native timber thinned so skilfully as to have the effect of the best landscape-gardening. It is a grand and lovely scene; and when I look at it, I do not wonder at one of the Consul's apothegms, namely, that the chief advantage of foreign travel is, that it teaches you that one place is just as good to live in as another. I imagine that the one place he had in his mind at the time was just this one. But that is neither here nor there. When candles came, we drew our chairs together, and he told me in substance the following story. I will tell it in my own words, — not that they are so good as his, but because they come more readily to the nib of my pen.

## II.

NEW YORK has grown considerably since she was New Amsterdam, and has almost forgotten her whilom dependence on her first godmother. Indeed, had it not been for the historic industry of the erudite Diedrich Knickerbocker, very few of her sons would know much about the obligations of their nursing mother to their old grandame beyond sea, in the days of the Dutch dynasty. Still, though the old monopoly has been dead these two hundred years, or thereabout, there is I know not how many fold more traffic with her than in the days when it was in full life and force. Doth not that benefactor of his species, Mr. Udolpho Wolfe, derive thence his immortal or immortalizing Schiedam Schnapps, the virtues whereof, according to his advertisements, are fast transferring dram-drinking from the domain of pleasure to that of positive duty? Tobacco-pipes, too, and toys such as the friendly saint, whom Protestant children have been taught by Dutch tradition to invoke, delights to drop into the votive stocking, — they come from the mother-city, where she sits upon the waters, quite as much a Sea-Cybele as Venice herself. And linens, too, fair and fresh and pure as the maidens that weave them, come forth from Dutch looms ready to grace our tables, or to deck our beds. And the mention of these brings me back to my story, though the immediate connection between Holland linen and Malibran's marriage may not at first view be palpable to sight. Still it is a fact that the web of this part of her variegated destiny was spun and woven out of threads of flax that took the substantial shape of fine Hollands; and this is the way in which it came to pass.

Mynheer Van Holland, of whom the Consul spoke just now, you must understand to have been one of the chief merchants of Amsterdam, a city whose merchants are princes, and have been kings. His transactions extended to all parts of the Old World, and did not skip over the New. His ships visited the harbor of New York as well as of London; and, as he died two or three years ago a very rich man, his adventures in general must have been more remunerative than the one I am going to relate. In the autumn of the year 1825 it seemed good to this worthy merchant to despatch a vessel, with a cargo chiefly made up of linens, to the market of New York. The honest man little dreamed with what a fate his ship was fraught, wrapped up in those flaxen folds. He happened to be in London the winter before, and was present at the *début* of Maria Garcia at the King's Theatre. He must have admired the beauty, grace, and promise of the youthful *Rosina*, had he been ten times a Dutchman; and if he heard of her intended emigration to America, as he possibly might have done, it most likely excited no particular emotion in his phlegmatic bosom. He could not have imagined that the exportation of a little singing-girl to New York should interfere with a potential venture of his own in fair linen. The gods kindly hid the future from his eyes, so that he might enjoy the comic vexation her lively sallies caused to *Doctor Bartolo* in the play, unknowing that she would be the innocent cause of a more serious provocation to himself in downright earnest. He thought of this himself after it had all happened.

Well, the good ship "Steenbok" had prosperous gales and fair weather across the ocean, and dropped anchor off the Battery with some days to spare from the amount due to the voyage. The consignee came off and took possession of the cargo, and duly transferred it to his own warehouse. Though the advantages of advertising were not as fully understood in those days of comparative ignorance as they have been since, he duly announced the goods which he had received, and waited for a customer. He did not have to wait long. It was but a day or two after the appearance of the advertisement in the newspapers that he had prime Holland linens on hand, just received from Amsterdam, when he was waited upon by a gentleman of good address, and evidently of French extraction, who inquired of the consignee, whom we will call Mr. Schulemberg for the nonce, "whether he had the linens he had advertised yet on hand."

"They are still on hand and on sale," said Mr. Schulemberg.

"What is the price of the entire consignment?" inquired the customer.

"Fifty thousand dollars," responded Mr. Schulemberg.

"And the terms?"

"Cash on delivery."

"Very good," replied the obliging buyer. "If they be of the quality you describe in your advertisement, I will take them on those terms. Send them down to my warehouse, No. 118 Pearl Street, to-morrow morning, and I will send you the money."

"And your name?" inquired Mr. Schulemberg.

"Is Malibran," responded the courteous purchaser.

The two merchants bowed politely, the one to the other, mutually well pleased with the morning's work, and bade each other good-day.

Mr. Schulemberg knew but little, if anything, about his new customer; but, as the transaction was to be a cash one, he did not mind that. He calculated his commissions, gave orders to his head clerk to see the goods duly delivered the next morning, and went on Change, and thence to dinner, in the enjoyment of a complacent mind and a good appetite. It is to be supposed that M. Malibran did the same. At any rate, he had the most reason, at least, according to his probable notions of mercantile morality and success.

### III.

THE next day came, and with it came, betimes, the packages of linens to M. Malibran's warehouse in Pearl Street; but the price for the same did not come as punctually to Mr. Schulemberg's counting-room, according to the contract under which they were delivered. In point of fact, M. Malibran was not in at the time; but there was no doubt that he would attend to the matter without delay, as soon as he came in. A cash transaction does not necessarily imply so much the instant presence of coin as the unequivocal absence of credit. A day or two more or less is of no material consequence, only there is to be no delay for sales and returns before payment. So Mr. Schulemberg gave himself no uneasiness about the matter when two, three, and even five and six days had slid away without producing the apparition of the current money of the merchant. A man who transacted affairs on so large a scale as M. Malibran, and conducted them on the sound basis of ready money, might safely be trusted for so short a time. But when a week had elapsed, and no tidings had been received either of purchaser or purchase-money, Mr. Schulemberg thought it time for himself to interfere in his own proper person. Accordingly, he incontinently proceeded to the counting-house of M. Malibran to receive the promised price, or to know the reason why. If he failed to obtain the one satisfaction, he at least could not complain of being disappointed of the other. Matters seemed to be in some little unbusiness-like confusion, and the clerks in a high state of gleeful excitement. Addressing himself to the chief among them, Mr. Schulemberg asked the pertinent question, —

"Is M. Malibran in?"

"No, sir," was the answer, "he is not; and he will not be, just at present."

"But when will he be in? for I must see him on some pressing business of importance."

"Not to-day, sir," replied the clerk, smiling expressively. "He cannot be interrupted to-day on any business of any kind whatever."

"The deuce he can't!" returned Mr. Schulemberg. "I'll see about that very soon, I can tell you. He promised to pay me cash for fifty thousand dollars' worth of Holland linens a week ago. I have not seen the color of his money yet, and I mean to wait no longer. Where does he live? for, if he be alive, I will see him, and hear what he has to say for himself, and that speedily"

"Indeed, sir," pleasantly expostulated the clerk, "I think, when you understand the circumstances of the case, you will forbear disturbing M. Malibran this day of all others in his life."

"Why, what the devil ails this day above all others," said Mr. Schulemberg somewhat testily, "that he can't see his creditors, and pay his debts on it?"

"Why, sir, the fact is," the clerk replied, with an air of interest and importance, "it is M. Malibran's wedding-day. He marries this morning the Signorina Garcia, and I am sure you would not molest him with business on such an occasion as that."

"But my fifty thousand dollars!" persisted the consignee. "And why have they not been paid?"

"Oh, give yourself no uneasiness at all about that, sir," replied the clerk, with the air of one to whom the handling of such trifles was a daily occurrence. "M. Malibran will, of course, attend to that matter the moment he is a little at leisure. In fact, I imagine, that, in the hurry and bustle inseparable from an event of this nature, the circumstance has entirely escaped his mind; but, as soon as he returns to business again, I will recall it to his recollection, and you will hear from him without delay."

The clerk was right in his augury as to the effect his intelligence would have upon the creditor. It was not a clerical error on his part when he supposed that Mr. Schulemberg would not choose to enact the part of skeleton at the wedding-breakfast of the young *Prima Donna*. There is something about the great events of life, which cannot happen a great many times to anybody, —

> " A wedding or a funeral,
> A mourning or a festival,"

that touches the strings of the one human heart of us all, and makes it return no uncertain sound. *Shylock* himself would hardly have demanded his pound of flesh on the wedding-day, had it been *Antonio* that was to espouse the fair *Portia*. Even he would have allowed three days of grace before demanding the specific performance of his bond. Now, Mr. Schulemberg was very far from being a Shylock, and he was also a constant attendant upon the opera, and a devoted admirer of the lovely Garcia. So he could not wonder that a man on the eve of marriage with that divine creature should forget every other consideration in the immediate contemplation of his happiness, even if it were the consideration for a cargo of prime linens, and one to the tune of fifty thousand dollars. And it is altogether likely that the mundane reflection occurred to him, and made him easier in his mind under the delay, that old Garcia was by no means the kind of man to give away a daughter who dropped gold and silver from her sweet lips whenever she opened them in public, as the princess in the fairy-tale did pearls and diamonds, to any man who could not give him a solid equivalent in return. So that, in fact, he regarded the notes of the Signorina Garcia as so much collateral security for his debt.

So Mr. Schulemberg was content to bide his reasonable time for the discharge of M. Malibran's indebtedness to his principal. He had advised Mynheer Van Holland of the speedy sale of his consignment, and given him hopes of a quick return of the proceeds. But, as days wore away, it seemed to him that the time he was called on to bide was growing into an unreasonable one. I cannot state with precision exactly how long he waited. Whether he disturbed the sweet influences of the honeymoon by his intrusive presence, or permitted that nectareous satellite to fill her horns, and wax and wane in peace, before he sought to bring the bridegroom down to the things of earth, are questions which I must leave to the discretion of my readers to settle, each for himself or herself, according to their own notions of the proprieties of the case. But at the proper time, after patience had thrown up in disgust the office of a virtue, he took his hat and cane one fine morning, and walked down to No. 118 Pearl Street, for the double purpose of wishing M. Malibran joy of his marriage, and of receiving the price — promised long, and long withheld — of the linens which form the tissue of my story.

> "The gods gave ear, and granted half his prayer:
> The rest the winds dispersed in empty air."

There was not the slightest difficulty about his imparting his epithalamic congratulation; but as to his receiving the numismatic consideration for which he hoped in return, that was an entirely different affair. He found matters in the Pearl Street counting-house again apparently something out of joint, but with a less smiling and sunny atmosphere pervading them than he had remarked on his last visit. He was received by M. Malibran with courtesy, a little overstrained, perhaps, and not as flowing and gracious as at their first interview. Preliminaries over, Mr. Schulemberg, plunging with epic energy into the midst of things, said, "I have called, M. Malibran, to receive the fifty thousand dollars, which, you will remember, you engaged to pay down for the linens I sold you on such a day. I can make allowance for the interruption which has prevented your attending to this business sooner; but it is now high time that it was settled."

"I consent to it all, monsieur," replied M. Malibran with a deprecatory gesture. "You have reason, and I am desolated that it is the impossible that you ask of me to do."

"How, sir!" demanded the creditor. "What do you mean by the impossible? You do not mean to deny that you agreed to pay cash for the goods?"

"My faith, no, monsieur," shruggingly responded M. Malibran. "I avow it; you have reason; I promised to pay the money, as you say it; but, if I have not the money to pay you, how can I pay you the money? What to do?"

"I don't understand you, sir," returned Mr. Schulemberg. "You have not the money? And you do not mean to pay me, according to agreement?"

"But, monsieur, how can I, when I have not money? Have you not heard that I have made — what you call it? — failure, yesterday? I am grieved of it thrice sensibly; but if it went of my life, I could not pay you for your fine linens, which were of a good market at the price."

"Indeed, sir," replied Mr. Schulemberg, "I had not heard of your misfortunes; and I am heartily sorry for them, on my own account and yours, but still more on account of your charming wife. But there is no great harm done, after all. Send the linens back to me, and accounts shall be square between us, and I will submit to the loss of the interest."

"Ah, but, monsieur, you are too good, and madame will be recognizant to you forever for your gracious politeness. But, my God! it is impossible that I return to you the linen. I have sold it, monsieur — I have sold it all!"

"Sold it?" reiterated Mr. Schulemberg, regardless of the rules of etiquette, — "sold it? And to whom, pray? and when?"

"To M. Garcia, my father-in-the-law," answered the catechumen blandly; "and it is a week that he has received it."

"Then I must bid you a good-morning, sir," said

Mr. Schulemberg, rising hastily, and collecting his hat and gloves; "for I must lose no time in taking measures to recover the goods before they have changed hands again."

"Pardon, monsieur," interrupted the poor but honest Malibran. "But it is too late! One cannot regain them. M. Garcia embarked himself for Mexico yesterday morning, and carried them all with him."

Imagine the consternation and rage of poor Mr. Schulemberg at finding that he was sold, though the goods were not! I decline reporting the conversation any further, lest its strength of expression and force of expletive might be too much for the more queasy of my readers. Suffice it to say that the *swindlee*, if I may be allowed the royalty of coining a word, at once freed his own mind, and imprisoned the body of M. Malibran; for in those days imprisonment for debt was a recognized institution, and I think few of its strongest opponents will deny that this was a case to which it was no abuse to apply it.

## IV.

I REGRET that I am compelled to leave this exemplary merchant in captivity; but the exigencies of my story, the moral of which beckons me away to the distant coast of Mexico, require it at my hands. The reader may be consoled, however, by the knowledge that he obtained his liberation in due time, his

Dutch creditor being entirely satisfied that nothing whatsoever could be squeezed out of him by passing him between the bars of the debtor's prison, though that was all the satisfaction he ever did get. How he accompanied his young wife to Europe, and there lived by the coining of her voice into drachmas, as her father had done before him, needs not to be told here; nor yet how she was divorced from him, and made another matrimonial venture in partnership with De B——. I have nothing to do with him or her, after the bargain and sale of which she was the object, and the consequences which immediately resulted from it; and here, accordingly, I take my leave of them. But my story is not quite done yet: it must now pursue the fortunes of the enterprising *impresario*, Signor Garcia, who had so deftly turned his daughter into a shipload of fine linens.

This excellent person sailed, as M. Malibran told Mr. Schulemberg, for Vera Cruz, with an assorted cargo, consisting of singers, fiddlers, and, as aforesaid, of Mynheer Van Holland's fine linens. The voyage was as prosperous as was due to such an argosy. If a single Amphion could not be drowned by the utmost malice of gods and men, so long as he kept his voice in order, what possible mishap could befall a whole shipload of them? The vessel arrived safely under the shadow of San Juan de Ulua; and her precious freight in all its varieties was welcomed with a tropical enthusiasm. The market was bare of linen and of song, and it was hard to say which found the readiest sale. Competition raised the price of both articles to a fabulous height. So the good Garcia had the benevolent satisfaction of clothing the naked, and making the ears that heard him to bless him at the same time. After selling his linens at a great advance on the cost-price, considering he had only paid his daughter for them, and having given a series of the most successful concerts ever known in those latitudes, Signor Garcia set forth for the Aztec City. As the relations of *meum* and *tuum* were not upon the most satisfactory footing just then at Vera Cruz, he thought it most prudent to carry his well-won treasure with him to the capital. His progress thither was a triumphal procession. Not Cortés, not General Scott himself, marched more gloriously along the steep and rugged road that leads from the seacoast to the table-land than did this son of song. Every city on his line of march was the monument of a victory, and from each one he levied tribute, and bore spoils away. And the vanquished thanked him for this spoiling of their goods.

Arrived at the splendid city, at that time the largest and most populous on the North American continent, he speedily made himself master of it, — a welcome conqueror. The Mexicans, with the genuine love for song of their Southern ancestors, had had but few opportunities for gratifying it such as that now offered to them. Garcia was a tenor of great compass, and a most skilful and accomplished singer. The artists who accompanied him were of a high order of merit, if not of the very first class. Mexico had never heard the like, and, though a hard-money country, was glad to take their notes, and give them gold in return. They were feasted and flattered in the intervals of the concerts, and the bright eyes of señoras and señoritas rained influence upon them on the off nights, as their fair hands rained flowers upon the *on* ones. And they have a very pleasant way, in those golden realms, of giving ornaments of diamonds and other precious stones to virtuous singers, as we give pencil-cases and gold watches to meritorious railway-conductors and hotel-clerks, as a testimonial of the sense we entertain of their private characters and public services. The gorgeous East herself never showered " on her kings barbaric pearl and gold" with a richer hand than the city of Mexico poured out the glittering rain over the portly person of the happy Garcia. Saturated at length with the golden flood and its foam of pearl and diamond — if, indeed, singer were ever capable of such saturation, and were not rather permeable forever, like a sieve of the Danaïdes, — saturated, or satisfied that it was all run out, he prepared to take up his line of march back again to the City of the True Cross. Mexico mourned over his going, and sent him forth upon his way with blessings, and prayers for his safe return.

But alas! the blessings and the prayers were alike vain. The saints were either deaf or busy, or had gone a journey, and either did not hear or did not mind the vows that were sent up to them. At any rate, they did not take that care of the worthy Garcia which their devotees had a right to expect of them. Turning his back on the halls of the Montezumas, where he had revelled so sumptuously, he proceeded on his way towards the Atlantic coast, as fast as his mules thought fit to carry him and his beloved treasure. With the proceeds of his linens and his lungs, he was rich enough to retire from the vicissitudes of operatic life to some safe retreat in his native Spain or his adoptive Italy. Filled with happy imaginings, he fared onward, the bells of his mules keeping time with the melodious joy of his heart, until he had descended from the *tierra caliente* to the wilder region on the hither side of Jalapa. As the narrow road turned sharply, at the foot of a steeper descent than common, into a dreary valley, made yet more gloomy by the shadow of the hill behind intercepting the sun, though the afternoon was not far advanced, the *impresario* was made unpleasantly aware of the transitory nature of man's hopes and the vanity of his joys. When his train wound into the rough open space, it found itself surrounded by a troop of men whose looks and gestures bespoke their function without the intermediation of an interpreter. But no interpreter was needed in this case, as Signor Garcia was a Spaniard by birth, and their expressive pantomime was a sufficiently eloquent substitute for speech. In plain English, he had fallen among thieves, with very little chance of any good Samaritan coming by to help him.

Now, Signor Garcia had had dealings with brigands and banditti all his operatic life. Indeed, he had often drilled them till they were perfect in their exercises, and got them up regardless of expense. Under his direction they had often rushed forward to the footlights, pouring into the helpless mass before them repeated volleys of explosive crotchets. But this was a very different chorus that now saluted his eyes. It was the real thing, instead of the make-believe, and in the opinion of Signor Garcia, at least, very much inferior to it. Instead of the steeple-crowned hat, jauntily feathered and looped, these irregulars wore huge *sombreros*, much the worse for time and weather, flapped over their faces. For the velvet jacket with the two-inch tail, which had nearly broken up the friendship between Mr. Pickwick and Mr. Tupman, when the latter gentleman proposed induing himself with one, on the occasion of Mrs. Leo Hunter's fancy-dress breakfast, — for this integument, I say, these minions of the moon had blankets round their shoulders, thrown back in preparation for actual service. Instead of those authentic cross-garterings in which your true bandit rejoices, like a new Malvolio, to tie up his legs, perhaps to keep them from running away, these false knaves wore, some of them, ragged boots up to their thighs, while others had no crural coverings at all, and only rough sandals, such as the Indians there use, between their feet and the ground. They were picturesque, perhaps, but not attractive to wealthy travellers. But the wealthy travellers were attractive to them: so they came together, all the same. Such as they were, however, there they were, fierce, sad, and sallow, with vicious-looking knives in their belts, and guns of various parentage in their hands, while their captain bade our good man stand and deliver.

There was no room for choice. He had an escort, to be sure; but it was entirely unequal to the emergency, even if it were not, as was afterwards shrewdly suspected, in league with the robbers. The enemy had the advantage of arms, position, and numbers; and there was nothing for him to do but to disgorge his hoarded gains at once, or to have his breath stopped first, and his estate summarily administered upon afterwards, by these his casual heirs, as the King of France, by virtue of his *Droit d'Aubaine*, would have confiscated Yorick's six shirts and pair of black silk breeches, in spite of his eloquent protest against such injustice, had he chanced to die in his Most Christian Majesty's dominions. As Signor Garcia had an estate in his breath, from which he could draw a larger yearly rent than the rolls of many a Spanish grandee could boast, he wisely chose the part of discretion, and surrendered at the same. His new acquaintances showed themselves expert practitioners in the breaking-open of trunks and the rifling of treasure-boxes. All his beloved doubloons, all his cherished dollars, for the which no Yankee ever felt a stronger passion, took swift wings, and flew from his coffers to alight in the hands of the adversary. The sacred recesses of his pockets, and those of his companions, were sacred no longer from the sacrilegious hands of the spoilers. The breastpins were ravished from the shirt-frills, — for in those days studs were not, — and the rings snatched from the reluctant fingers. All the shining testimonials of Mexican admiration were transferred with the celerity of magic into the possession of the chivalry of the road. Not Faulconbridge himself could have been more resolved to come on at the beckoning of gold and silver than were they, and, good Catholics though they were, it is most likely that Bell, Book, and Candle would have had as little restraining influence over them as he professed to feel.

At last they rested from their labors. To the victors belonged the spoils, as they discovered with instinctive sagacity that they should do, though the apothegm had not yet received the authentic seal of American statesmanship. Science and skill had done their utmost, and poor Garcia and his companions in misery stood in the centre of the ring, stripped of everything but the clothes on their backs. The duty of the day being satisfactorily performed, the victors felt that they had a right to some relaxation after their toils. And now a change came over them which might have reminded Signor Garcia of the banditti of the green-room, with whose habits he had been so long familiar, and whose operations he had himself directed. Some one of the troop, who, however "fit for stratagems and spoils," had yet music in his soul, called aloud for a song. The idea was hailed with acclamations. Not satisfied with the capitalized results of his voice to which they had helped themselves, they were unwilling to let their prey go, until they had also ravished from him some specimens of the airy mintage whence they had issued. Accordingly the Catholic vagabonds seated themselves on the ground, a fuliginous parterre to look upon, and called upon Garcia for a song. A rock which projected itself from the side of the hill served for a stage as well as the "green plat" in the wood near Athens did for the company of Manager Quince, and there was no need of "a tiring-room," as poor Garcia had no clothes to change for those he stood in. Not the Hebrews by the waters of Babylon, when their captors demanded of them a song of Zion, had less stomach for the task. But the prime tenor was now before an audience that would brook neither denial nor excuse. Nor hoarseness, nor catarrh, nor sudden illness, certified unto by the friendly physician, would avail him now. The demand was irresistible; for, when he hesitated, the persuasive though stern mouth of a musket hinted to him in expressive silence that he had better prevent its speech with song.

So he had to make his first appearance upon that "unworthy scaffold," before an audience, which, multifold as his experience had been, was one such as he had never sung to yet. As the shadows of evening began to fall, rough torches of pine-wood were lighted, and shed a glare such as Salvator Rosa loved to kindle, upon a scene such as he delighted to paint. The rascals had taste; that the tenor himself could not deny. They knew the choice bits of the operas which held the stage forty years ago, and they called for them wisely, and applauded his efforts vociferously. Nay, more, in the height of their enthusiasm, they would toss him one of his own doubloons or dollars, instead of the bouquets usually hurled at well-deserving singers. They well judged that these flowers that never fade would be the tribute he would value most, and so they rewarded his meritorious strains out of his own stores, as Claude Duval or Richard Turpin, in the golden days of highway robbery, would sometimes generously return a guinea to a traveller he had just lightened of his purse, to enable him to continue his journey. It was lucky for the unfortunate Garcia that their approbation took this solid shape, or he would have been badly off indeed; for it was all he had to begin the world with over again. After his appreciating audience had exhausted their musical repertory, and had as many encores as they thought good, they broke up the concert, and betook themselves to their fastnesses among the mountains, leaving their patient to find his way to the coast as best he might, with a pocket as light as his soul was heavy. At Vera Cruz a concert or two furnished him with the means of embarking himself and his troupe for Europe, and leaving the New World forever behind him.

And here I must leave him, for my story is done. The reader hungering for a moral may discern, that, though Signor Garcia received the price he asked for his lovely daughter, it advantaged him nothing, and that he not only lost it all, but it was the occasion of his losing everything else he had. This is very well as far as it goes; but then it is equally true that M. Malibran actually obtained his wife, and that Mynheer Van Holland paid for her. I dare say all this can be reconciled with the eternal fitness of things; but I protest I don't see how it is to be done. It is "all a muddle" in my mind. I cannot even affirm that the banditti were ever hanged; and I am quite sure that the unlucky Dutch merchant, whose goods were so comically mixed up with this whole history, never had any poetical or material justice for his loss of them. But it is as much the reader's business as mine to settle these casuistries. I only undertook to tell him who it was that paid for the *Prima Donna* — and I have done it.

## V.

"I CONSIDER that a good story," said the Consul, when he had finished the narration out of which I have compounded the foregoing, "and, what is not always the case with a good story, it is a true one."

I cordially concurred with my honored friend in

this opinion, and if the reader should unfortunately differ from me on this point, I beg him to believe that it is entirely my fault. As the Consul told it to me, it was an excellent good story.

"Poor Mynheer Van Holland," he added, laughing, "never got over that adventure. Not that the loss was material to him, — he was too rich for that, — but the provocation of his fifty thousand dollars going to a parcel of Mexican *ladrones*, after buying an opera-singer for a Frenchman on its way, was enough to rouse even Dutch human nature to the swearing-point. He could not abide either Frenchmen or opera-singers all the rest of his life. And, by Jove! I don't wonder at it."

Nor I, neither, for the matter of that.

University Press, Cambridge: John Wilson and Son.

www.ingramcontent.com/pod-product-compliance
Lightning Source LLC
Chambersburg PA
CBHW020226240426
43672CB00006B/432